GU01006448

Champions

Trade Unions and LGBT Rights in Britain

Champions of Equality

Trade Unions and LGBT Rights in Britain

Peter Purton

Lawrence & Wishart
London 2017

Lawrence and Wishart Limited
Central Books Building
Freshwater Road
Chadwell Heath
RM8 1RX

Typesetting: e-type
Cover design: Andrew Corbett

ISBN 9781912064588

British Library Cataloguing in Publication Data.
A catalogue record for this book is available from the British Library

Contents

Acknowledgements and bibliographic references   vii

A word on language   x

List of organisations and abbreviations   xii

Champions of equality: Trade unions and LGBT
rights in Britain, Foreword by Frances O'Grady   1

Introduction: Champions of equality   2

1. Early interactions with the labour movement   10

2. Coming together in the 1970s   25

3. Breakthrough: The early 1980s   54

4. Old and new issues, continued progress and laying
    firm foundations   85

5. Trade union champions of equality   115

6. Global outreach   150

7. LGBT+, trade unions and new challenges   163

Index   184

Acknowledgements and bibliographical references

Where use has been made of printed sources, bibliographical information is given in the relevant endnote. Most of the documentary sources for the book came from papers preserved in archives, in the personal files of the many people interviewed for the work, who have generously given me access to them, or in files accumulated while I was working at the TUC. From my own collection, in particular, are those produced by the Labour Campaign for Lesbian and Gay Rights.

I wish to record sincere thanks to the staff at the Women's Library at the LSE which holds the Hall-Carpenter Archive. References in the endnotes identify these folders by 'HCA/...'. I also wish to thank Jeff Howarth and James Goddard at the TUC Library at London Metropolitan University. Andrea Peace, Information Manager at the TUC, has greatly helped in providing access to the large collection of files at Congress House which are currently awaiting archiving. Other TUC staff have willingly assisted me, particularly my successor as disability and LGBT officer, Huma Munshi, and Owen Tudor, who is head of the international department.

However, the greatest acknowledgement is to the people who helped make the history described here and who gave freely of their time to answer my questions. There are many others with stories to relate who I was not able to reach and should any of them feel offended, I can only offer genuine apologies. There were also a few who have died and their own stories must go unheard. In alphabetical order, the following is the list of people without whom this history could not have been written – and without whose efforts there would have been much less of a story to tell. I interviewed them on the dates given below.

Paul Amann, 3 November 2016
Carl Banks, 15 December 2016

Mark Beresford, 6 February 2017

Mike Blick, November 2016

Ruth Blunt, 10 November 2016

Pat Carberry, 30 January 2017

Sarah Coldrick, 31 January 2017

Terry, Theresa Conway, 25 October 2016

Chris Creegan, formerly Eades, 16 December 2016

Ian Davies, 2 December 2016

Angela Eagle, MP, 26 October 2017

Shane Enright, 1 August 2016

Maria Exall, 13 December 2016

Betty Gallagher, 25 January 2017

Jean Geldart, 18 November 2016

Katie Hanson, 11 January 2017

Mary Hanson, 13 December 2016

Geoff Hardy, 5 October 2016

Ron Harley, 11 November 2016

Diana Holland, 26 July 2016

Richard Humm, 18 November 2016

Philip Inglesant, 29 December 2016

Alan Jackson, 23 August 2016

Mike Jackson, 25 October 2016

Jon Johnson, 26 January 2017

Dan Jones, 21 November 2016

David Lascelles, 9 March 2017

Jackie Lewis, 25 June 2016 and 24 August 2016

John Lindsay, 21 November 2016

Tim Lucas, 10 August 2016

Lesley Mansell, 26 November 2016

Angela Mason, 23 January 2017

Ros McNeil, 2 September 2016

Phyll Opoku-Gyimah, 10 February 2017

Paul Penny, 6 February 2017

Derek Relph, 21 November 2016

Peter Roscoe, 5 October 2016
Dave Samuel, 30 January 2017
Sue Sanders, 8 August 2016
Brian Shaw, 22 December 2016
Laurie Smith, 23 November 2016
Carola Towle, 31 October 2016
Michael Walker, November 2016
Yvonne Washbourne, 'Wash', 22 December 2016
Jessica Webb, February 2017 and October 2017

A word on language

Using the right words is always important, especially when describing someone's identity. A problem in writing about LGBT+ history is that the language and referential terms have often not been simultaneously accepted by different participants in the community, and the language used has continued to change over the years. The changes have, of course, been striking since the nineteenth century, and now people tend not describe themselves as an 'invert' or as belonging to 'an intermediate sex', as they were referred to then. Some people, however, do continue to lay claim to terms such as 'homosexual' or 'queer', and disagree with other terminology.

I have opted to use the terms lesbian, gay, bisexual and transgender, and thus to use the acronym LGBT. Very recently, certain organisations and individuals have shifted this acronym, to recognise more fluid identities. In some cases this has been reflected in the addition of further letters to the end of LGBT, e.g. LGBTQQI (Lesbian, Gay, Bisexual, Trans, Queer, Questioning, Intersex). Others, including the TUC, have instead added a '+', to create LGBT+. I use this only in the last chapter to reflect current usage.

In 1970, it was usual practice for most campaigners to use either 'homosexual' (as in the name of Campaign for Homosexual Equality, CHE) or 'gay' (as in the Gay Liberation Front, GLF). There was little concern or, perhaps, much awareness at the time that this might reinforce the exclusion of women (let alone trans people). Lesbians became linguistically incorporated into these groups over the following decade, as women asserted their voices. Although a few of the more progressive participants in lesbian and gay groups recognised that bisexuals were still excluded from their titles, it was several more decades before the formula took them on board with any kind of regularity. In an overlapping but distinct battle, trans people also finally came to participate in these circles – although there continue to be problematic debates around trans inclusion.

In using LGBT and then LGBT+ in this book, then, I am following the usage of trade unions and the TUC. In this too I have used the titles adopted by the trade union self-organised structures as they followed the same chronological journey of shifting names from being just 'gay' groups to becoming more inclusive.

List of organisations and abbreviations

Name	Full title/description
ACTT	Film technicians' union, now part of BECTU
Amicus	Union formed by the merger of AUEEW and MSF
AEEU	Amalgamated Engineering and Electrical Union
APEX	Association of Professional, Executive, Clerical and Computer Staff
ASLEF	Train drivers' union
ASTMS	Association of Scientific, Technical and Managerial Staffs, merged with TASS into MSF
ATL	Association of Teachers and Lecturers
AUE(E)W	Amalgamated Union of Engineering Workers, (AUEW), merged with electricians to become AUEEW, then MSF to form Amicus, then TGWU to form Unite
AUEW-TASS	The Technical, Administrative and Supervisory Section of the Amalgamated Union of Engineering Workers, separate to the AUEW
BGMAG	Black Gay Men's Advisory Group
BIFU	Banking, Insurance and Finance Union
BiUK	Bisexual UK
BMRB	British Market Research Bureau Ltd
BT	British Telecom
CAB	Community Advisory Board (Pride London 2013-)
CARE	Christian Action Research Education
CCSU	Council of Civil Service Unions
CGT	Confédération Générale du Travail – French General Confederation of Labour

Name	Full title/description
CHE	Campaign (originally Committee) for Homosexual Equality
COHSE	Confederation of Health Services Employees, now in UNISON
Commonwealth Foundation	International organisation funded by Commonwealth states, aiming to work for greater civil society engagement in politics and society
CPGB	Communist Party of Great Britain
CPSA	Civil and Public Services Association
CPSAGG	Civil and Public Services Association Gay Group
CPSGG	Civil and Public Services Gay Group
CSP	Chartered Society of Physiotherapy
CSU	Civil Service Union
Cutting Edge Consortium	Alliance of organisations aiming to promote equality and human rights across faiths
CWU	Communication Workers' Union
DPAC	Disabled People Against Cuts
DTI	Department for Trade and Industry
DWP	Department for Work and Pensions
EAT	Employment Appeal Tribunal
EETPU	Electrical, Electronic, Telecommunications and Plumbing Union, became part of AUEEW
EHRC	Equality and Human Rights Commission
EI	Education International
EIS	Educational Institute of Scotland, union for Scottish teachers
Equity	Actors' union
EOC	Equal Opportunities Commission
ET	Employment Tribunal
ETUC	European Trade Union Confederation
Evangelical Alliance	Body representing a range of evangelical churches
FA	Football Association
FoL	Festival of Light, a Christian fundamentalist organisation
FBU	Fire Brigades Union
FCO	Foreign and Commonwealth Office in the UK government

Name	Full title/description
FDA	First Division Association, union for senior managers and professionals in public service
FGG	Federation of Gay Games
FFLAGS	Families and Friends of Lesbians and Gays, support group
FNV	Federatie Nederlandse Vakbeweging, Dutch trade union federation
Friend	A national support group for lesbians and gay men established in the 1970s
Gay Switchboard	LGBT telephone helpline
The Gay Youth Movement	There are now many LGBTQ groups for young people, usually locally based in larger cities
GC	General Council of the TUC
The Gender Trust	Charity promoting support for trans people and understanding of gender identity issues
GEO	Government Equalities Office in the UK government
GLAD	Gay Legal Advice
GLC	Greater London Council
GLG	Gay Labour Group, which became LCGR then LCLGR and now LGBTLabour
GMB	Originally the General and Municipal Boilermakers, previously GMW and GMBATU, now a freestanding acronym
GMB Shout!	GMB gay group
GMBATU	General, Municipal, Boilermakers and Allied Trades Union, became the GMB
GMW	General and Municipal Workers, became the GMB
GPTW	Gay Post and Telecom Workers' group
GRAW	Gay Rights at Work
GTG	Gay Teachers Group
HLRS	Homosexual Law Reform Society
Icebreakers	Support group for gay and bisexual men
ILEA	Inner London Education Authority
ILGA	International Lesbian, Gay, Bisexual, Transgender and Intersex Association

Name	Full title/description
ILO	International Labour Organisation, part of the United Nations
IMG	International Marxist Group
IPCS 1	Institution of Professionals, Managers and Specialists
IPCS 2	Institution of Professional Civil Servants
IPMS	Institute of Professionals, Managers, Scientists, now Prospect
IRSF	Inland Revenue Staff Federation, now part of PCS
IS	International Socialists, forerunner of the SWP
IT	Industrial Tribunal (now called Employment Tribunal)
ITF	International Transport Workers' Federation
ITUC	International Trade Union Confederation
J-FLAG	Jamaican Forum for Lesbians, All-Sexuals and Gays – a non-profit NGO working for LGBT rights in Jamaica
Kaleidoscope	UK international LGBT rights lobby group
KAOS GL	Kaos Gey ve Lezbiyen Kültürel Araştırmalar ve Dayanışma Derneği – Turkish gay and lesbian group
LAGER	Lesbian and Gay Employment Rights
LAGIM	Lesbians and Gays in MSF
LAPC	Lesbians Against Pit Closures
LCGR	Labour Campaign for Gay Rights
LCLGR	Labour Campaign for Lesbian and Gay Rights
LGAC	Lesbian and Gay Advisory Committee
LGCM	Lesbian and Gay Christian Movement
LGL	Lithuanian national LGBT rights organisation
LGSM	Lesbians and Gays Support the Miners
LGSP	Lesbians and Gays Support the Printworkers
Liberty	Previously the National Council for Civil Liberties
MBS	Manchester Business School
MSF	Manufacturing, Science and Finance, formed from a merger of ASTMS and TASS. Now part of UNITE (via Amicus)
NALGO	National and Local Government Officers' association, now UNISON
Nalgay	National and Local Government Officers' gay group

Name	Full title/description
NAPO	National Association of Probation Officers, union for probation and family court workers
NASUWT	National Association of Schoolmasters Union of Women Teachers
NATFHE	National Association for Teachers in Further and Higher Education, now part of UCU
NCCL	National Council for Civil Liberties, now Liberty
NCU	National Communications Union, now CWU
NGA	National Graphical Association, then GPMU, now part of Amicus
NEC	National Executive Committee
NLGC	National Lesbian and Gay Committee (NALGO)
NUCPS	National Union of Civil and Public Servants, now part of PCS
NUJ	National Union of Journalists
NUM	National Union of Mineworkers
NUPE	National Union of Public Employees, now in UNISON
NUPEGG	National Union of Public Employees Gay Group
NUR	National Union of Railwaymen, now RMT
NUS (1)	National Union of Seamen
NUS (2)	National Union of Students
NUT	National Union of Teachers
OLGA	Organisation for Lesbian and Gay Action, formed in response to Section 28 in 1988 but shortlived
OPAL	Out and Proud African LGBTI
Operation Black Vote	Non-partisan group working to increase black participation in elections
OPZZ	Ogólnopolskie Porozumienie Związków Zawodowych – Polish trade union confederation
OutRage	Queer direct action campaign group founded 1990, of which Peter Tatchell is a prominent spokesperson.
PCS	Public and Commercial Services Union, formed from the merger of a number of civil service unions
PFA	Professional Footballers' Association
POEU	Post Office Engineering Union, now part of CWU

Name	Full title/description
Press for Change	Campaign and support group for trans people
Prospect	Union formed from several mergers, for engineers, scientists etc
Proud	Combined LGBT group, from groups in NUCPS and IRSF after their merger into PCS
PSI	Public Services International, an international union federation
Rank Outsiders	Campaigned to end the ban on lesbians and gay men serving in the armed forces
Rainbow International Fund	UK trade union-based campaign raising money to support LGBT communities internationally
RMT	Rail, Maritime and Transport workers union
Runnymede Trust	UK race equality think tank
SCPS	Society of Civil and Public Servants, now part of PCS
SHC	Scientific Humanitarian Committee
SOGAT	Society of Graphical and Allied Trades, then GPMU, now part of Amicus
Social and Community Planning	Predecessor to NatCen (National Centre for Social Research)
Scottish Minorities Group	Scottish equivalent of CHE
Shout!	See GMB Shout!
Stonewall	Campaigns for the equality of lesbian, gay, bisexual and trans people across Britain
SWP	Socialist Workers' Party
TUAS28	Trade Unions Against Section 28
TGEU	Transgender Europe
TGWU	Transport and General Workers' Union, now part of UNITE
TUC	Trades Union Congress the federation to which all British unions are affiliated
UCATT	Union of Construction, Allied Trades and Technicians

Name	Full title/description
UCU	University and College Union, formed of a merger of AUT and NATFHE
UCW	Union of Communication Workers
UKBP	UK Black Pride
UNISON	Public service union, formed from a merger of COHSE, NALGO and NUPE
UNHCR	United Nations High Commission for Refugees
UNITE	Formed from merger of TGWU and Amicus
UPW	Union of Postal Workers
USDAW	Union of Shop, Distributive and Allied Workers
Young Socialists	Youth wing of the Labour Party, 1965-1993

Champions of equality: Trade unions and LGBT rights in Britain

Foreword by Frances O'Grady

The British trade union movement has made great strides forward on the equality agenda. One of the highlights for me is how trade unionists have fought for – and won – many rights for LGBT+ people.

Peter Purton led on LGBT+ and disability rights at the TUC for eighteen years. During that time, he and our LGBT committee made sure that LGBT equality was a key part of our work. I am grateful to them all for their campaigning to tackle homophobia in football, to highlight the mental health needs of LGBT people, to support the Pride marches across the country, and to campaign for equal survivor pensions for lesbian and gay couples.

It is because of the many individuals identified in this book that we have come so far. Their insistence that a trade union has a duty to represent *all* its members, even when popular hostility was at its height – such as during the AIDS crisis – is inspiring. No less inspiring was their understanding that trade unions offer a home to all working people, even when they did not live up to that ideal of equality. Now, I am proud that we do.

As this book points out, the battle for equality is still not won, and dark clouds on all sides pose threats to the world which we all share. It is now more important than ever to have a stronger labour movement which lives by the old trade union principle: an injury to one is an injury to all.

Frances O'Grady
General Secretary, TUC
February 2017

INTRODUCTION

Champions of equality

There is a big hole in histories of the struggle for lesbian, gay, bisexual and trans equality in Britain: there is little discussion of the part played by the labour movement, in particular trade unions, in the development of this movement and in the successes achieved.[1] This book will fill this gap, and will argue that this struggle is very far from complete, even in Britain, and that unions can continue to play a vital part in completing the job in the future.

For many years, trade unionists have taken part in, and set up stalls at London Pride and many other Pride events around the country, to promote the benefits of trade union membership to LGBT people. Too often, the puzzled responses have been: what's a union, or, what have unions got to do with my rights?

The correct answer to the second question is: a great deal. But for a trade unionist, the bitter truth behind both questions is located in the success of all governments since that of Margaret Thatcher's in 1979. Governmental political agendas have caricatured trade unionists as dinosaurs who come from an extinct age of collectivism and who are obstacles to progress and modernisation, opponents of individual choice, and who are greedy disrupters of public services into the bargain (usually with references to all being under the unfettered control of 'evil' politically motivated 'union barons' plotting to hold the 'public' to ransom).

Such crude ideas are in fact the opposite of the truth. It is true that trade unionists sometimes (actually, very rarely in recent years) take industrial action to protect services and jobs against attempts by employers and the government to cut them. Protecting the jobs and living standards of workers, and protecting services provided for the public, against those who wrongly believe that everything is better when delivered for private profit, are the main functions of trade unions. In a country in which growing numbers of people are finding themselves locked into insecure jobs that inhibit their participation in society, one might have thought that anyone who wanted a fairer society would applaud and endorse the role unions can play in working for that. However, alongside this need for unions to be able to carry out their fundamental and original functions, a more accurate picture of the real role of trade unions in modern society is demonstrated by the part that they have played, working collectively as well as at an individual level, in achieving the rights for people who are LGB and T. This work with the LGBT movement has occurred at the same time as unions have participated in fights for gender, race, disability and age equality. And, far from being the modern equivalent of feudal relics run by power-hungry robber barons as many parts of the media would have it, every trade union elects its leaders and its executives and makes its policies through democratic structures.

The invisibility of the union contribution to equal rights struggles is not just a result of the demonisation of trade unions by politicians willingly supported by almost the entire national press (although they carry a major responsibility); it is also the consequence of deliberate choices made by self-appointed spokespersons for the LGBT movement. During the 1990s and 2000s, the lobbying organisation Stonewall made a massive contribution to the victories achieved for LGB equality (they decided, happily, in 2015/16 to include trans people for the first time). LGB people have much to thank them for, and many do so through generous donations (they are not able to influence policy). But sadly, for many years, anyone reading their website, publications or media releases as the only source of information would be forgiven for thinking they had achieved all the results single-handed. This monopolisation of credit has been assisted by journalists wanting a single point of contact for a quote. Every time there is a story about LGB(T) issues, the quick option is to call Stonewall.

Much smaller and less well financed groups are campaigning on particular issues: the continued challenges of hate crime, domestic abuse, housing shortages, mental health, the exclusion or marginalisation of bisexual people, trans people, multiple prejudices still faced by black LGBT people and many other issues, that all add up to a powerful warning against the complacency that equal rights have now been completely won, and the battle is over. While many in the community recognise the problems, I have witnessed (and heard personal accounts from many colleagues) a climate of hostility against 'introducing politics into Pride' – as if the history of LGBT struggle had nothing to do with today. Many campaigners have generally welcomed trade union alliances, but their voices have also gone mostly unheard. Government austerity policies since 2010 have also silenced them; many have closed or shrunk because of funding cuts, and their charitable statuses often prevent overtly political campaigning.

As well as a concern with historical accuracy, there are other more important reasons for offering a balanced account of the history of LGBT rights. The first is that the struggle for LGBT liberation (not just legal equal rights, but inclusion and acceptance in a much more equal society) continues in Britain, in Europe and globally. The widespread belief that victory has been won and we can all go and party, particularly strong after the introduction of same-sex marriage, is false and potentially very dangerous.

One reason for this is that LGBT rights and liberation do not stand alone, but are necessarily part of a much larger picture. Economic and social policies impact as strongly on LGBT people (or at least, the majority of LGBT people who are not rich enough to excuse themselves from the daily struggle for existence) as on any other part of society, and in some cases more so – due to ongoing social and economic exclusionary practices and violence. LGB and T people share with each other only their sexuality or their gender identity; they also share with many others their class origin, employment status, education, gender, race, (dis)ability and many other facets making up each individual. They are not immune from the consequences of climate change, or military conflicts.

The labour movement can offer a specific response to problems people encounter every day in most areas of their lives. The labour movement offers solutions that are collective, not just individual. It encourages people to work together to resist attacks or to move forward together towards brighter futures. As global capitalism undergoes more and deeper crises (and their recurrence is inherent in the very nature of capitalism) more people will discover that individual solutions are not adequate. Collectively, resistance is stronger and progress can be made more rapidly. In the crisis-ridden world of the early-twenty-first century, collective organisation of 'ordinary' people is more necessary than ever. And this is especially the case in the face of another response to these crises, the rise in Europe and the USA of extreme right-wing populist political forces and dangerously demagogic leaders: events that should shred any illusions that racism, xenophobia – and sexism and the scapegoating of minority rights – have been driven from western 'civilisation'. Trade unions are an already existing form of collective action. That, put simply, is the other reason why LGB and T people who are not members of the club of the super-rich need to be trade union members. That is the answer to the first puzzled question – what is a union? – posed by too many LGBT people when approached by trade unionists at Pride festivals.

This history will trace the story of how the modern trade union movement in Britain became a champion of LGBT equality. This includes a longer history, in the heroic efforts of pioneers in the nineteenth century to win understanding and support, to end the inherited legal and social oppression that recognised the legitimacy only of heterosexuality and strict gender norms. These early champions were of various political persuasions, of course, but many did look to the then young labour movement and political parties of the left to be their allies. But that small progress was put back in its box for five or six decades by the global crises resulting in and from the First and Second World Wars, the impact of the rise to power of reactionary and fascist nationalist movements, and the re-criminalisation by Stalin of homosexuality after the hope offered by the early repeal of repressive laws by the Bolshevik government following the Russian Revolution. It is not possible to know what progress might have been made to build on these links without such world-changing events.

In Britain, in conditions where even the words to describe homosexuality were taboo, and where the majority of those who were homosexual would see campaigning to end this situation as hopeless, and indeed most likely to lead to even more severe consequences, people instead tried to live out of sight of society. It took a small handful of individuals of immense courage to pick up, in the 1950s and 1960s, where the early pioneers had left off, and to ever so gradually win a place on the political agenda. The organisation they created, the Campaign for Homosexual Equality (CHE) is still working today. But while there were then a few links with trade unionists and the labour movement, in the 1970s, in a process linked to the emergence of Gay Liberation (itself a result of the youth rebellions of the 1960s and the movements for women's liberation and for black civil rights in the USA), that some LGBT workers in Britain began to organise inside their own unions. The aim was to win the unions over to the idea that they should take up the (lack of) rights for their lesbian, gay, bisexual and trans fellow workers. This would take place at the same time as extending union struggles against racism and sexism, themselves only recently introduced into the mainstream concerns of trade unionism. It was hard work for a long time. Small groups of LGBT workers set about seeking recognition from their own unions, sometimes working with campaign groups outside, and increasingly supported by far-sighted union officers who grasped that the historic trade union principle that 'an injury to one is an injury to all' should equally be applied to this group of members who, in addition to facing massive prejudice, also had no protection at all against discrimination on the grounds of their sexuality or gender identity. A number of such groups began to make progress but very little concrete was achieved in the 1970s. However, the work itself was vital: important foundations were laid, connections were established, research was done to provide evidence to back the arguments for unions to take up the issue. Alliances were created that helped to ensure that, during the following decade, the first significant victories were achieved both inside the unions, and outside.

The 1980s were also a time when Labour local authorities, driven by progressive Labour Party activists, began to work more effectively to win support for equality within that party, with a view that a future Labour government would legislate for equal rights. The links between the party and the trade union movement (although of course not all unions were or are affiliated to Labour) were vital too in gaining a wider platform for the issue. It remained true that many party leaders were afraid to speak out, but it became harder to ignore debates staged – and victories gained – at both the Trades Union Congress in September 1985 and the Labour Party Conference itself in October 1985, with both events then being televised live.

A significant boost to the reach and the visibility of the message was generated by the magnificent display of solidarity created by the small group of LGBT activists who set up Lesbians and Gays Support the Miners (LGSM) and Lesbians Against Pit Closures during the strike of 1984-85. These groups delivered that other key principle of trade unionism: solidarity. This has now been commemorated in the brilliant film *Pride*, but what matters is that it was not just as history, but also as a call to action that was still relevant in the new century.

The struggle continued, and it was many more years before the first concrete steps towards legal equality were taken in parliament. Relentless pressure led to the first breakthrough on the legal front since the Sexual Offences Act of 1967, when John Major's Conservative government reduced the gay male age of consent to eighteen, although they did not equalise it with heterosexual ages of consent. The vigour of the opposition to this tiny step was indicative of the resistance there would be to legislating for actual equality.

Trade unions (working effectively through the TUC from 1998) played a big part in the laws introduced under the Labour governments led by Tony Blair from 1997 onwards, although they faced internal as well as external obstacles. Having been closely involved in these discussions with ministers myself, I can offer an informed interpretation of how progress was achieved.

But there is another side to the role of unions here. Trade unions exist primarily to support their members and, alongside lobbying and campaigning for new rights, trade unions were to be found winning workplace rights – often before they became legal requirements – and defending individual LGBT members. This is a critical part of this story, both for the people whose lives were directly affected, and as part of a highly significant process of social change. Over less than twenty years, popular attitudes towards LGBT people were turned from majority hostility to an equally large majority acceptance (or at least toleration – an important distinction). We have now, finally, put an end to the too-long lasting notion that we were dealing with Oscar Wilde's 'love that dare not speak its name'. It is inconceivable that the Conservative Party, most of whose members voted to retain the notorious Section 28, would have legislated same-sex marriage ten years later without these enormous shifts in public opinion. The work and campaigning done by trade unionists and trade unions, alongside Stonewall, LGBT groups in all the major political parties and other allies, was critical to driving this transformation.

Trade unions are voluntary associations – still the largest in the country – and this gives them many opportunities to influence developments locally, regionally, nationally and internationally, and on LGBT issues (as on many others) they have done just that. But being voluntary associations seeking to recruit as many workers as possible in any workplace, to strengthen their hand when negotiating with an employer, unions face the same challenges as any other organisation of taking their members with them when they adopt new policies that are not always popular with everyone at the outset. Even while fighting for new equality laws and to defend individuals from discrimination, unions have also had to face resistance from their own members. The history in this volume will not shy away from this reality, but will emphasise how often this initial opposition was overcome and transformed into support. However, in a world where the media is positively seeking to make trouble for unions, too often narratives about the overall progressive role of trade unions have been compromised by the reactionary views of individual members, the ignorance of a shop steward, a paid official's failure to act, which have provided easy opportunities for those hostile to trade unionism to criticise. The reality is that an organisation of nearly six million members contains all kinds of people. As such, it has never been a surprise to an active trade unionist that some members are homophobic: trade unionists are human beings sharing the views – and prejudices – which have been learnt and which may be reflected and consolidated in their local communities. There will always be such prejudices, but it has been and still is the work of unions to win over these members. That represents one of the most significant parts that unions play today, in turning legal rights into real acceptance. This is another hidden part of the history of the trade unions as champions of LGBT equality.

The outline summary given here is traced back to its distant origins in the nineteenth century, in the first chapter of this volume. Chapters Two, Three and Four then focus particularly on the struggles of small groups of committed activists to challenge prejudice and lack of understanding in their unions through the 1970s, 1980s and 1990s. The successful outcomes of these efforts will be explored through the words and memories of those that did the work. The particular part played by unions in winning legal equality under the leadership of the TUC brings the account into the twenty-first century in Chapters Five and Six. The final chapters explore the warning that the battle has not yet been won. At a time when the dominant culture argues that anyone can be successful in their life if they just 'work hard', regardless of their other circumstances or the obstacles they face, it is essential to present the case (once widely accepted but currently written out of history) that true equality also depends on economic and social factors, and is more easily achieved – in fact, can only be achieved – in a society that is much fairer (much less unequal) than Britain is today. Trade unions' present weakness is a problem because it hinders their role in helping to win a better, fairer, more equal world in which LGBT+ people must have their own – equal – place. This is something yet to be achieved and only to be secured as part of wider changes.

NOTES

1. There are numerous UK books on the history of the movement for LGBT equality, but few have references to trade unions in their indexes. The situation is better in the USA, where there are both close parallels, and striking differences, in the ways in which unions in that country took up and related to LGBT members and issues. This is not surprising given the differences in scale, numbers, political systems and cultural traditions between the two countries. For a recent view, see Miriam Frank, *Out in the Union: A Labor History of Queer America,* Philadelphia: Temple University Press, 2014.

1

Early interactions with the labour movement

Men who had sex with other men, women who had sex with other women, or men and women attracted to sexual relations with any gender, had always existed, in every age and every kind of society. The behaviours were recognised and have been identified by historians (see below). With a few exceptions – of which classical Greek acceptance of (strictly limited) adult male with male child sex is the best known – same-sex physical acts had usually been condemned by religious institutions and, following their lead, state laws and social norms. Such sexual acts were condemned as unnatural, against the divine order, impure, or threatening to the future of the race, and the fact that some people's behaviour was overlooked because of their rank or position did not change the overall situation. Laws penalised the behaviour of individuals rather than an identified group of people, and so the focus remained on the individual. However, in the nineteenth century, homosexuality became identified as a medical or psychological defect, and those who practised it (or wished to) were for the first time identified as a specific social group.

Arguably, this development was connected with the enormous changes that occurred as capitalism replaced previous types of economies (first in the western world) and generated fundamental social change as a result. Dramatic industrialisation that began in the eighteenth century transformed traditional societies; this was a change led by Britain but rapidly repeated across the rest of Europe and the United States. This is not the place to analyse how these changes interacted to create a distinctly different world from what had gone before, but, evident by the middle of the nineteenth century, was the recognition and characterisation – both by themselves, and by wider society – of a group of people identified by their same-sex attractions. Big cities such as London had seen the emergence of subcultures for men who enjoyed sex with men (the 'molly houses') during the eighteenth century, who had themselves followed on from subcultures of the century before.[1]

However, it was during the Victorian period that scientists tried to explain this phenomenon, starting a trend towards the medicalisation of 'variant' sexualities (and in due course gender identities) that still survives (albeit decreasingly accepted) today. Along the way, homosexuals became a distinctly identified group of people. The overwhelming focus was on male behaviour. Women were socially oppressed, denied many of the rights enjoyed by men of all classes; among men there was a broad consensus that woman's role was to have children and to raise them, as homemaker, with very few exceptions of women who were able to break through these barriers, usually limited to specific areas of life such as the arts and literature. These oppressions meant that the notion that women might develop same-sex attractions was rarely if ever recognised. The link between oppression on grounds of gender and oppression on grounds of sexuality remains insufficiently understood despite the impact of feminism on (parts of) the modern world. Gender oppression has continued to be a fraught issue for the LGBT community to this day, provoking vigorous debate, as witnessed by the violence of exchanges around whether a transwoman is entitled to the same rights as ciswomen, that exploded in Britain in 2015-16 and continues even now (see Chapter Seven).

While scientists looked for reasons and for 'cures' for this 'condition', in the nineteenth century, the objects of such enquiry set about challenging the prevailing culture, which treated them as anathemas, as perverted practitioners of sin. These individuals' willingness to stand up to hostile opinions that were shared across every class, every social group, every nationality, and every religion, formed a heroic backdrop to the beginnings of a movement for liberation. Their names today are largely forgotten even by LGBT rights activists, and that is a travesty. They deserve recognition as the pioneers of our movement in their own right, but also because many of them inclined towards radical political views sharing a critique of capitalist society. They shared these views with the trade unions and socialist groups that were developing and organising at the same time, which enabled them to resist then challenge the class oppression that still lies at the heart of capitalist relations. In a few cases, a direct link between groups was achieved that would prefigure the connections that have contributed to achievements in more recent times.

The working class emerged alongside the mass industrialisation of economies. In Britain, this led to urbanisation at an unprecedented rate, as millions were drawn from the countryside to feed the incessant demands for labour in the new factories. The ghastly conditions in which people worked and were forced to live was rapidly recognised as a problem. From the start, liberal social reformers among the ruling class, appalled by what they saw as an unacceptable price for Britain's economic pre-eminence, had called for government to intervene to legislate the most basic rights, and some advances were achieved during the course of the nineteenth century. But this was top-down. It was the creation of trade unions by workers (alongside short-lived political movements such as the Chartists) that gave the workers themselves their own voice. This was where working people joined together to protect themselves against the worst exploitation, to call for better working conditions and for better wages. Initially repressed by law (the Tolpuddle Martyrs were among the first working class heroes, transported to Australia in 1834 for the crime of organising a union), changes were (slowly) secured, and unions won limited freedom to organise.

In 1868, at the Mechanics' Institute in Manchester, a number of unions came together to form the Trades Union Congress (TUC) to provide a single voice for this new movement. The founders were from small, craft-based unions, and their aim was to achieve 'respectability' within the existing social order. Politically, they looked to the Liberal Party, then dominated by William Gladstone (1809-1898), to achieve rights for working people. In the last decades of the century, new mass membership unions, created by unskilled workers (such as the dockers) transformed the trade union movement into a body much wider in its reach and more radical in its approach. Still thriving successors of these first large general unions were the modern General, Municiple and Boilermakers' union (GMB), and the Transport and General Workers' Union (TGWU, one of the main participants in the amalgamations constituting Unite the Union).

Repeated attacks on unions' rights that greatly limited their ability to protect their members were only ultimately overturned in the early years of the twentieth century, by a Liberal government. This was the first parliament in which the Labour Party was represented, and the successes won there for unions survived until the anti-union laws introduced under Margaret Thatcher in the 1980s (taken further by recent coalition and Conservative governments).

In 1899, the annual Congress of the TUC voted to instruct its parliamentary committee to meet with socialist societies and the co-operative movement, to discuss obtaining direct representation of working people in parliament: it was time for workers to acquire their own voice in the seat of political power. From this meeting came the Labour Representation Committee and, in the 1906 general election, the first twenty-nine Labour members of parliament were elected (following an electoral pact with the much larger Liberal Party). At this time, the executive of the new party was dominated by trade union nominees, and the programme was deliberately modest, seeking basic reforms in trade union rights and some social improvements. Despite the contemporary high profile votes-for-women campaigns by the Suffragettes, trade unions at this time were reluctant to take up such issues. Indeed, it would be some time before the prevalent majority opinion that a woman's place was in the kitchen and raising the children would be challenged within the trade union movement, which still falsely viewed women workers as a threat to male jobs and wage levels. It was therefore inconceivable in such circumstances that either the new political voice for working people (the Labour Party) or their voice in the workplace (the unions) would raise the question of the legal oppression of those attracted to their own sex.

THE EMERGENCE OF HOMOSEXUAL IDENTITIES

Fortunately, there were other people who rejected this narrow focus and whose work during the nineteenth and early-twentieth centuries opened many people's eyes. Karl Ulrichs (1825-1895) may have been the first, writing compendiously in the 1860s and 1870s, to challenge the persecution of same-sex love, and significantly influencing the following generation of campaigners. He called LGB people 'Uranians'. In 1869, Dr Benkert (a Hungarian) coined the word 'homosexual' (a strange linguistic construction of a word made from both classical Greek and Latin) and challenged a contemporary attempt to criminalise same-sex behaviour with the argument that it was absurd to punish a natural condition.

In the next generation, the key figure was the German doctor Magnus Hirschfeld (1868-1935). He created the Scientific Humanitarian Committee (SHC) in 1897, to win rights for what he deemed 'the intermediate sex'. This was initially conducted through a petition calling for the repeal of Paragraph 175 of the German legal code of 1871, a measure that reflected a common trend across some European states of actively criminalising (at least male) same-sex relationships. One of the petition's active supporters was a leader of the German Social Democratic Party, August Bebel, who tried (and failed) to introduce it in the German parliament in 1898. The SHC continued its work until it was crushed by the Nazis soon after they gained power (see below). The German Social Democrats also continued to campaign on this issue and another leading figure, Eduard Bernstein, wrote extensively in support of repealing the repressive law.

In England, Havelock Ellis (1859-1939), a champion of women's rights and sex education, published *Sex Inversion* in 1897. During the same period, in the USA, the poet Walt Whitman (1819-92) devoted a whole section of his greatest work *Leaves of Grass* (beginning with the edition published in 1860) to praising same-sex love. This was widely influential in promoting awareness of the issue among some sections of society.[2] It also generated further discussion and political action; among those influenced by Whitman was the English socialist Edward Carpenter.

In Britain, a small number of individuals (such as Ellis) had taken up the cause of liberation by echoing Ulrich's argument that it was wrong and absurd to attempt to criminalise a natural characteristic. Among these, the person with the closest connections with the labour movement was Edward Carpenter (1844-1929). His influence at the time was significant, in particular on the growing and confident working-class movement, which, through trade unions, the Labour Party or socialist society organisations, was increasingly involved in discussing political and social issues. Carpenter, who has recently and deservedly attracted some renewed recognition of his role after decades of being ignored, was a profound thinker, brilliant educator and powerful advocate for liberation for all those suffering oppression in the capitalist and imperialist world. This included not only those with same-sex attractions (whom he called 'inverts', deriving from the idea that this was an inversion of the majority sexuality), but also women (his advanced view understood their social position and how it was intimately linked with the organisation of capitalist society), working people as a whole (exploited by their bosses and the capitalist system), and the victims of empire (chiefly the British empire – his correspondents included Mahatma Gandhi). He was an 'invert' and from 1898, he lived openly with his partner, George Merrill, a young man from the slums of Sheffield, in a cottage near that city that became an open centre for debate and education.

Carpenter's libertarian socialist vision was expressed through many publications and through delivering numerous lectures to audiences of all kinds, including at trade union meetings. His first book on homosexuality, *Homogenic Love*, was unfortunately scheduled for publication in the same month as the sensational trial of Oscar Wilde in 1895. As a result, no publisher would touch it and it appeared only in a small private edition. However, the text was included in a more extended work, *The Intermediate Sex* (he had absorbed many of the ideas of Magnus Hirschfeld), which was published in 1908; this took place without any public scandal and it began to make an impact. In 1913, he was a founder member of the British branch of Hirschfeld's Society for the Study of Sex Psychology.[3]

Carpenter's overall contribution was recognised when the TUC General Council sent him a manifesto signed by every one of its members on his eightieth birthday in 1924. Soon after this, the TUC librarian, Herbert Tracey, wrote a tribute to Carpenter as an interpreter of 'the deepest thoughts and aims of the democratic movement' which had:

> helped to make the Labour Movement. Its [the labour movement's] humane and generous spirit, its hatred of tyranny, its contempt for snobbery [...] its belief in the good impulses of the common people [...] its faith in the future, its interest in education derive in great part from the work of Edward Carpenter.[4]

It is now impossible to know how aware Tracey was of Carpenter's sexuality and his domestic arrangements, but it seems implausible that he could be entirely ignorant of the fact that the subject of his eulogy was in a relationship with a man.

Shortly after this, another scandal led to trade union engagement. In 1928, well-known novelist Radclyffe Hall's latest publication, *The Well of Loneliness,* narrating 'the life of a woman who is born an invert', attracted violent hostility from the *Sunday Express* and the *Daily Express.* Their calls for the novel to be banned were fulfilled when the fundamentalist home secretary got involved; a consignment of the books were confiscated by customs, and a court hearing found that the book breached the 1857 Obscene Publications Act. This was resisted on the grounds of free speech, however, and among the supporters were the pro-Labour *Daily Herald,* a paper originally launched by radical trade union leaders and by now backed by the TUC (it would become, ironically, *The Sun* in 1964 before being acquired by Murdoch), which called for support for Hall. Letters of support were indeed received from the National Union of Railwaymen and the South Wales Miners' Federation.[5] There was no concealing that the book was a sympathetic account of lesbian relationships, but apart from public sympathy, there was no sign that the trade unions' leading body would actively campaign for equality.

It is evident that during the last decades of the nineteenth and the beginning of the twentieth centuries, there was some overlap between the first representatives of a movement for the liberation of those we now describe as LGB (the question of gender identity was not reflected in its modern sense at that time, and would have been confused in any case with the issue of 'cross dressing', which was present), and people associated with socialist and workers' organisations. However, despite this, the progressive stance of the German Social Democrats (who were a major political force in national life) was an exception to the general political disinterest in 'LGB' rights. In relation to communism, Friedrich Engels wrote a letter to Karl Marx, indicating his awareness of Ulrichs' work, but did not apply his and Marx's own historical materialist approach to sexuality but simply shared Victorian prejudices.[6]

It is not possible now to guess whether the progress that began in these decades might have led to a genuine breakthrough. It might have achieved the repeal of hostile laws such as Germany's Paragraph 175, or, in Britain, the Labouchère amendment which, following a routine public uproar about 'immorality', had added to a criminal justice law in 1885 a much stronger offence of 'gross indecency' that chiefly impacted on homosexual men. Had such a breakthrough occurred in Britain there would necessarily have been an open public debate that would have demonstrated the depth of resistance to change across all sections of contemporary society. This conservatism was responsible for profound prejudice even in countries where there was not a specific legal ban, as was the case in many states whose civil legal systems were based on the Code Napoleon from a century before, which was silent on the issue of same-sex relationships. In France, the revolutionary government had abolished the criminal offence of sodomy in 1791 and it was not revived at any time, but other discriminatory laws could be and were invoked. However, what happened over the following decades ended any prospect of immediate progress for gaining rights for people with same-sex desires.

THE IMPACT OF THE WORLD WARS

The wide-ranging consequences of the first global war and the upheavals and economic crises that followed in the 1920s and 1930s powerfully contributed to progress towards recognising women's rights and partial success for the suffrage movement in Britain (not least because of the part played by women in sustaining the war effort). However, in 1918, despite initial hopes that it would be possible to pick up where things had been left in 1914, this actually proved to be a false dawn for LGBT rights.

In Germany, the SHC – its membership much depleted by casualties of the war – backed the failed 1918 revolution led by German Bolsheviks, and then continued its work under the Weimar Republic that replaced the German empire, optimistically spreading its campaigns internationally, with Hirschfeld still the leading advocate. Socially, a liberated bohemian culture developed in Berlin during the Weimar republic, well exemplified in the writings of visitors such as Christopher Isherwood, whose 1939 novel *Goodbye to Berlin*, was adapted into *Cabaret*, initially a powerful musical (first produced in 1966) and then a film (1972). In this culture, what would now be called a 'homosexual subculture', prospered despite its continued illegality. But neither the public campaign nor the urban subculture could survive the march to power of the far-right, led by the Nazi Party with its vicious ideology focussed on racial purity and Aryan superiority. Homosexuals were evidently not the primary target (unless, like Hirschfeld, they were also Jewish) of Nazi violence, but were rather collateral damage, seen as pathetic specimens, impure and incapable of procreating future generations of the master race. Hirschfeld's Institute of Sexual Science (in Berlin) was described by the Nazis as an 'unparalleled breeding ground of dirt and filth' and was raided by storm troopers (6 May 1933) and its contents seized and burnt. Direct persecution followed the elimination of Hitler's early lieutenant Ernst Röhm (homosexual leader of the Nazi Brownshirts) in the Night of the Long Knives (1934). The inclusion of homosexuals among the many groups sent to the concentration camps was the inevitable consequence of Nazi policy. It was additionally reflective of the depth of social hatred that these people – who were identified by a pink triangle – were also held in contempt by their fellow prisoners. (The pink triangle was subsequently adopted as a badge of defiance by post-war campaigners.) With Paragraph 175 in place, the Nazis did not even need new legislation to commit these abuses, although the law was broadened to provide a veneer of legality to the persecution. The largest, best organised and most socially progressive labour movement in Europe was eliminated at the same time.[7]

In Russia, in the days immediately after the Bolshevik revolution, the old Tsarist laws criminalising homosexuality were abolished by decree (December 1917) along with much other repressive legislation. Russian delegations visited Hirschfeld and his colleagues in Berlin and reported favourably on what they saw. They insisted that there was no hint here of anything other than Russian revolutionaries embracing a wider concept of a new society, and showing the openness to new understanding that the revolution had fostered. But this early promise did not last. Ten years later, Joseph Stalin, consolidating his control as the new leader of the Soviet Union, re-imposed regressive laws as part of a policy to consolidate the 'new Soviet family'. This included re-criminalising homosexuality. Legal repression was accompanied by periodic purges of gay meeting places followed by mass prosecutions, and homosexual people were sent to the gulags.[8]

Here then, the early links between LGBT liberation and the labour movement and political left were brutally severed. Communist parties in other countries loyally followed the lead of the Soviet Union in their policies. Tragically, in the following decades, it was not unknown for leftists to seek to damage the reputations of opponents by implying that they were homosexual.[9] In Britain, unlike much of the rest of Europe where communist parties were strongly entrenched in the trade unions, the native version of the Communist Party was always comparatively small, so the damage caused by its following of Kremlin policies was limited. But despite its relative lack of numbers, it was influential in the trade union movement, where its activists offered committed leadership in key industrial battles and earned positions of authority as a result. With Labour's own lack of interest in 'social issues' during this time, the gains that might have appeared possible while people like Carpenter were still alive seemed no longer to be on the agenda. The impact of the 1930s great depression on ordinary working people left little space for trade unionists and socialists to think about anything other than mass unemployment and grinding poverty and there is no evidence of broader thinking in the movement in this period.

Work to win a hearing for the cause of LGBT rights within British society, and trying to win over the trade unions and labour movement to support such a cause, had to begin anew after the end of the Second World War. This then took place during a period of harsh post-war economic austerity accompanied by a dominant cold war ideology. But begin they did, with the coming together of campaigners to create the Homosexual Law Reform Society (HLRS), a small centralised group based in London. A local group based in Manchester became the North West HLRS under the committed guidance of local gay man, also briefly a Labour councillor, Allan Horsfall. Operating publicly from an address in a traditional mining community, this group eventually transformed itself into the first national organisation working for equal rights as the Campaign for Homosexual Equality (CHE).

The HLRS organised the first post-war public meeting in Britain on homosexual rights in 1960, the goal of which was to persuade parliament to act on the Wolfenden Report. This report had been published in 1957, and was a very modest proposal for partial decriminalisation of same-sex male relationships. It was commissioned because of a spate of highly publicised scandals that had generated much public concern during the 1950s: the arrests of well-known political and artistic figures for homosexual offences during periodic purges carried out by the police, and the use of threats of blackmail by the Soviet secret service that had led to the defection of British spies Guy Burgess and Donald Maclean in 1951, at the height of the cold war. Parts of the British establishment woke up to the continuing danger posed by the blackmail of leading public figures or government employees who were homosexual, and the reform proposals were motivated by that consideration, and not to support equal rights. But the first effort to turn the report into law was resisted by the government and the whole of the Conservative Party, although (positively) it attracted strong support from Labour MPs.

THE 1960S AND 1970S

Ten years later and under a Labour government (during Harold Wilson's second term as prime minister) in 1967, Wolfenden was enacted in the form of the Sexual Offences Act. This legalised same-sex relationships between two men, over the age of twenty-one, in private. The government allowed time for a private member's bill rather than a government bill, which suggests that there was concern regarding the public reaction. The other constraints on same-sex relationships were untouched (some were strengthened) and there were many exemptions to the law, as a result of the many deals the bill's sponsor, Leo Abse MP, had to make with opponents.[10] Numerous ways in which LGB people faced discrimination remained unchallenged. Lesbian and bisexual women were not affected in the same way by the criminal law (which partially explains the male domination of groups like HLRS and CHE, given that their primary focus was the age of consent), but they faced the dual problems of prejudice based on both sexuality and gender, resulting in both social and institutional denial of equal rights across all areas of life, work and family, and they had seen no recognition of their struggle for acceptance.

Trans people did not feature at all in these debates and while many felt an affinity for the gay movement, this was as much down to a feeling of being similarly isolated, friendless and widely misunderstood as to having common objectives. It would be a while before trans people created their own organisations to support individual members (for example, to seek out gender reassignment surgery that was extremely hard to obtain in Britain) and to campaign for rights. The Beaumont Society was set up as a support group in 1966.

The decision by a majority of trans people to ally with LGB people during the coming decades would go on to contribute significantly to the victories achieved by both groups.

The many parliamentarians who believed that the Sexual Offences Act had finally dealt with the issue and that it would now go away were in for a surprise. The 1967 act did not represent equality, and many people within the LGBT communities, including CHE which replaced the HLRS in 1969 and emerged as a dominant campaigning voice, were not prepared to tolerate this. What the act actually achieved, contrary to the intentions of many of those who voted it into law, was to raise the public profile of the issue of lesbian and gay rights to one fit for political debate, to challenge the unequal status of a whole social group, and to allow a modest but important step in enabling LGBT people to speak for themselves as a result of the campaign and the publicity around it. Far from putting the question to bed, it inspired people to believe it was now possible to go further. It had also informed and gained the active support of numerous Labour Party parliamentarians and supporters, amongst whom it was seen as an issue of social justice. This raised awareness re-imported the question into the broader labour movement. CHE prepared a draft bill for homosexual equality that it promoted to politicians in the hope that a progressive government might enact it; this was the first (and not the last) attempt to prepare a blueprint for equal legal rights around which the groups could organise campaigning and work to obtain commitments of support from public figures.

In the aftermath, then, of this act, that represented historic but limited legal progress, CHE continued to work both to challenge many outstanding inequalities, and to provide a much needed support network for homosexual people. CHE groups were set up in many towns and cities, alongside the existing (sub)culture of bars and clubs which were usually the only places where lesbian and gay people could meet one another with a degree of safety and privacy, although they continued periodically to be subject to police raids. It was one of the negative side effects of the Sexual Offences Act that the new older legal limits on gay sex actually encouraged greater police attempts to catch gay men in particular acting outside of the law, and some police chiefs rejoiced in their ability to arrest and expose 'perverts' who overstepped what was allowed by the 1967 act.

It was, however, just such a police raid that provoked the next step forward, this time as a result of one that took place in the US, when the New York police raided the Stonewall bar in June 1969. The predominantly trans clientele fought back, this time leading to a riot which inspired participants and supporters to create the Gay Liberation Front (GLF). A British version was established in November 1970, by activists who rejected what they saw as the too-polite, quiet lobbying approach of CHE. In 1972, the first Gay Pride march took place in London. This was 'in your face' liberationist struggle, emerging from the same background as: youth movements against the Vietnam War; struggles by feminists against sexism and for women's liberation; and black people challenging racism, following the lead of the older civil rights movement in the USA.

For those marching at Gay Pride, the slogan was 'gay is good' and the message was: we are not asking for favours, we demand our liber-ation. One of the key demands that GLF placed on its supporters was 'coming out', seen as a critical step both in achieving self-respect and identity, and in challenging oppressive society itself. Many other lesbians and gay men continued to reject this approach, and GLF as an organisation with no formal structure and no official leaders had a very short existence, but its ideas were far reaching and activated new generations of campaigners.

Some of these more 'in your face' campaigners were also workers who were active in the trade union movement, just as many of the members of CHE and its local groups were workers and members of trade unions. From this time in the early 1970s, it is possible to trace in an unbroken chain a series of battles: first the fight to gain trade unions' recognition that the oppression of LGBT people was a legitimate trade union concern; then to get the unions to offer their LGBT members the same individual support as was the entitlement of all trade union members; then to get them to campaign publicly for equality, a task in which they would make a critical difference. From the outside, this may have looked like an improbable outcome from how things stood in 1970. But the people who undertook the struggle shared with Edward Carpenter a faith in the inherent commitment of the labour movement to equality, fairness and social justice, which would triumph. They were right to have this commitment.

NOTES

1. There are many excellent studies, such as: John Boswell, *The Marriage of Likeness: Same-Sex Unions in Pre-Modern Europe*, London: Harper Collins, 1994; Alan Bray, *Homosexuality in Renaissance England*, London: Gay Men's Press, 1982; Kent Gerard, Gert Hekma (eds), *The Pursuit of Sodomy. Male Homosexuality in Renaissance and Enlightenment Europe*, New York: Harrington Park Press, 1988; and Michael Goodich, *The Unmentionable Vice: Homosexuality in the Later Medieval Period*, Dorchester: Dorset Press, 1979.

2. For more on these pioneers, see: J. Lauritsen and D. Thorstad, *The Early Homosexual Rights Movement (1864-1935)*, New York: Times Change Press, 1974. Two of Bernstein's articles were translated by Angela Clifford in *Bernstein on Homosexuality. Articles from 'Die Neue Zeit' 1895 and 1898*, Belfast: Athol Books, 1977.

3. See my *Sodom, Gomorrah and the New Jerusalem: Labour and Lesbian and Gay Rights from Edward Carpenter to Today*, London: Labour Campaign for Lesbian and Gay Rights, 2006. Carpenter's *The Intermediate Sex* was reprinted with other works in Noël Greig (ed.), *Edward Carpenter Selected Writings, Vol. 1: Sex*, London: GMP Publishers, 1984. Sadly, this was the only volume published. There is now an excellent biography of him: Sheila Rowbotham, *Edward Carpenter. A Life of Liberty and Love*, London/New York: Verso, 2008.

4. In *The Labour Magazine*, October 1924, p243-5.

5. M. Baker, *Our Three Selves. A Life of Radclyffe Hall*, GMP: Heinemann, London, 1985, pp205, 223-35, 237. I am indebted to Angela Mason for the reference. Sadly, the book does not identify the source for these letters.

6. As reflected in a letter from Engels to Marx having seen a pamphlet by Ulrichs, in 1869, quoted in Graham Robb, *Strangers: Homosexual Love in the Nineteenth Century*, London: Picador, 2003, p170.

7. Lauritsen and Thorstad, *op. cit.*, pp38-45. There is an extensive literature on the Nazi persecution of homosexuals. See Heinz Heger, trans. David Fernbach, *The Men with Pink Triangles*, London: Gay Men's Press, 1980; Günter Grau, trans. Patrick Camiller, *Hidden Holocaust. Gay and Lesbian Persecution in Germany 1933-45*, London: Cassell, 1993; Richard Plant, *The Pink Triangle. The Nazi War Against Homosexuals*, Edinburgh/New York: Mainstream Publishing, 1987. Hirschfeld himself moved to France (where he died in 1935).

8. For a thorough survey based on Soviet sources, see D. Healey, *Homosexual Desire in Revolutionary Russia: The Regulation of Sexual and Gender Dissent*, Chicago: University of Chicago Press, 2001.

9. I recall a leading anti-fascist publication in the 1970s 'exposing' the homosexuality of a leading figure in the National Front, for example.

In this they were continuing a trend followed by some German socialist papers that used Röhm's homosexuality to bait the Nazis in the early 1930s.

10. The parliamentary battle is well described in Stephen Jeffrey-Poulter, *Peers, Queers and Commons. The Struggle for Gay Law Reform from 1950 to the Present*, London/New York: Routledge, 1991.

2

Coming together in the 1970s

The 1970s was a decade of ferment, in which many of the traditionally accepted norms of society were challenged. There was a new movement, for the first time in British history, for people to come out, identifying themselves as having a different sexuality or gender identity. While the numbers of people involved were small when compared with the feminist movements, or even fewer when seen against the millions of trade union members involved in industrial action in these years, the challenge this movement posed was distinctive, and the horrified reaction it provoked in many quarters raised the stakes still higher. If at the beginning of this decade the possibility of the trade union movement being involved in any way with the movement for LGBT rights appeared a fantasy, by the end of the 1970s, the foundations had been laid for extending the equality agenda of the labour movement, which would come to fruition in the 1980s.

The world of the 1970s was very different from that of the twenty-first century. Idealistic young people in Britain were inspired by the youth rebellions of the late 1960s in the USA, and by the events of Paris (May 1968), which were emulated in other West European cities. And there were many causes in the UK for them to support, from national liberation movements challenging right wing dictators in Latin America or Apartheid regimes in Africa, to the continuing war being waged by the US government in Indochina. Across the western world, feminists were using many channels to demand women's liberation. In Britain (as in the USA) black people were organising in local communities against pervasive racism – particularly virulent in the form of neo-Nazi groups like the National Front – but also faced every day at work and in the streets. Laws passed, such as the Sex Discrimination Act and the Race Relations Act, recognised the problems of discrimination and prejudice without eliminating the root causes of them.

The trade unions were at a peak in terms of membership and were at a high point of struggle for better pay and working conditions. By 1980, there were eleven million members of unions affiliated to the Trades Union Congress (TUC). Governments had to make time to talk to trade union leaders, and Labour governments in particular tried to work out policy together with them. Massive demonstrations of workers protested against any laws designed to weaken unions' ability to act on their members' behalves, and did so successfully on a number of occasions.[1]

But the main issue for the trade unions in the 1970s was pay: the underlying problem was high inflation, which continually ate into workers' living standards. One of the most well-organised and militant unions, the National Union of Mineworkers (NUM), already successful in strike action in 1972, campaigned for a pay rise the following year. This was based on a recommendation by an independent commission following the earlier dispute, and took the form of a ban on overtime that led Conservative Prime Minister Ted Heath to impose a three-day week on industry in December 1973. In response, the miners voted for an all-out strike. Heath called a general election, asking people 'who governs?', and lost (February 1974).[2] The miners got the pay rise they had been recommended. Organised labour had demonstrated its power.

CHE AND GLF

This was the context in which those working to remove the inequalities faced by lesbian, gay, bisexual and trans people had to place their strategies for achieving success. More than one way forward was available, and the choice between these might be quite personal, depending on one's own life experiences, or on a political philosophy, or on where one lived. The leaders of the Campaign for Homosexual Equality (CHE) pursued a strategy of legal change, which they aimed to achieve by convincing politicians and those people who were thought to influence public opinion, of the justice of the cause, and defeating prejudice with information. Establishing a method to bring this about was not easy, given deep-rooted opposition, a reluctance to even use the word 'homosexuality', a hostile media, fear of voters' reactions even among already supportive Liberal and Labour politicians, and the absence of strong allies whose voices might help swing the balance in favour of reform and progress. CHE continued to work for its objectives throughout the 1970s, but it also had to find a way to maintain its existence at a time when even finding a venue for a meeting might lead to refusals from the owners or violent hostility from local newspaper editors. But they pressed on. Members were signed up, which provided the finance to keep CHE running. Local groups were established, and at their meetings, people could meet others of the same sexuality in relative safety. By 1972, there were already thirteen local CHE groups in London alone and there was one in each of the major British cities. CHE groups provided an essential facility enabling LGBT people to come together. There were ways in which these people (and gay men in particular) had been able to meet for (often anonymous) sex, and these continued. But you could not build a movement for social and political change by cottaging,[3] and the CHE structure not only helped people meet socially, thereby creating a lifeline for isolated individuals by demonstrating that they were not alone, but also enabled the kind of local campaigning – letters to local papers, trying to meet local politicians, offering to send speakers to other organisations – that gradually wins allies and supporters. Campaigning at a national level was the prerogative of the CHE executive committee, elected at annual conferences. For CHE's leaders and many of its active members, the right approach was seen to be to convince others that homosexuals represented no threat but were respectable citizens. At the annual conference, a draft bill to remedy the defects of the 1967 Act was created that CHE hoped would be taken up by Wilson's new government in 1974. Initial signs from this government were hopeful: those who had been reformers in 1967 wished to make amends for the compromises that had been required in order to win that vote, and the injustices that these had led to. They thus brought forward proposals, including one to reduce the male age of consent (albeit only to eighteen). However, this was blocked by a majority in the House of Lords in 1978, at the same time as a major backlash against (what we would now call) LGBT rights was underway.

During this time, CHE also identified the importance of winning over trade unions and took conscious steps that through a number of avenues encouraged and promoted the creation of union lesbian and gay groups (as most then were called, though many groups simply subsumed everyone under the title 'gay'), as discussed below.

To many of the activists who embraced liberation via the Gay Liberation Front (GLF), the CHE approach of making oneself appear respectable in order to get listened to effectively amounted to a betrayal of the cause. The GLF programme consisted of a charter of demands formulated when the group was established in November 1970. These were focussed around the assertion that 'gay is good', which directly challenged the common belief in the opposite. Practical campaigning issues raised in the charter, not surprisingly, were remarkably similar to those championed by CHE: ending discrimination by the law, by employers, and – a particular target in these times – by psychiatrists, who were attempting to 'cure' people of their homosexuality; as well as demanding the freedom to meet, to advertise, to hold hands and kiss in public. These demands were taken to the public not via politely argued letters in the columns of the local newspaper, but by public protest, for which the first Pride march in the UK in London, in June 1972, set the tone. In that year, the paper *Gay News* also appeared for the first time; it became, as it proudly proclaimed on its masthead, 'the world's largest circulation newspaper for homosexuals', appearing fortnightly and serving as a vital source of information for many people.

GLF also initiated the team that went on to launch the telephone advice service Gay Switchboard, which started in 1973. Denis Lemon (who became editor of *Gay News*) and Martin Corbett were key figures in this. John Lindsay, founder of the Gay Librarians Group, was central to the process of collating the information given to people who called the line. He remembers that the advice given at the outset to LGBT callers with employment problems was to seek help from CHE or Friend (a national support group for lesbians and gay men), not from a trade union.

GLF initially functioned through weekly open meetings held in Notting Hill in London, but the difficulty in achieving anything effective with no formal structures, in a room of up to 400 people, rapidly led to its abandonment. Andrew Lumsden, one of GLF's founders, wrote that 'Wednesday in Notting Hill has become more of an admin-cum-cruising ground than a policy meeting for a movement'. Lesbian members walked out, writing that 'sexism within the movement had pissed off a lot of us to the point where it was felt that working with gay men, who are not infrequently as oppressive as their straight counterparts, was [...] just so much wastage of time and energy'. They decided instead to participate in the women's movement. CHE, too, faced repeated difficulty making itself relevant to or comfortable for lesbian and bisexual women.[4]

Within a year GLF structures changed to local groups with a central team of volunteers working from a basement office in London's Caledonian Road, under Housmans bookshop. They coordinated and dealt with enquiries, and produced a weekly news diary. Interestingly, the same issue of the GLF newsletter *Ink News* that reported these issues at GLF meetings also carried a page-long article discussing (sympathetically) the 1972 Miners' Strike and the closure of the Saltley coke works by flying pickets from the NUM.[5] This was the type of militant political action most likely to appeal to many GLF activists. Many GLF members were young people, not in paid employment, who had rejected CHE's commitment to 'respectability'.

Not only did lesbians find it difficult to work inside GLF with gay men, but so did trans people. In a telling echo of the arguments still being heard in the twenty-first century, a leaflet entitled 'Transvestites Transsexuals Come Out' pointed out that the trans person who was among those arrested at the GLF disruption of a Festival of Light event (see below), was the only one facing a prison sentence. The (anonymous) leaflet went on 'whenever we bring up the subject at a gay lib meeting people complain we're wasting their valuable time', and 'A transvestite or transgender should not have to demonstrate or prove to lesbians, individually or collectively, that she's a sister'.[6]

The open appearance of LGBT people in public and their demands for equality inevitably stirred up opposition. Seeing themselves as the last bulwark of decency against a tide of filth, the Festival of Light (FoL), Christian fundamentalists whose spokesperson was the charismatic and prejudiced Mary Whitehouse, campaigned vigorously against anything and anyone who dared to question their profoundly exclusionary views, labelled by their victims as 'Victorian values'. While the BBC, with its sometimes daringly radical programming including occasional gay content was a favourite FoL target, 'queers' in general were another even easier group to attack, given their lack of popular acceptance by society in general. The appeal to defend 'family values' and to prevent the 'corruption' of young people found widespread backing, in precisely the anticipated locations – the occupants of the House of Lords, who dutifully prevented any further legal progress for two decades. But these narratives were also popular among newspaper owners, who relished the chance to sell papers by continuing to publish anti-gay stories, especially where they could expose prominent individuals. The FoL achieved one of their goals when in 1977, they had Denis Lemon and *Gay News* prosecuted for the anachronistic offence of blasphemous libel, and, despite a vigorous defence campaign run by LGBT activists,[7] succeeded. Lemon and the paper were found guilty and fined. Lemon received a (suspended) prison sentence which was quashed on appeal, but the verdict was upheld. A community fund-raising campaign paid the fines and the paper continued to publish until 1983.

GLF's list of demands had included ending discrimination in employment. They soon had a cause through which they could show their solidarity with the labour movement: the Industrial Relations Bill, which was designed to reduce union rights and establish an Industrial Relations court. The TUC (led by Vic Feather) was totally opposed and a major national demonstration took place on 12 January 1971. For the first time, the GLF banner was brought out in solidarity with trade unionists. Angela Mason remembers crosstalk such as 'we don't want you behind us' which was ironic since GLF was indeed right at the back of the protest.[8] However, their partici-pation did confirm that GLF members saw the left as allies.

Another GLF campaign in the world of work was directed against newspaper owners. In 1973, a GLF working group organised a campaign aimed at encouraging print workers to challenge their bosses to write non-oppressive copy about LGBT people. The GLF produced a leaflet – as usual, a duplicated low quality typewritten page of A4 – that mentioned several appalling newspaper stories as examples of crude misrepresentations of gay people (plate 3).[9] The leaflet was distributed to people working on Fleet Street, including in pubs at the end of the working day. The newspapers covered by the leaflet were *The Sun*, which had a policy of not reporting any GLF actions and not printing letters discussing homosexuality, the *News of the World* ('these creatures who children should be warned against'), the *Spectator* for celebrating the death of Noel Coward, the *Evening Standard* for printing 'rants against queers' by Lord Arran (who was actually a supporter of law reform), and *The Guardian* and

The Times for printing without comment articles on chemical castration, or failing to report GLF actions without insulting comments. The leaflet wisely added that they were not asking workers to risk their jobs in pursuit of this action. The impact of the campaign is not recorded although Angela Mason recalls no hostility.[10] It may be that isolated LGBT print workers were alerted to GLF's existence by seeing the leaflet. That GLF believed print workers could influence the content of what their newspapers printed suggests a certain naivety, but the decision to approach workers was encouraging.

THE ROLE OF THE 'FAR LEFT'

Print workers were organised; their unions for the most part were specialist craft unions with some superficial resemblance to the medieval guild, very effective at protecting their own. But if anyone reading the GLF leaflet had asked a shop steward about it, they would probably not have had a positive response, even if the workplace representative was a member of the Communist Party. One of the papers cited among the villains in the GLF leaflet was, shockingly, the Communist Party's *Morning Star,* which had previously described the aristocracy as pervaded with 'fornication, sodomy and drunkenness' – as the GLF quoted. But, by 1973, the parties and groups on the British left were beginning to pay attention to the LGBT movement, often at the behest of their own LGBT members. They had to first shake off the legacy left by Stalin's legislation and the ideology behind it that saw homosexuality as a bourgeois perversion that would disappear with the socialist revolution. The Communist Party of Great Britain (CPGB) finally adopted a comprehensive pro-gay policy in 1976.

Organisations originating in the minority Trotskyist opposition to Stalin also took time before challenging this part of their inheritances.[11] LGBT members of the Young Socialists (the youth wing of the Labour Party) who tried to raise the topic were denounced by members of the dominant Militant tendency who ran the YS. National Association of Teachers in Further and Higher Education (NATFHE) activist Bob Cant joined the International Socialists (IS, the forerunner of the Socialist Workers Party, SWP) in 1973 and became part of the IS gay group but failed to get his branch to discuss the subject. Around the time Bob left (1976), the (then) SWP recognised the issue, and switched to becoming an active promoter of lesbian and gay rights across the trade union movement (a process well remembered by GLF activist John Lindsay who joined the party in that year).[12] The SWP's trade union members, organised in 'rank and file' groups at this time,[13] were of great assistance to fledgling LGBT trade union groups in getting established and moving on to being recognised. It is important to remember that while groups like the CP (by far the largest of the organisations to the left of Labour) and groups from the Trotskyist tradition like the Militant, SWP, Workers' Revolutionary Party and the smaller International Marxist Group had, at best, some thousands of members, and often only in the hundreds, their talented, committed and hardworking members often achieved elected office in workplaces and unions and could often drive policies and practices forward quite disproportionately to the actual numbers of their groups.

UNION ORGANISING BEGINS

Nalgay

Meanwhile, amidst these frequent conflicts being waged in the courts, on the streets, in debating chambers and meeting halls, the first trade union LGBT groups came into existence. Early pioneers were often people who had been active in CHE groups, and those who came through GLF; the pressing necessity of raising LGBT rights in a workplace setting was obvious to these campaigners. At the very start, people may have thought that the only way to organise in the workplace was to link up with one of the existing lesbian and gay organisations, and the CHE executive committee had discussed writing to trade unions about challenging workplace discrimination as early as June 1973 (although this project took some years to come to fruition).[14] Meanwhile, union members were already taking up these issues. John Lindsay recalled seeing an article in the newsletter of Camden National and Local Government Officers' Association (NALGO) talking about CHE as early as 1972. Camden NALGO, with a deserved reputation as a large, militant and progressive branch, continued to be a significant contributor to the progress of LGBT rights inside that union. Following a strikingly similar trajectory, self-organisation of LGBT workers in the National Union of

Teachers (NUT) began with the setting up of the Gay Teachers Group (GTG) in the first years of the 1970s. Although formally open to members of all the teaching unions, its membership came to be predominantly drawn from the NUT, although there was also an important presence of members from NATFHE.

However, with members from local government, the health service and other (then) public services such as gas, NALGO was the first union to see people coming together to set up a group and then a national network of LGBT members. The first (informal) meeting for the NALGO group 'Nalgay' was organised in Nottingham, through the work of Howard Hyman, a member of the NALGO Nottingham Health Service branch, who had written a letter announcing it to the union journal *Public Service*. *Nalgay News* No. 1 was dated October 1974 (plate 1), published in his name, and was a single sheet of text announcing that it was 'for all homosexuals, bisexuals, transvestites, transsexuals and any other sexuals', adding 'except child molesters or rapists'. This statement, the first public announcement of a trade union LGBT group, was careful to distinguish its membership from those too often associated by the media (and public perception); gay men (in particular) were all too often imagined into the same category as paedophiles. The other point to note was that the first NALGO gay group was deliberately presented as being for all those people who would now fall within the rubric of LGBT+ (see Chapter Seven). This was an inclusive approach that was quickly abandoned, and would afterwards take decades to recover.

Notes of the next meeting (the first formal gathering) that took place in Nottingham on 30 November 1974 show that just eleven people were present. These were the president of CHE, two members of the Transsexual Action Organisation, a social worker, a member of the Open University Gaysoc, one member each from London and Northampton and four from Nottingham. Despite the lack of numbers, the meeting set out a clear agenda for moving ahead. It intended to approach the union's general secretary to seek protection against discrimination at work, and at the same time a motion would be drafted for branches to send to the union's annual conference. Announcements of the formation of Nalgay would be sent to CHE, *Gay News* and the Scottish Minorities Group (the organisation in Scotland that was the equivalent of CHE in England and Wales). It was decided that anyone seeking practical support would be referred on to Friend or CHE. Finally, an article would be drafted for *Public Service*, and a request made for a stall at the annual conference.[15]

Early members of the group included people from the far left as well as from the CHE tradition (and both 'wings' of the early gay rights movement), and John McKay and Lionel Starling were prominent – John's name would feature in many LGBT initiatives over the years to follow. Another who joined Nalgay at the beginning was Peter Roscoe,[16] also a member of IS, who worked as a social worker in London and participated in the quickly established London branch of Nalgay. He recalls that younger members wanted to remove Howard, but despite this, he continued to edit *Nalgay News* for some years to come. It is through his meticulous reports that the progress and the obstacles faced – and overcome – can most easily be traced.

Within months, membership stood at more than 100 and Nalgay's letter to the general secretary, Geoffrey Drain, produced a positive response, which was printed in *Nalgay News*: 'the Association's policy in relation to discrimination is one of opposition, whatever the grounds'.[17] However, there had been problems with the main union journal, *Public Service*, which had refused to publish an advertisement for the gay group in March 1975.[18] No doubt assisted by members of Nalgay who were also in the IS/SWP, to help win support for the national conference motion, the group decided to enlist the support of one of the political factions operating within the national union, the NALGO Action Group, which was the name adopted by the 'rank and file' group in NALGO. The decision of the journal editor was reversed and Nalgay placed a notice in *Public Service* of its first national conference, which led to a steady stream of enquiries from union members.

The conference took place on 25 October 1975, and those attending included Mike Rowland, representing the Gay Labour Group (GLG), and Mike Notcutt, who was struggling to set up an equivalent group in the National Union of Public Employees (NUPE), another large public sector union. The conference made the structure of the group more democratic, by electing a steering committee. It also agreed the text of the motion that it intended to send to the NALGO national conference, calling on the union to ensure its negotiators strove to add sexual orientation to employers' equal opportunities policies.[19] Mike Blick, who became NALGO's first out gay president in 1991, proposed the motion at the Nalgay meeting, from which it was circulated to branches expected to be sympathetic, and he spoke to it at conference.[20] The motion, submitted by the Camden NALGO branch, was carried in June 1976, and NALGO became the first significant national trade union to adopt a policy on lesbian and gay rights, at least on paper.

Nalgay members had thus secured the support of their union within eighteen months of the group's establishment, a remarkable achievement. A number of factors can be seen as having led to this rapid progress. Evidently, the sympathy of the union's leader, the general secretary, was of great importance – he had also intervened to tell Howard Hyman's branch that it was fine for Nalgay to use the union name in its title. But the political backing of activists was also significant, not only the Nalgo Action Group (the only one identified in the records) but also the more mainstream political currents from the CHE tradition, as epitomised by Howard Hyman himself, and the support brought by people in the Gay Labour Group (who were from the same background). Perhaps the most important factor, however, was the clear line of action agreed by all the activists in the group, whichever part of the LGBT movement they identified with. The steering committee elected in 1976 was a politically inclusive group (but sadly lacked gender balance) comprising Howard Hyman, John McKay, Alan Deighton and Raymond Corvello. Winning the vote at a union national conference was far from a certain outcome, but it seems likely that the political and social composition of NALGO activists was such that they were more likely to have rejected rampant popular and media prejudices against gay people than in other unions at the time. That there was some opposition among NALGO members was only to be expected, as this would reflect the popular mood, but evidently it was already a minority; all the members I interviewed who were open and active at this time have confirmed this. For example, in the same year, Richard Webster reported that the Nottingham County Council branch had agreed to allow Nalgay representation on the branch executive committee, with just four votes against. He wrote in the newsletter that he was now convinced that he had the support of the entire branch.[21]

Nalgay then faced the challenge of turning this policy into action, and sustaining interest in their meetings and campaigns. Peter

Roscoe noted how attendance at what were meant to be London-wide meetings dropped to a mere handful. These small numbers limited what work could be done, with a consequent further drop off of interest. John McKay set about reactivating work in London with a successful re-launch of the group at regional level in July 1977, and the institution of regular meetings. Nalgay had, from the start, relied on the voluntary work of a network of regional convenors and their names and telephone numbers were published in the newsletters. Initially, these had been the activists who had turned up to meetings. By 1976, they were listed on a regional basis: London and the South East was covered by Gerry Edwards, the South by Sally Dee, Wales, Central and Eastern England by Barry Hillman, Scotland by David Samson – and the North West by Alan Horsfall, the stalwart initiator of the legal reform work of the Homosexual Law Reform Society (HLRS) and then CHE.[22]

Tower Hamlets Council, 1976

The level of support for NALGO members was put to a very real test in the London Borough of Tower Hamlets, in 1975. The raw facts can be set out most simply in a timeline:[23] Ian Davies was arrested for 'gross indecency' in a public toilet in West London in a classic act of police entrapment. The next morning (9 October 1975) he was fined £25 at Marlborough Street magistrates' court. Davies was a senior social worker for Tower Hamlets, managing one of seven social work areas, and had worked for the council without complaint for twelve years. Following what turned out to be bad advice from a friend, he pleaded guilty and decided to inform his manager of the conviction. On 5 November, he was sacked by a disciplinary panel (and re-employed at a lower grade in another department which did not involve contact with the public). At this panel, he was accompanied by a NALGO officer and they lodged an appeal, which the council refused to hear, and, after several weeks of delay, they also refused to allow the matter to be taken to arbitration. At this point, Davies decided to take a claim to the Industrial Tribunal (IT, now called the Employment Tribunal, ET) with the backing of the union. Tower Hamlets asked the IT to adjourn the hearing, but this was refused, and on Friday 16 July 1976, the council was found guilty of unfair dismissal and (unusually) ordered to reinstate Davies in his former role. The Tribunal reluctantly agreed to a council request for a month in which to consider their position. On Monday 9 August, the Administration Committee of the council voted by a majority of one – eight votes to seven – not to accept the IT recommendation. Had the claim been one of discrimination, it would have failed, there being no protection in law against it, but the Tribunal had found the council's procedures to be unfair.

Over the following days, thanks to the firm support of the union, the issue exploded into a full dispute. The very next day, Tuesday 10 August 1976, Davies's team of social workers met and voted for immediate strike action, and the branch executive endorsed the strike later that day, agreeing to call a full branch meeting. The striking members prepared a petition and union reps were asked to explain what had happened to their members across the council, which they did in a series of meetings. After the weekend, strike action was also taken in three other social work areas, and a petition with 665 signatures was presented to councillors. On 19 August, a meeting of the branch executive donated £200 to the strike fund, set up a strike committee and instructed all NALGO representatives to consult members to see if there was support for extending strike action. The strike committee prepared leaflets explaining the facts and a poster lobbying the NALGO Metropolitan District and the national executive to argue for official backing. Meanwhile, a meeting of the whole social services department had agreed to call for a one day all-out strike. A motion to this effect was prepared for a full members' meeting at Bethnal Green Town Hall on 18 August, where it was proposed by branch chair Barry Howe. Also present were representatives of NUPE and the National Council for Civil Liberties (NCCL). Howe's speech covered the failure of the council to distinguish between homosexuality and pederasty, and referred to the union's very recent national conference policy. One person spoke against the motion, defending the council's right not to employ someone with a 'particular sexual orientation' who must have a 'certain attitude to life'. Other speakers stressed how the council's rejection of an Industrial Tribunal ruling was a fundamental trade union issue. Ian Davies himself spoke, pointing out that homosexuals were treated differently by the law, praising the support of his colleagues and stating his strengthened determination to fight for equality. The closing speech was from another member of his team expressing total support for Davies. The overwhelming majority of the 270 members present voted in support of the motion.[24] Within days the Metropolitan (i.e. London region) district council had voted (by 150 votes to one) to support the action and the NALGO national executive had made the dispute official, supporting a strike on 3 September and subsequently a rota of strikes if the council did not back down. Many hundreds of pounds were donated to the strike fund by other NALGO branches and by individuals (plate 2).

With the involvement of national union officials, negotiations took place with council leaders on 2 September, and they agreed to recommend reinstatement to the Administration Committee if the strike was called off. The union agreed to defer action and reinstatement was accepted by the committee on 7 September. It was a total victory; the council insisted on the caveat that Davies would not do personal casework, but this had not been part of his job previously.

Much can be learnt by looking at the details of what happened during these few weeks. These events at Tower Hamlets Council attracted widespread press attention. Few council workers or residents of the borough can have been unaware that the original cause of the dispute was a case of what the Sexual Offences Act 1967 still called 'gross indecency' – something that (as was regularly pointed out in some of the coverage) would not have been illegal if it had involved a heterosexual act. Every national newspaper reported the strike and its roots. Most space was devoted by the *Daily Telegraph*, in which the reports were mainly factual, but on the day before the branch meeting (16 August) it devoted editorial space to the dispute and ended by asking whether, if the strikers could not see the council's point of view, 'are they fit to be social workers?' BBC Radio Four's *Today* programme interviewed councillor John Riley, chair of the Administration Committee, on the same day who said: 'We are worried that he could corrupt anybody that required help. Rather than help them, he could corrupt them'. Similarly ignorant and prejudiced views were occasionally expressed in letters published in local papers and in a few cases were stated by other social workers, following articles supporting Davies in professional journals including *Social Worker* and *Community Care*. As expected, left-wing papers (*Morning Star, Socialist Worker, Militant*) carried pieces backing the strike, and London-wide publication *Time Out* printed a feature article entitled 'Hamlets Homophobia' giving full backing to Ian Davies, and quoting Councillor Riley again:

> he was concerned at a gay person 'being employed in a capacity where he's dealing with children. A normal sort of person wouldn't get involved in that sort of offence [...] As far as I'm concerned he needs help himself'.

This article, and others, further reported on the fact that another employee, a lavatory attendant who had been convicted of the same offence within weeks of the Davies case, had escaped with a reprimand thanks to the pressure of his union, NUPE. The *Hackney Gazette* (issue of 7 September) printed a column asking whether 'in these enlightened days [...] should a man with homosexual tendencies be victimised for this in his job. Or a woman, for that matter, who may have lesbian inclinations?' and concluded with the resounding answer 'to banish any reliable worker because he may be homosexual is a completely misguided rule in a modern society'. *Gay News* (issue 103) welcomed Davies's reinstatement in a front page leading article, which pointed out (using Davies's own words) that the condition adopted by Tower Hamlets (that his work would not involve a personal caseload) was meaningless because that had always been his job role.[25]

Most industrial disputes are messy – people approach them with different viewpoints and take part in them with a variety of motives and this one was no different. Talking to branch officers and representatives at the time, and to Ian Davies himself, it was evident that a similar variety of reasons lay behind the massive support branch members gave to Ian. It is significant that there had not been any activity by members of Nalgay inside this branch to prepare the ground. The branch had a reputation for militancy. But there were 1300 members in the branch and many working in other parts of the council workforce who did not necessarily share this. Among these, branch representatives reported that they sometimes decided to emphasise the issue of the council's rejection of the Industrial Tribunal recommendation as a basic attack on employment rights, rather than the gay rights issue. Howard Hyman, writing of the dispute and the victory in *Nalgay News* a month later, saw it as a victory won on this basis 'so it cannot really be seen as a victory which would help other [lesbian or gay] social workers [facing discrimination]'. The national attention paid to the issue undoubtedly did advance awareness of the arguments involved, and was a great morale-booster for campaigners across the trade union movement. The case featured in a motion backing Nalgay that was carried at the NALGO Action Group conference aiming to build on the successful outcome, and Ian Davies featured at CHE's employment conference in April 1977.[26]

This case remains the only example of a trade union branch organising at first unofficial, but later official strike action in support of a member victimised because he had been convicted of an offence that applied only to homosexual men. The branch officers, and Ian Davies himself, had worked to win backing at all levels of the union, and from other members of the branch, and had succeeded without any significant opposition. This was trade unionism at its best. But there were some respects in which Howard Hyman's misgivings were to be found to be only too accurate, and trade unions at this time were faced with several other cases of victimisation by employers, in which the outcome was not so positive. A common feature of many of these cases was that the worker was employed in a profession involving contact with 'vulnerable people' – as social workers were – and especially children. Underlying homophobia asserted that being LGBT meant being unnatural, evil, or at least undesirable, and thus that children and young people were vulnerable to being corrupted or recruited to an unhealthy lifestyle. This prejudice was deeply rooted in popular consciousness, and similar prejudices continue to the present day, of course. Although surveys suggest they have now been reduced to a minority, throughout the decades from the beginning of the movement for LGBT rights to the end of the millennium they would be repeated thousands of times in the pages of local or national media, again and again from the benches of both Houses of Parliament; it is important to understand that the views expressed in Tower Hamlets by (Labour) councillor Riley were shared by millions of people, that these included large numbers of working people and, inevitably, trade union members, and that those who stood up to them and eventually won were taking on a formidable range of foes. That the members of Tower Hamlets NALGO did so deserves recognition as a historic action. The branch leaders and activists – and especially Davies himself, who refused to accept his demotion, which would have been the easy step often followed by others who found themselves in a similar predicament – stand out as modest and unassuming but genuine champions of equality, recognising that an injury to one is an injury to all.

Teachers' unions and the Gay Teachers' Group

LGBT teachers form the second group of workers who had to confront the prevalent opinion that young people were at risk of being converted into homosexuals if they encountered an openly homosexual adult at school or college. This prejudice is rooted in the belief that even if people who were LGBT should not face discrimination, it remains an inferior option, and that children could be seduced into it even against their 'nature' (the debate about how sexuality emerges remains unresolved, of course). Sadly, this continues to be a problem, demonstrating that the battle against prejudice has not yet been won. Back in the mid-1970s, protecting children was the battle cry of a popular majority, at least insofar as it was reflected in the overwhelming majority of the media.

The Gay Teachers' Group (GTG) was formed under the leadership of Paul Patrick (who had come through GLF) and Peter Bradley in late 1974, following the announcement in *Gay News* (issue of 18 July 1974) from the head of the Inner London Education Authority (ILEA), Sir Ashley Bramall, that the Authority would not discriminate against homosexual teachers. Shortly after this, Patrick received a letter from John Warburton reporting that he had been refused employment in December 1974 because he was openly gay. Warburton (who was not initially a member of the NUT) had simply responded to pupils' questions about his sexuality, but was now being told he could only work if he signed an undertaking never to discuss it again. He had refused to do so. Bramall, despite the ILEA's announcement, refused to meet a delegation from GTG, which then decided on a campaign that involved a number of actions: petitions for teachers and non-teachers to sign to express their support for Warburton, motions to union branches, and gaining publicity for the issue. 2000 teachers signed the petition that was presented to the ILEA full council meeting on 24 June 1975, and it was accompanied by a vigorous picket of London's County Hall where the meeting took place. The issue was referred to a sub-committee which decided (the following April, 1976) that teachers should be allowed to respond openly to 'the natural curiosity and anxiety that this topic [homosexuality] will arouse'.[27] But John Warburton, who was by then training as a librarian, was still not accepted as suitable to be a teacher. Many branches of his union, the NUT, supported the motion backing him, but the union officers, including deputy general secretary Doug McAvoy, advised him to accept the ILEA conditions. There was clearly still some way to go before this body recognised that an injury to one is an injury to all.

The dispute was all the more bizarre because at the time it was going on, other teachers and union members working under ILEA's jurisdiction were openly gay at school – including Paul Patrick – and several 'came out' as a result of the campaign, with none of them being required to sign a similar undertaking. One of these was Geoff Hardy, an early member of the GTG, who had been openly gay without any problem at all while teaching at Charlton secondary school from 1975. He was a member of GLF and when a photograph of him picketing a Larry Grayson event was published in the local press, he reports, the subsequent discussion with his pupils was 'fantastic'.[28] Another was Alan Jackson, who taught at the same school in Putney for thirty-three years. He joined GTG at the time of the Warburton case, and was a NUT branch officer as well as being a supporter of the 'rank and file' group. He noted the wide impact of the case and would later play his part in the decisive battles to win full union policy in 1983.[29] ILEA's failure to impose similar constraints on other out teachers suggested that the campaign had registered at least one level of success. Many of the teachers concerned also reported that they had received positive backing from their head teachers, but the ILEA did not budge on Warburton.

One issue faced by the GTG was that it was initially organised only in London, which began to be solved when union activists (almost all from the NUT) set up groups in other cities. One was quickly established in Bristol for the south-west. Tim Lucas, who began teaching in Lewes (Sussex) in 1976, and was already a union branch officer, met Paul Patrick and Peter Bradley, and shared the frustration at the failure of the union properly to support Warburton.[30] Among the plans agreed by the activists was to repeat the successful strategy pursued by Nalgay, and to get a hearing at NUT national conference. This required motions submitted by branches to go through a process of being prioritised for the agenda – there were always more motions submitted than conference time to hear them all. Several attempts would be made to achieve this before success was eventually achieved (see Chapter Three). At about the same time, the capture of control of the Greater London Council and ILEA by a new generation of left-wing Labour Party activists would transform the position of equality in general, and LGBT rights in particular, in Britain's capital city during the 1980s.

Nonetheless, despite continuing successful campaigning through gaining union recognition and active backing during the 1980s and 1990s, it was always a problem that a significant proportion of LGBT teachers refused to be open at work. The individuals who formed the GTG and who would continue campaigning – not just in the NUT, but increasingly in the other teaching unions as well – remained a small minority. The consequent invisibility of LGBT people in so many schools had a negative effect on the ability to challenge homophobic and transphobic attitudes and practices among young people, and made it less likely that heterosexual colleagues would challenge prejudiced statements. This continues to be a problem even today.

Another teaching union where LGBT activists came together at this time was NATFHE (which is now part of the University and College Union, UCU). The gay group in this union was formed in 1975, and within a year had won support at the union's 1976 national conference, supported by the union's 'rank and file' group. However, no publicity was given to the conference policy of support and no action taken to carry it out by the union nationally. It was not until 1980, when there was a GLF-type campaign of actions protesting NATFHE's decision to organise its annual conference in Scarborough, where the Council was known for refusing to host CHE's conference, that a significant change of approach was secured.[31] Once again, this was a union where a higher than usual proportion of the lay member activists came from backgrounds that might encourage them towards radicalism, but problems turning union support into practical backing demonstrated that there was a lack of support and training for union officers. A publication by the Teachers in Further and Higher Education Gay Group (costing 10p), undated (but probably from 1982) (plate 5b) described the experience of two NATFHE members, John Shiers and his partner, when they danced together at Wythenshawe College of Further Education's Christmas social in 1975. They received hostile responses from other members, and were 'investigated' by their employer but found the union branch secretary completely at sea when they were approached for support.[32]

Gay groups in other unions and the support of CHE

Alongside these professional, white collar unions, what was happening in their sister organisations where manual workers formed the predominant membership? The presence of members of NUPE alongside NALGO members in the Tower Hamlets dispute has been mentioned, and a close connection between the two unions was inevitable, if only because they would frequently find themselves negotiating with the same employers in local government and other services. A key figure in the creation of the NUPE Gay Group, known as NUPEGG, was Mike Notcutt, who was also an active member of CHE. He and Lilian Lishman were listed as the contacts for the NUPE group in an undated (possibly 1975) Information Sheet announcing the formation of the group 'to campaign to end discrimination in employment on sexual orientation' and to bring together 'homosexual or bisexual men or women [...] and assist any member victimised or discriminated by an employer or for that matter by the union'. A press release containing the leaflet went on to state 'most NUPE members are of a working class background and as a result will find it exceptionally difficult to "come out" to their friends and colleagues, let alone employer and/or union'. NUPEGG, it stated proudly, 'is the first working class union-based gay group to be formed'. The release was sent to other organisations for publication because NUPE itself had refused to give publicity to the group in its journal, *Public Employee*. The assistant general secretary, Bernard Dix, had replied to their letter saying 'it has never been the policy of the union to assist in the formation of separate groups'.[33]

The references to class in the group's message were significant, of course. One would not find many university-educated workers among NUPE members, but it was not necessarily the case that this made it more difficult for lesbian or gay members to be open than it was for workers in white collar jobs, although the attitude of the union at the time presumably did not encourage it. Among union members, there was no lack of willingness to fight for what they saw as right, as witnessed in spectacular fashion during the public sector pay disputes that led to the 'winter of discontent' in 1979.

NALGAY was happy to provide information about NUPEGG to its members in the hope they might pass it on to NUPE colleagues. The contrast between NUPEGG's experience with *Public Employee* and the routine coverage now provided (through the support of the leadership) by the NALGO journal was stark. This would not be reversed for several years, when another high profile case of employment discrimination – that of Susan Shell – led the NUPE leadership to convert to a much more positive approach (Chapter Three).

Also in 1975, both Nalgay and NUPEGG pressed the TUC itself to include sexual orientation in the model equal opportunities clause it had adopted for unions to use. *Nalgay News* No. 6 printed the reply to the group's letter on this topic. In it, the Secretary of the TUC's Organisation and Industrial Relations department, K. Graham, had stated that the model clause was intended:

> to promote equal opportunities [...] and eliminate discrimination of all forms. I recognise that the clause refers only to the most frequent grounds [...] but we will [...] be reviewing the operation [...] with affiliated unions and we will bear in mind the point you raise.[34]

To those familiar with TUC communications, this message cleverly suggested both that action might be taken, but insisted it must have the backing of member unions, and that it would take some time. At the time it was written, of course, no union had adopted a national gay rights policy and even those that did would not have given any priority to raising it with the TUC. As a result, it would indeed be a long time before the TUC attitude was revisited. When this eventually did happen, it took yet more time to use the TUC's influence and leadership to turn words into action. Activists' focus had to be on establishing themselves within their own unions, recruiting sufficient members to set up regional structures, and putting on pressure to defend members facing discrimination. It was entirely understandable that, although far-sighted people understood that securing TUC backing was a highly worthwhile objective, it remained a distant prospect while attitudes in their own union had yet to be changed.

Meanwhile, gay groups continued to form inside other white collar unions: one that would go on to become an important campaigning group was the Civil Service Gay Group that was founded at a meeting at the (CHE) Gay trade union conference on 2 April 1977. This group announced its four-month anniversary in July 1977, at which point it already had 200 members. A key campaigning message set out at the first meeting planned to challenge government departments that insisted that being gay represented a security risk. This was, of course, precisely the 'risk' that the 1967 act had been designed to eliminate, but it was no surprise that the conservatism of state bureaucracies refused to recognise this (and would continue to do so for a long time to come). The group invited other members of civil service unions to come and meet them at CHE annual conference again that year.[35] Under an employer with numerous small unions represented, it made sense to try to form a single group, but many obstacles lay in the way, not least the reluctance of the unions themselves to take up or even recognise, at this time, the issue confronted by LGBT members. This civil service group would go through a number of incarnations before eventually triumphing, ultimately in the form of PCS Proud (as will be seen in the following chapters).

The gathering at the CHE conference highlights the practical and supportive role played by non-labour movement organisations in promoting the establishment of LGBT groups inside trade unions. The overlap in membership offered CHE some in-house expertise. Following a decision of the CHE annual conference in 1974 to set up gay groups in trade unions (to use the language of the time), the CHE executive committee set up a sub-committee to work on this project and it spent considerable time debating how effectively to set about this daunting challenge. David Dancer, a member of the GTG and of the CHE Executive, took on the preparation of the initial leaflets, which were to be agreed with the Gay Labour Group before publication. This took place over December 1975 and January 1976. The result was two leaflets that were sent to local CHE groups.

The first leaflet invited lesbian and gay trade unionists to contact a 'central clearing scheme' run jointly by CHE and the GLG. The scheme was to be advertised through the media, gay rights groups and advertisements and would collect names of people to be listed, categorised by union. Once sufficient numbers had been reached, and the union's rules had been checked to confirm there was no problem with the next step, the registered members were to be invited to attend a meeting and form a (self-organised) union lesbian and gay group. The second leaflet was aimed at trade union members and explained trade union structures, gave advice on getting speakers invited to branch meetings, and recommended discussing:

> gay rights in terms relevant to the membership. It is a denial of civil liberties to a large minority of the population and one which often affects the rights of the worker [...] an approach in these terms is more likely to gain support than an intellectual discussion about sexism [...] Talk practicalities.[36]

Worthy though the intention of the project was, it does not seem that it produced any great results. At the time of the Gay Labour Group AGM on 10 January 1976, fifty-one responses had been logged, but they were from twenty-three different unions, far too few from any single union to lead to the intended next step of encouraging people to attend a meeting.[37] Certainly, although several of the union groups that were established during these early years owed at least part of the initiative to active members of CHE, the creation of viable groups had to be the work of LGBT workers themselves. Some will have seen the advice on how to raise the issue in unions as patronising (if they saw it at all), while the majority of LGBT members who were not out were unlikely to see the leaflet in the first place.

Working across unions

In parallel with this campaign, the approach of bringing LGBT trade union activists together in national conferences was pursued both by CHE and by GLF. For a couple of years, gay workers' conferences were a feature of the calendar. It is hard to identify the benefits of these gatherings from the scanty reports that survive, although as always *Nalgay News* was diligent in printing advance notices and short news items. The conferences led to people sharing experiences and encouraged attendees to use the lessons learnt in their own work, as well as sometimes acting as inspiration.

There was a gay workers' conference at London's Conway Hall on 11 October 1975 (the leaflet promoting it was headed 'Are you a degenerate bourgeois pervert or a gay worker?'). Leeds GLF (no doubt with overlapping participation) organised conferences under the title of the Gay Working People's Campaign in May 1975 and February 1976. The women's journal *Spare Rib* printed a report by Sarah Benton of the first of these, held in Leeds on the weekend of 10 and 11 May 1975. Fifty people attended, about one quarter of whom were women, and most were trade union members, coming from the Association of Professional, Executive, Clerical and Computer Staff (APEX), the Amalgamated Union of Engineering Workers (AUEW), the Electrical, Electronic, Telecommunications and Plumbing Union (EEPTU), the NUT, the Transport and General Workers' Union (TGWU), and the Union of Postal Workers (UPW). It is notable that, except the NUT, none of these unions had a LGBT group at the time (and GTG was not officially only for NUT members, i.e. it was not officially an exclusive union LGBT group), and none would see one established for some years yet. It would seem that most attendees were or had been members of far left groups, as Sarah Benton noted the presence of CPGB, IS and International Marxist Group (IMG) members, as well as people from the Labour Party. It was probably inevitable that such a meeting would show as many differences as there were agreements, that its organisation would be described as chaotic, and that some would be alienated by the style and politics of the debate. *Nalgay News* said it was 'a lot of the same old arguments […] not constructive'. But Benton identified that although it had not attempted to address deeper questions of the roots of oppression (which was not its stated purpose), it did identify the debt that lesbians and gays owed to the women's movement, and it did agree to prepare a gay workers' charter. The follow-up conference took place at Leeds Polytechnic on 14-15 February 1976. Here, a charter was adopted, recognising that winning the labour movement was vital, that creating a link between women and gay struggles was critical, but not providing any clear idea of how to achieve these objectives. The position adopted by the conference included an explicit criticism of CHE and was amended to include affiliation to the Working Women's Charter campaign, which was then being promoted by the left.[38]

The positive feature of all these meetings was that they brought together activists from many different unions, and, although the political direction chosen by the GLF-inspired campaign was far to the left of the work that CHE was doing, on the ground the practical differences were much smaller. The former, GLF-style route was adopted by activists who met in December 1979. Members from NALGO, the National Union of Journalists (NUJ), National Union of Railwaymen (NUR), National Association of Probation Officers (NAPO), the civil service unions and postal workers unions agreed to constitute a Gay Rights at Work (GRAW) committee and to call a national conference for March 1980.

The CHE and GLG employment campaign continued and they wrote to every union head office directly. The replies were collated and published in the booklet *What About the Gay Workers?* in September 1981. Just nineteen unions responded, including five of the eight that had by then included sexual orientation in their policies, and they gave mixed answers to CHE's questions. The most promising signal was that even those with no policy stated (with one exception) that they would support a member who was facing discrimination on grounds of sexual orientation.[39]

During the decade of the 1970s, LGBT people had forced their way onto the public agenda so effectively as to generate a significant backlash. They had done so through the active leadership of an extraordinary group of 'ordinary' people no longer prepared to put up with being silent, with pretending to be what they were not, and who were thus willing to challenge the prejudice and discrimination they found everywhere around them. Many of these people understood that they shared the experience of discrimination with many others in society and they joined in to support campaigns against racism and fascism, in solidarity with women's rights and with international causes. Sometimes they initially met with (prejudice-based) rejection but generally, they quickly overcame this.

The issue of *Gay News* that carried a photograph of Ian Davies on its front page also printed photographs showing GLF, Gay Teachers Group and CHE banners with the IS Gay Group on a London demonstration to mark the third anniversary of the CIA-supported coup that led to the bloody overthrow of the elected government in Chile. On page three of this issue of *Gay News*, was pictured an obviously homemade 'Gays for the Right to Work' banner carried by a contingent of lesbians and gay men on the Right to Work campaign's London to Brighton march. In 1977, CHE banners were seen on a protest march against the National Front in Lewisham, and considerably further left on the political spectrum, SWP members set up 'Gays against the Nazis', who were welcomed into the newly-created Anti-Nazi League. In his introduction to *What about the Gay Workers?* CHE chair Mike Jarrett recognised the parallel work done by GRAW and the NCCL and noted that 'all sides are agreed about the absolute need to involve trade unions in the fight against discrimination'.[40] He went on to identify how the CHE survey confirmed what a challenge this still was, but affirmed the battle could be won 'through gay groups acting within the union movement'. That he was right would be confirmed by the events of the following decade.

NOTES

1. For example, 140,000 took part in a TUC rally against the Industrial Relations Bill on 21 February 1971. Robert Taylor, *The TUC from the General Strike to New Unionism,* Basingstoke: Palgrave, 2000, p193.
2. The result was no overall control by any party. But Heath could not form a majority with other parties, so Labour's Harold Wilson returned to lead a minority government. In October, he called another general election and Labour returned to office with a tiny majority of three MPs. The government continued (under Jim Callaghan) until it was defeated in the 1979 general election that brought in Margaret Thatcher for her first term.
3. Cottaging was a gay male practice of seeking sexual partners in public toilets. For some people it was simply the only way to meet others of the same sexuality, for some the experience added excitement to sexual encounters, and its anonymity was often welcome to participants, particularly if they were also hiding their sexuality and were married. Since the 1967 Act (see Chapter One) had added the words 'in private' to same-sex relationship laws, during this period some police forces made a practice of posting young male officers (out of uniform) in toilets to entrap gay men.
4. See next note.
5. All in *Ink News*, 25 February 1972, pp4, 5 and 6. HCA/GLF/15.
6. HCA/GLF/15. The leaflet is undated but predates October 1973, when meetings of TV/TSG group appeared in the listings.
7. This was the first national campaign that I was involved with, acting on behalf of Oxford CHE. Other members of this group resented being involved in political activity, and I and the chair, Peter Grant, were sacked as officers of the group at the next opportunity.

8. Angela Mason had joined GLF when it began. She was not sympathetic to the lesbian walk-out. Angela Mason, interviewed 23 January 2017.
9. GLF print worker leaflet: HCA/GLF/1. All the quotations from the papers listed here and in the next paragraph are taken from this leaflet.
10. Angela Mason, as note 8.
11. Peter Tatchell has spoken often of the bad experience of trying to raise lesbian and gay rights with the organised left in the early 1970s, nationally and internationally. In contrast, and significant also because many members of the 'new' left groups were students, the National Union of Students was among the first national organisations to adopt a fairly comprehensive gay equality policy (April 1973). Also prominent among other early allies of LGBT rights was the National Council for Civil Liberties (NCCL – today's Liberty) which began a long and honourable history of support with an inquiry into police harassment early in 1972.
12. Bob Cant, 'Normal Channels', in Bob Cant and Susan Hemmings (eds), *Radical Records. Thirty Years of Lesbian and Gay History,* London/New York: Routledge 1988, pp206-21; John Lindsay, interviewed 21 November 2016.
13. At this time the SWP had decided to recruit workers to their organisation by persuading activists to take part in workplace groups led by their own members but pitched as a structure able to act free from the control of the union's official structures.
14. CHE Executive Committee minutes 10 June 1973 – HCA/CHE/9/62.
15. *Nalgay News* No. 1; *Nalgay News* No. 3 (December 1974): both in HCA/CHE/9/62.
16. Peter Roscoe, interviewed 5 October 2016.
17. *Nalgay News,* No. 6 (April/May 1975): HCA/CHE/9/62.
18. *Nalgay News,* No. 5 (February/March 1975); HCA/CHE/9/62.
19. *Nalgay News,* No. 7 (June/July 1975): HCA/Ephemera 197, with minutes of the Nalgay conference.
20. Email correspondence between the author and Mike Blick.
21. *Nalgay News,* September/October 1976: HCA/Journals/280 (miscellaneous).
22. *Nalgay News,* September/October 1977, HCA/Journals/280 (miscellaneous). *Nalgay News,* October 1976 (regional convenors): HCA/Ephemera/327.
23. I am deeply grateful to Ian Davies himself both for his memories but also for providing access to a copious collection of documents and reports, and to former Tower Hamlets branch officers or representatives Jean Geldart, Dan Jones, Derek Relph and Richard Humm (interviewed or corresponded with the author, November 2016). These form the evidence for the following paragraphs. Davies was a member of CHE and had links with NCCL, and told me that following a Westminster CHE meeting, he discussed his case in the pub with Terry Munyard, and it

was decided to set up Gay Legal Advice (GLAD)'s 24-hour helpline for those having similar problems with unequal laws.

24. Report of speeches at branch meeting as given in the branch newsletter *Tower Power*, Vol. 38, September 1976.

25. All the press cuttings were collected by Ian Davies in several folders which he kindly allowed me to read.

26. HAC/Ephemera/327.

27. Quoted in the booklet published by the Gay Teachers' Group, *Open and Positive: An Account of How John Warburton Came Out at School and the Consequences*, London, 1978, with a foreword by Paul Patrick and a retrospective by Peter Bradley. It reprints John Warburton's correspondence with ILEA and the NUT. Paul Patrick's untimely death in 2008 was a tragic loss to the cause of equality and the continuing struggle within education, for which he had been a passionate lifelong advocate.

28. Geoff Hardy interviewed by the author 5 October 2016.

29. Alan Jackson interviewed by the author 23 August 2016. Sue Sanders, who went on to lead Schools Out! with Paul Patrick, was teaching at the time in Hammersmith College, and remembers supporting the Warburton petition. Sue Sanders, interviewed 8 August 2016.

30. Tim Lucas interviewed 10 August 2016.

31. Bob Cant, 'Normal Channels', in Bob Cant, Susan Hemmings (eds), *op. cit.,* pp212-14.

32. The pamphlet, *Gay People in NATFHE,* was found in HCA/ Ephemera/105.

33. HCA/Ephemera/111 – NUPEGG information sheet, press release. The formation of the group was mentioned in *Nalgay News*, No. 7 (June-July 1975): HCA/Ephemera 197.

34. HCA/CHE/9/62.

35. HCA/GLF/15 (founding of group) and HCA/Ephemera/114 (invitation to meet at CHE conference).

36. HCA/CHE/9/62: Letter (ND) from Mike Rowland, secretary, GLG; CHE leaflet; paper for CHE Executive, 14 December 1975.

37. Minutes of GLG AGM, 10 January 1976, pp4-5 (from my records). The largest number of responses were from education unions: AUT (lecturers) with six, and NUT with five. The minutes noted that GLG had two trade union branches affiliated (Charlton GMW, and Holborn APEX).

38. Information about these various conferences was found in: *Nalgay News* No. 6, April-May 1975; *Spare Rib,* No. 37, 1975, p22; HCA/ CHE/9/62: Report of Leeds GLF Conference 10-11 May 1975; Gay Workers' Conference, 14-15 February 1976, motion and amendment; Gay Workers' Newsletter. I have not found a report of the CHE conference on 11 October 1975 except that the speakers (if this was the same

event – the record is undated) were Mike Notcutt, Howard Hyman, Mike Rowland from the GLG, and Jon Bennett speaking about discrimination in the army (where being gay was then illegal).

39. *What About the Gay Workers? A Report of the Commission on Discrimination,* London: CHE, 1981. The report was compiled by Mike Daly, Ken Davison, Bruce Galloway, Howard Hyman, Mike Jarrett, Rosemary Johnson, John Meredith and Bill Neal. It began with a long list of cases of employment discrimination.

40. *Ibid.,* p.3

3

Breakthrough: The early 1980s

Margaret Thatcher became Prime Minister in 1979, and she was determined to tilt the balance of power that had developed during the previous decade back in favour of capital. This involved crushing the Labour Party at the polls but, no less importantly, also a strategy of defeating the unions, because they had successfully resisted policies that could be detrimental to the lives and living standards of working people. Initially, she chose to tread with some caution, backing down from a potential dispute with the National Union of Mineworkers (NUM) early in her first government.[1] But this early experience led her to later formulate a well-prepared campaign to smash the power of this union. Thatcher's economic policies aligned with the neoliberal agenda of US President Ronald Reagan (1981-89). She deliberately drove up unemployment, and began a programme of undermining the welfare state; her policy of selling off council houses served as well to undermine traditional support for the Labour Party. In order to accomplish this agenda, carried out over three terms (the Conservatives were re-elected in 1983 and 1987, and again in 1992 under John Major), it was necessary to remove the block represented by organised labour. This was achieved through both new laws reducing trade union rights, and politically-motivated industrial conflict initiated by employers who were then fully backed with the resources of the state.

Meanwhile, following the electoral defeat of the increasingly right-wing Labour government in 1979, there was a left wing backlash led by Tony Benn MP, whose supporters took control of parts of the party without ever achieving a majority among Labour MPs.[2] The 'gang of four' left Labour to set up the Social Democratic Party which eventually merged with the Liberal Party. The divided Labour Party and the ineffective leadership of veteran left-winger Michael Foot contributed to Thatcher's victory in 1983, alongside the Conservatives' jingoistic exploitation of her war with Argentina over the Falkland Islands (1982). In contrast to Labour's parliamentary party, Labour leftists won elections in a large number of local government bodies; prominent among them was Manchester City Council, and the Greater London Council, where Ken Livingstone became leader in 1981. Equality issues thus took centre stage in local government for the first time.

This background strongly influenced the progress of LGBT equality. Thatcher was not much interested in social policy and did not care whether any of her loyal supporters were homosexual, but the level of hostility to LGBT people displayed by the media and most of her party had not changed. The by-election in the previously safe Labour seat of Bermondsey (London) in 1983, where the local party had selected an 'out' radical, Peter Tatchell, as candidate, turned into the most bitterly (and sometimes physically violent) homophobic campaign in history.[3] This atmosphere combined with the Conservative Party's own resistance to reforms that would benefit LGBT people meant that there was never the slightest prospect of any step being taken to reform the relevant laws under Thatcher's premiership – the only legal changes (most significantly 'Section 28/2A') would be negative. The only exceptions were the result of external actions, such as the positive rulings of the European Court on cases extending the provisions of the 1967 Act to Scotland in 1980 and Northern Ireland in 1982.

Despite this, however, these years witnessed an eventually unstoppable momentum in the progress of LGBT equality policies and activity through the trade union and labour movement, progress which survived the defeats suffered by organised labour and led to victories for equality in subsequent decades. This chapter summarises the progress during this period inside trade unions and the labour movement, describes the significant turning points at two union conferences, and highlights the combination of factors including solidarity in the miners' strike that placed LGBT rights on the policy agenda of the whole labour movement for the first time.

WORKPLACE DISCRIMINATION AND NEW RESPONSES

As Thatcher came to power, for the first time cases of workplace discrimination attracted widespread public attention for victims' attempts to use sex discrimination law to challenge their dismissals. John Saunders had been sacked by a Scottish residential children's camp in 1979 for no reason other than being gay. Legal challenges were made in the following year but both the Industrial Tribunal (IT) and the appeal court (the Court of Sessions) ruled the dismissal fair. The Scottish Minorities Group and the National Council for Civil Liberties (NCCL) organised a petition that attracted celebrity support and the signatures of many trade unionists but the fact remained that there was no protection from discrimination on grounds of sexual orientation. This meant that by law, no court could rule against such dismissals, and there was no legal protection if an employer was prejudiced against homosexuals working with children or 'vulnerable people'.

The other high profile cases in the late 1970s and early 1980s were Susan Shell, who was sacked by Barking Council (in east London) after revealing her homosexuality in conversation, in May 1981. She was a care assistant. So too was Judith Williams, who was sacked a year later, in 1982, by Berwyn College, a home run by Care Concern for adolescent girls who were placed there by many local authorities. Williams's case was the basis of four motions to the National and Local Government Officers' association (NALGO) annual conference in 1982; even though she was not a union member, the union enthusiastically supported the defence campaign run by Gay Rights at Work (GRAW) and others. The union also called on its members to boycott Care Concern until she was reinstated. Thus NALGO was responsible for both the first and second union actions against an employer guilty of discrimination.[4]

These three cases were also significant because of the level of trade union interest and response. The decision of a group of trade union LGBT activists to organise what became GRAW was immediately justified by these examples of workplace discrimination. Even though John Saunders was not a union member, Nalgay member Bob Deacon had ensured that a motion protesting the sacking was submitted by NALGO to the Scottish TUC, where it was carried. The Saunders and Shell cases became causes célèbres for campaigners and featured prominently in early GRAW conferences. The press release for the conference held on 27 March 1982 (at Digbeth Civic Hall in Birmingham) highlighted both cases as demonstrating the need for the conference. GRAW's 'Action Sheet' No. 1 was devoted to the Saunders case. The Birmingham conference was opened by Paul Mackney, president of Birmingham Trades Council, who was a rising star of the trade union movement (he went on to become general secretary of the National Association for Teachers in Further and Higher Education, NATFHE), and who here represented important public support from a heterosexual ally.[5] GRAW also produced (June 1980) a pamphlet, 'Gays at Work', which sold for 25p, explaining recent cases of discrimination (Ian Davies, John Warburton, Louise Boychuk – sacked for refusing to stop wearing a 'Lesbians ignite!' badge – and John Saunders). It offered practical information for workers facing discrimination, arguing that they should try to claim unfair dismissal, and listed current union gay groups and contact information for NCCL and the Campaign for Homosexual Equality (CHE).[6]

The Shell case had an impact too where it mattered most: at the very top of Susan Shell's own trade union. The struggle of the National Union of Public Employees Gay Group (NUPEGG) to gain a voice had finally overcome its obstacles and a gay rights policy had been adopted at NUPE's annual conference in 1980. The union had offered every assistance to Susan Shell but could not win the battle with her employer for two main reasons. The first concerned the law, or lack thereof, and this was understood. It helped the union towards a positive policy on equality. The second was unwillingness of other members to take action in her support.

The policy change partly originated elsewhere in the labour movement: NUPE was actively involved in the Labour Party and in 1981 the party's National Executive published a ground-breaking document (for a political party), *The Rights of Gay Men and Women*. Tony Benn MP had come out publicly in support of lesbian and gay rights in 1981 and his supporters on the NEC were behind the document. While it was largely based on CHE's draft bill, it made explicit reference to the Saunders and other cases. The document reached the National Executive of NUPE in 1982 and the minutes of that meeting are worth citing:

Item 7(b) NUPE Gay Rights Policy. [Noted resolution carried at 1980 conference.] It was also pointed out that NUPE had a special interest [...] in that a number of the cases of dismissals on grounds of sexual orientation had occurred in the public services and, in particular, in NUPE areas of work, such as with the Susan

Shell case. [Paper from the NUPE office] proposes support for the Labour Party document, to press employers and the TUC to include sexual orientation in equal opportunity clauses, help build a campaign of education. *Agreed* and to circulate document for discussion and education among NUPE branches.

The attached paper from NUPE researchers stated:

1.2 Susan Shell's sacking resulted purely from the prejudices that often exist against gay people rather than any complaint about her work.

1.3 [and that this was not] a peripheral issue for NUPE […]

1.4 While NUPE officers strongly supported Susan Shell […] low level of support from NUPE members in her branch […] illustrates the need for much more explanation and education.

Tom Sawyer, the union's deputy general secretary, wrote to the general secretary of the Labour Party (Ron Hayward) on 23 April 1982 welcoming the party's discussion document, fully supporting its recommendations but asked why it had not been given a higher profile. He concluded by saying 'The Labour Party should show its commitment to gaining equality for gay people and ensuring that it is discussed throughout the movement. It is important that such policies become part of the Labour Party manifesto before the next election.'[7] The latter was a vain hope at this time as the party itself had no policy.

However, it is worth noting the turnaround that had taken place in this manual workers' union in just a few years. Also, there was no attempt at pretence. The Executive paper honestly recorded that Shell had not received the kind of warm support from her own colleagues that Ian Davies had secured from his. There was evidently no prospect of them taking industrial action in her support. But the union officers had done their duty and more, and were committed to challenging prejudices among their own members. NUPE later became the first major trade union to affiliate to the Labour Campaign for Lesbian and Gay Rights (LCLGR) in 1984, and its votes at conference would help to achieve the first policy commitments from the party a year after that.

CIVIL SERVANTS AND POSTAL WORKERS

Before looking at the most significant advances for LGBT rights inside the trade union movement in the early 1980s it is useful to understand other, less high profile developments that demonstrate that a general process of forward movement was underway. The early struggles of civil service LGBT workers to set up a group and win a hearing in the 1970s continued into the new decade. At a meeting in Birmingham (13 January 1979) a new name was agreed (the Civil and Public Services Gay Group, CPSGG) and new officers were chosen. The aims of the group continued to be: getting branches to send motions to union annual conferences; reporting cases of discrimination; writing to MPs; setting up regional support groups; and notifying external organisations of their existence (CHE and the short-lived Gay Activists Alliance that had grown out of the campaign to defend *Gay News* were listed). A newsletter was established. Lack of resources continued to be an issue, however, and only twelve people attended the London AGM in 1981. The secretary was Richard Nurick and the chair, Don Street. Despite small numbers, the group was involved in GRAW (through Eric Hinton) and had three members on the CHE Commission that had published *What About the Gay Workers?* But only one member turned up for a national meeting in Manchester and the chair had resigned. The newsletter appealed for volunteers to take over.

However, on the positive side, fifteen to twenty gay delegates had attended an event at the Civil and Public Servants Association (CPSA) annual conference, where a gay rights motion had been on the agenda – although it was not taken. In the issue of the CPSGG newsletter that reported these conference events, it was also noted that although two civil service unions, First Division Association (FDA) and Institution of Professional Civil Servants (IPCS – predecessor of today's Prospect) had not responded at first to the CHE discrimination commission's letters, they had now decided to do so, which indicated that progress was being made. In an interesting note, the group secretary felt it necessary to out himself as a Conservative supporter in this newsletter. The CPSGG was gradually extending its influence; it quickly reached out to members in several more civil service unions (at this time there were eight). They campaigned for anti-discrimination policies and won in all the larger civil service unions – CPSA, the Society of Civil and Public Servants (SCPS), IPCS and FDA – by 1982.

The February 1983 CPSGG newsletter advertised a social in the traditional gay London pub the City of Quebec, and put out an appeal for a banner for that year's Pride march, which it reported had been successful in June. Significant political developments were announced in its June issue. At the CPSA annual conference that year, lobbying had gained the support of both the Broad Left (the coalition of supporters of left wing groups and individuals) and the 'moderates' on the union's national executive, to oppose a hostile amendment to the gay rights policy (which in the end had not been debated by the end of the conference). The persistence of an old problem in winning support among members was confirmed by the story behind this amendment, which was reported in the October newsletter; there had been correspondence between the CPSGG and the branch behind the proposal. Their explanation for their position was that while they had not meant to be hostile, their problem with the gay rights policy was that 'paedophilia is also a sexual orientation'.

The group's newsletters continued to reflect the political difficulties faced by civil servants and their unions. It was deemed appropriate by CPSGG, for example, for support to be offered to the campaign (launched April 1984) to defend the London community bookshop *Gay's the Word*, which had been the subject of a Customs and Excise raid and prosecution for importing a wide range of LGBT literature (including material published and widely available in Britain). However, in contrast, it was decided to leave to individuals whether or not to support Lesbians and Gays Support the Miners (August 1984), this being a cause not specifically LGBT as well as being politically divisive.[8]

Union leaders' lack of response to the CHE questionnaire was also an issue for the slowly developing LGBT group of post office workers. The original Union of Communication Workers (UCW) gay group had been launched at a meeting in London's Drill Hall in April 1978 – The Gay Post and Telecom Workers' group (GPTW) – and it reached its third newsletter in December 1981. It reported efforts to organise a social event in London, and noted a campaign in which a member had successfully persuaded a Post Office welfare officer to include in the information provided for new apprentices details about support groups for young gay people. Ann Mckinley from the Oxford Day Telephonists Branch wrote in the newsletter 'I worry about our Executive Council', and described routine ridiculing of male telephonists' sexuality in her branch. The journal of the UCW refused to carry advertisements from CHE. The officers of the GPTW at this time were London-based Rosemary Franklin and Paul Wilkinson, and John Jenkinson from Brighton. Little progress was being made.

Subsequently, issues of the GPTW newsletter during 1982 reported that the UCW union journal had finally carried a letter from the group secretary complaining about the advert ban. The summer 1982 issue printed a letter from a member in Battersea (London) complaining that 'in my office, the word queer is one of the most frequently used "playful" abuse words. I feel hurt and angry each time I hear it.' The positive news was the UCW had supported a gay rights motion at the Scottish Labour conference in 1981.

This account demonstrates how far there was still to go in many traditional working-class unions. The lack of support for LGBT rights from their union leaders at this time was a critical missing ingredient in challenging prejudice among members. The small group of active LGBT members in the UCW was evidently working hard in difficult circumstances to support lesbian and gay members where it had contacts, but the problem of reaching out to most parts of the union had not yet been solved. The scale of the resources problem is best shown by the GPTW accounts for 1981/2: during a whole year, their income totalled just £232.[9] The difficulty of sustaining the entirely voluntary effort required to run such groups was immense – this group's treasurer combined his financial role with producing the newsletter. He stood down after four years, and the newsletter was then taken on by the membership secretary. Apart from the simple fact that what they were trying to achieve was right and necessary, the sense of progress elsewhere may well have served as an incentive – there was a postal worker at the meeting that first established GRAW.

A TALE OF TWO CITIES: NUT AND NALGO 1983

In 1983, the stubbornness of two large unions' leaders unexpectedly propelled the issue of LGBT rights firmly onto their respective agendas, providing the foundation for official recognition, continuing self-organisation and accelerated progress. Both events happened in the same year and they arose because the National Union of Teachers (NUT) had decided to hold its annual conference on Jersey, and NALGO had booked its event on the Isle of Man. Homosexuality was still illegal on these two islands, which were self-governing crown dependencies. Despite the remarkable parallels between the two campaigns each one took a different form.

For the teachers, members of the Gay Teachers' Group (GTG) had already drawn to the national union's attention the risk posed to gay members and their partners by holding the conference in a place where their relationships would be illegal. GTG member Tim Lucas had written to the general secretary of the NUT in 1981 and the union's solicitor had confirmed that this was the legal situation with regard to gay relationships in Jersey. When the NUT decided not to change its plans, Lucas sought to refer this back (that is, send it back for reconsideration by the Executive) at the 1982 conference but the decision was upheld. The GTG thus had a year to prepare its campaign, and it did so carefully, including a strong lobby of the executive meeting in March 1983 (which coincidentally enabled it to also lobby the NATFHE executive because they were meeting in the same building). That the NUT had ignored the issue provided GTG with plenty of ammunition through which it was able to get a number of branches to submit motions for the Jersey conference. Peter Bradley, Alan Jackson and Tim Lucas were elected as delegates, while Geoff Hardy went along to provide practical back up. The next event was also carefully planned: after the normal formality of a welcome address from a local dignitary, traditionally followed by a 'vote of thanks' to the speaker, Peter Bradley rose to oppose the vote of thanks (as was permitted by conference rules). No sooner had he stated that he was speaking as a gay man than the conference chair refused to let him continue, causing uproar (GTG had already distributed a leaflet explaining the issue so people were aware in advance). The next day, GTG members handed out a copy of Bradley's intended speech to delegates.

Rarely has an undelivered speech achieved so much. Bradley's measured and well-argued words (he had not intended to ask delegates to vote against the thanks in any case) had a great impact among the majority of delegates who had not previously had a view on the issue. National press coverage of the unprecedented furore helped too. Sue Reid of the *Daily Express* wrote 'Would you want your children taught by these people?' The GTG held daily planning meetings, and the (far left) Socialist Teachers Alliance (STA) allowed them to use its photocopying facilities; delegates were leafletted every day, with the pamphlet entitled 'Where to go next year? Sunny Jo'burg' (i.e. apartheid South Africa) being particularly well received. Geoff Hardy's idea of asking people to dance in same-sex couples at the Young Teachers' disco was put into effect with brilliant results as many heterosexual members did so, and the same thing happened, but spontaneously, at the STA disco. Delegates were asked to wear rapidly improvised pink triangles made by Hardy and hundreds did so out of solidarity. Tim Lucas and Alan Jackson raised gay rights in speeches on (respectively) the lack of pension rights and exclusion from equal opportunities policy. Jackson's was the first speech completely devoted to LGBT rights in education at a trade union conference. A first edition of the LGBT equality in education publication *School's Out* was launched at a fringe meeting held jointly with the STA where executive member Bernard Regan also spoke.[10]

The GTG was rightly proud of its impact. Geoff Hardy remembered it as being like 'a spark igniting'. It had demonstrated how to turn the initial indifference of the union's executive and the ignorance of much of the membership into a political triumph. From a small network predominantly based around a few activists in London (where it had achieved backing from the union regionally), it had been catapulted into national news headlines. The issue of gay rights had moved from being treated as insignificant to being a key feature of the conference. Every delegate who attended was expected to deliver a report on proceedings to their branch so the impact rippled out still further over the weeks ahead. Both throughout the conference and after, there was still opposition from some delegates, as was expected, but a majority had been won to the cause of equality.

The leadership of the NUT immediately recognised the new reality as well. Shortly after the conference, the (new) National Executive Committee (NEC) set up an ad hoc national working party on lesbian and gay rights, which included Tim Lucas and Gill Spraggs from Leicester along with half a dozen (all women) members of the Executive. The union's equal opportunities department provided the necessary support. The working party went through a number of changes, becoming a task group before eventually turning into a committee.

There was still a way to go before effective action began to be taken across the union, but the course had been set. By the time of Section 28 in 1988, the GTG itself had disappeared, and Peter Bradley left teaching. The GTG's work inside the union was continued by official structures while its broader campaigning activity was taken over (along with much of its personnel) by *School's Out* led by Steve Bonham, Sue Sanders and Paul Patrick from the 1990s.

The impact and immediate consequences of action on lesbian and gay rights at the NALGO conference held a few weeks later in Douglas, Isle of Man, were also significant. NALGO had agreed a lesbian and gay rights policy in 1976, but this did not prevent it from booking its conference venue on this island where homosexuality was still illegal. Ironically, in 1978 it had refused to meet in Scarborough because of that council's persistent refusal to allow CHE to meet there. The external focus of the NALGO campaigners made it different from the NUT experience, but the impact was similarly dramatic.

The lead role in the NALGO developments was played by activists from the Metropolitan District (i.e. London) Lesbian and Gay Group. They organised motions and amendments to motions that condemned the choice of venue and they prepared a campaign to be carried out on the island. The motion condemning the choice of venue was carried by the conference, but one on sexual orientation discrimination was not voted on, but referred back to the national executive. Alongside this, the lesbian and gay activists promoted a petition to be submitted to the Isle of Man parliament (the Tynwald) which was well supported by delegates. This was then the objective of a demonstration through the streets of Douglas one lunchtime, and hundreds of conference delegates joined in. As is still the case with demonstrations by UNISON members, the procession was enlivened with balloons and stickers produced to deliver the message to participants and bystanders. There were many bystanders, and Manx politicians were convinced to turn out to receive the petition, an event recorded with detailed accounts and photographs of the demonstration. The threat of losing the income from hosting union conferences was serious, although some Manx newspaper correspondents thought it was worth it to avoid corruption. Nothing like this demonstration had ever been seen before on the island. A packed fringe meeting (200 delegates) was addressed by John McKay and Jackie Lewis. It was organised by the union's national Equal Opportunities Committee (EOC), of which Lewis had been a part. Through this official structure a survey of examples of sexual orientation discrimination was later carried out.

Although the approach was completely different, like the Jersey conference, the effect was electric (although it had no impact on the law on the Isle of Man which was not reformed until 1992). Within the year, NALGO had convened its first national lesbian and gay conference and over the years ahead, with occasional setbacks (which will be discussed subsequently) significant progress was made in 'mainstreaming' lesbian and gay rights in the union's concerns. Having the first formally recognised national lesbian and gay conference (even if its precise status remained somewhat ambiguous for a while) represented another huge leap forward for trade union commitment to the cause of equality. Organisers remember other problems with this first event, including the union insurers refusing to cover it because of 'moral risk', until the branch stepped in, and it having to be held in a nursery in London's King's Cross Family Centre (booked through Sarah Coldrick, a member of the Camden branch who worked there), so everyone was perched on tiny chairs.[11] Coldrick recalled the sense of excitement at being involved in setting up the first trade union lesbian and gay conference: 'it felt like we were breaking new ground, an incredible feeling'. Having previously been involved in the branch's women's group, this was her first experience of working with gay men ('a challenge but a great joy'). Fifty people from all over the country took part, and many heterosexual members of the branch helped out with the crèche and the catering – for many of them it was the first time they had met out lesbians and gay men. This event produced the first national lesbian and gay group, which went on to organise future conferences with Chris Eades (now Creegan) as secretary (once the Metropolitan District had happily handed over the responsibility at the second conference, Manchester 1984), which helped to establish a genuinely national structure.

Those involved recognised that there were a range of ways that these achievements had come about. The activists who were involved were not just single-issue advocates but respected trade unionists in their own right: Sarah Coldrick had started work in Camden social services and became a workplace rep; she and the others had been involved in their branches and had earned their respect. Some had been building a base of support and understanding for many years, and had negotiated inclusive equal opportunities policies with their local authority employers – helped, of course, where these were now run by progressive Labour councillors, as in many urban areas. They had established crucial alliances with other equality campaigners within the union, especially those working for women workers' and black workers' rights. By participating in formal structures such as the Equal Opportunities Committees at both regional and national level, they were creating understanding and locating allies. There was also a clear strategy in place among those elected to lead the work that was rooted in the reality of the union.[12]

Subsequent practical steps included the preparation of an activist pack through the EOC – which had itself been given a training seminar in lesbian and gay issues in January 1984 – written by its support officer Tess Woodcraft, with the support of its chair, Rita Donaghy (who is now [2017] a member of the House of Lords). The pack focussed on key issues for NALGO members: their rights at work and creating the conditions to enable people to come out and be openly gay at work. It provided the practical tool for taking issues of LGBT rights around the whole union and was used to achieve that dissemination in the years ahead. This was the 'bottom up' part of the strategy.

However, the lesbian and gay group in NALGO also recognised the importance of national policy and action. To ensure the momentum created by the Isle of Man was not dissipated, a composite motion drafted by Angela Mason was debated and carried at the following year's national conference (1984).[13] It was carefully prepared. Meetings took place with other lesbian and gay delegates, and leaflets were produced for conference delegates. The motion was moved by Jackie Lewis from Lambeth NALGO and seconded by Angela, and it proved to be perfectly judged. It focussed on discrimination at work and in the union, introduced the idea of 'heterosexism', highlighted the legal position, and included reference to the idea of self-organisation. It went on to argue that it was the responsibility of the union as a whole to create a climate in which lesbians and gay men could come out at work, and concluded by stressing that lesbian and gay rights must be an integral part of the equal opportunities agenda. This motion set the framework for action for a long time to come. There was a speaker against, but it was carried with a large majority.

Accounts of the debate showed a pattern which was now developing at trade union conferences. Firstly, in general, leaderships continued to be worried about having the discussion. On this particular occasion, they tried to weaken the motion with an amendment, which they eventually withdrew before the vote. Secondly, delegations included some people who were simply prejudiced. At this 1984 conference, a speaker representing a branch in British Gas delivered a (by now) familiar rant about paedophilia, threats to children and society drifting into immorality – and encountered a great deal of hostility from the rest of the conference, which was a gratifying sign of the progress that had now been achieved for lesbian and gay rights. Another feature of debates in unions where much work had been done was that such opposition was actively welcomed because, where once much of the audience might have been influenced by the argument, by now it had the opposite effect of strengthening support for equality. The strategic priority was to win policy commitments before plunging into debates on structures; this same 1984 NALGO conference failed to recognise the inappropriateness of an almost-all-white race equality working group, which was evidence of the ground still to be made up on recognising the importance of allowing people facing discrimination to speak for themselves.[14] What can be said in summary, perhaps, is this: whereas NALGO had (twice) before voted through a policy against sexual orientation discrimination, the union nationally (as opposed to activists in particular in the larger urban branches) had done little to implement it.[15] Since the events on the Isle of Man had been consolidated by an effective campaign at the conference immediately after, and with a self-organised body of activists committed to ensuring continuing progress, Sarah Coldrick and Ben Benson made a presentation to the union's national executive (1984) to educate them on the experience of being lesbian or gay. In theory, from here, there would be no limitations on the creation of a union genuinely committed to this cause.

RUGBY

NALGO's commitment to lesbian and gay rights at work was quickly put to the test when the council running the small town of Rugby

(Warwickshire) voted in September 1984 to remove the reference to sexual orientation from the recently adopted equal opportunities policy. The official NALGO report of the campaign, which was written in September 1985, reproduced the key papers, and this is the basis for the following information. The motivation behind the vote was that to include it suggested Rugby 'positively welcomed child molesters and perverts'. The margin was a single vote; the Labour group supported the inclusion of the reference and its leader Jeff Coupe was a stalwart advocate throughout the campaign. The Chief Executive told the press that 'it does not mean we will discriminate against homosexuals but it does mean there is no guarantee that we will not [...] There may or may not be discrimination, who knows?' The leader of the council reinforced this with many homophobic statements on television and radio and in the press.

Most of the media was critical of this position, with the exception of *The Sun*, which hailed Rugby as a 'brave little town' standing up to the tide of 'filth'.[16] NALGO (which had a branch of 260 members in the council) was part of the protests at branch, district and national levels. When the next council meeting did not reconsider the vote, a protest march was organised that took place on 10 November 1984. Coachloads of protesters came from Scotland, Yorkshire, Bristol, Manchester and London with banners from the CHE, the Gay Switchboard, the Gay Youth Movement and the Labour Campaign for Gay Rights (LCGR). The march was led by the NALGO West Midlands banner and NALGO branches taking part included Lambeth, Camden and Leeds. 1000 people supported the march; Rugby (like Douglas) had never seen anything like it. Mike Blick, representing the union's local government committee, spoke at the rally and denounced the council's decision as 'bigotry and prejudice of the worst kind'. Another remarkable feature of the rally was that this was where Chris Smith, MP (elected in 1983 for Islington South and Finsbury in north London, later Lord Smith of Finsbury) came out in a moving speech, and became the first openly gay Member of Parliament. He had come with the Labour Campaign for Gay Rights (LCGR) contingent from London and this attracted most media attention, understandably.

The council backed down in February 1985. It was an industrial issue and after the demonstrators had left NALGO negotiators were evidently well-placed to deliver victory. The campaign between a range of organisations broke the council's resistance and NALGO got the final capitulation in writing. It was a magnificent display of solidarity between Labour councillors, party activists and lesbian and gay campaigners and organisations. But for the first time, this resistance had a trade union at its core. NALGO too learnt the importance of bringing its own members with it (members in Rugby would never have encountered such bigotry in this way before) and the union subsequently used it as a case study in its organising pack.[17]

THE MINERS AT WAR WITH THE GOVERNMENT AND THE IMPACT ON LGBT EQUALITY

The government agency that ran coal mines, the National Coal Board, led by Ian MacGregor (who had been appointed by Thatcher following his 'success' in halving the workforce at British Steel), announced the closure of twenty pits in March 1984, including several that were still profitable. It is now known that he planned a short term closure of seventy-five pits, and that the government was behind the plan.[18] Yorkshire miners began immediate strike action to defend their jobs, which were usually the only employment available in their communities, and the majority of NUM members followed their lead. The union's leaders – Arthur Scargill, Peter Heathfield and Mick McGahey were the senior officials – called an all-out strike. The sudden announcement of closures meant the action was urgent, without time to ballot the membership; this was used as justification by less militant areas such as the East Midlands – where miners (falsely, as it turned out) believed their jobs were safe – to continue working. Alongside advance planning by the government, who had created stockpiles of coal, importing large amounts from abroad, and mounted massive police action to protect non-striking miners against union pickets, this ultimately led to the failure of the strike after twelve months. It was one of the most bitter and divisive disputes in British history. Other unions were unwilling to take industrial action in solidarity, which would have been illegal because of changes to trade union law and the failure to ballot provided a reason (or excuse, depending on your point of view), this meant that the government was able to endure the strike despite a number of close calls. Thatcher's government was determined to defeat the miners and it succeeded, with her victory being seen by fellow politicians, the media and public opinion, as well as by many workers, as decisive.

Many other groups understood the significance of this struggle and rallied to support the striking miners. There were various methods used to show this support, such as: 'xxx Support the Miners' groups, which sprung up in towns and villages across the country; collections were made to raise money and provide necessities; and working links were set up between supporters and mining communities. Of these, one was to play a particular part in advancing the equality agenda. The activities of the people who came together to form Lesbians and Gays Support the Miners (LGSM), and, a little later, Lesbians against Pit Closures, have now been given national and international recognition in the magnificent film *Pride* (2014). This film was made with direct input from the survivors of the 1984-6 LGSM group who reconstituted themselves in 2014-15 with the intention of using the anniversary to recreate the original message of solidarity; they organised numerous events across the country, and internationally, working with the TUC and NUM and hundreds of trade union, Labour Party and community groups to ensure that this history was not lost.

The film however is not an entirely reliable guide to what happened, having been modified for extra dramatic effect. An original group gathered in Mark Ashton's London flat on 15 July 1984 for the first meeting of LGSM;[19] there were twelve people present (all men). They decided to produce a leaflet drafted by Mark Ashton for the LGBT community, explaining the link between the strike and lesbian and gay liberation. The plan was: to start leafletting pubs and clubs; to communicate with other LGBT organisations; to organise a benefit concert; to open a bank account; to elect officers (Mike Jackson became secretary); and to adopt a colliery: Dulais in South Wales. Through connections with LCGR contacts had already been made with Dulais and the office space used by LCGR in London was chosen as the group's postal address. Secretary Mike Jackson wrote to the Neath, Dulais and Swansea miners' support group and LGSM was well received on a women's demonstration on 8 August when the new banner was displayed. Word quickly spread amongst the group's contacts, and money came in from the collections.

Dai Donovan (actually a member of the Transport and General Workers' Union, TGWU) came to London, and spoke at a meeting at The Bell pub, a gay venue on Pentonville Road in London, on 6 September 1984, bringing solidarity from the miners to the LGBT community, and he invited LGSM to Dulais. Twenty-seven people from LGSM travelled down on 26 October 1984, arriving late at night. They went to stay among local families and on the night of Saturday 27 October, they took part in a local rally at the Miners' Welfare Hall. Other banners present included that of Haringey NALGO and the print unions, but LGSM's was the most conspicuous: everyone applauded. Siân James (later MP for Swansea East) read out the letter, then an open discussion began about sexuality. A few people were hostile but the great majority were welcoming – the reality was that no one there had ever met an openly lesbian or gay person. There were four visits to Dulais in all, and LGSM's fundraising and solidarity continued every week. Other LGSM groups sprang up spontaneously in other cities: there were eleven in all.[20] Two communities inhabiting very different worlds met and established a common cause.

When the strike was over, LGSM organised a conference – called 'The Way Forward' – before winding up their activities and closing the group. The conference was held at the London Lesbian and Gay Centre on 30 March 1985, and was backed by a range of left-wing organisations including the Campaign Group of (Labour) MPs and the NUM itself. A letter of thanks from Scargill, Heathfield and McGahey was read out. 100 people attended, and with the strike defeated, this was, in some respects, one of many left-wing gatherings where the already-converted talked to each other.

One of the decisions made by LGSM at the conference was to press for a role at the forthcoming London Pride. This was dramatised in *Pride*, but the truth behind it was real. The committee running the Pride march refused to allow political views attacking the government to be voiced at the demonstration, so LGSM organised a protest that was supported by the left-wing LGBT campaigns but also signed by non-party political groups such as Icebreakers and Friends of Lesbians and Gays (FLAGS).[21] The presence of the NUM with LGSM on the march highlighted that the 1985 Pride Committee had abandoned the goals and purpose of LGBT Pride as had originally been recognised by the Gay Liberation Front (GLF) just thirteen years before. Their decision reflected the growing reality that many sections of the community enjoyed the benefits of greater

openness and commercial opportunities, which had been hard won
by the pioneers of lesbian and gay liberation, but that many were
unwilling to directly challenge continuing inequality, prejudice and
oppression.

The significance of LGBT solidarity with striking miners and
their communities was even more far-reaching than the money that
it generated, important though this was – more than £22,000 was
raised by the London group alone. The NUM's decision to repay the
support they had been offered with their own solidarity is insepa-
rable from the other progress made in this period, but it was a hugely
important contribution.

THREE MORE IMPORTANT CONFERENCES

In the 1980s, lesbian and gay trade unionists were encouraged by
recent successes to take the next step, from their own unions to the
national platform of the TUC. In the same period, Labour activists
in the then-called Labour Campaign for Lesbian and Gay Rights
(LCLGR, formerly LCGR) planned to commit the Labour Party
to a lesbian and gay rights policy by winning a debate at the party's
annual conference, where trade union votes would be critical. As had
been found in many unions, winning a place on that agenda was not
easy – especially when the organisers would have been very nervous
at hosting such a debate. Despite strong presences at Labour conferences every year, sufficient motions from Constituency Labour
Parties to produce a debate were only achieved in 1985, and the first
debate was scheduled on the conference agenda.

Both the National Association of Probation Officers (NAPO,
which had a strong LGBT group) and NALGO submitted gay rights
motions to the TUC Women's Conference early in 1985. NALGO's
was based on that carried at its own 1984 conference. They were
well received, and carried by the Women's TUC. This was not a
guarantee that the forthcoming full TUC Congress would vote the
same way. Not all unions sent delegations to the Women's TUC. But
it was a good indicator of the way things were going. The motion for
Congress highlighted that workplace discrimination made lesbian
and gay rights a basic trade union issue. It referred as well to the
need for equality legislation, and specified the problem of discrimination in pension provision. A fringe meeting was held the day

before the debate at the full TUC Congress in September 1985, for which NALGO had distributed an attractively printed flyer arguing that 'Lesbian and gay rights are as much a trade union issue as any other area of discrimination'. The NALGO National Executive had agreed to second the motion. Ms J. Crabtree made the speech, the motion having been moved by J. Cove for NAPO. L. Broadbent, an out lesbian member of the entertainment union ACTT, spoke in support, and it was carried after a short debate in which there was one speaker against, Mr F. Sweeney from the Union of Construction, Allied Trades and Technicians (UCATT) whose short contribution ended with the words 'these people are absolutely vile. They corrupt everything and anything they touch'. Fortunately, Congress did not agree with him.[22]

For the first time, the national body of the British trade union movement had a policy in favour of lesbian and gay rights. Unlike the vote of the women's conference, which was advisory, this was binding. As we have seen, a growing number of unions – especially but not exclusively in the public sector – had already agreed gay rights policies themselves, and these unions would have supported the motion. Others that had not agreed such policies were given reason to think about the issue. Some would remain opposed for some time to come. But large unions like the TGWU, one of the largest in the country, which had not yet adopted their own policy (see Chapter Four), saw themselves as progressive, so voted in favour. The vote was not recorded so it is now impossible to identify how each delegation voted: but it was usual practice for each union dele-gation to decide before the conference what its attitude would be to every item on the agenda, usually acting on the advice of its general secretary. After the solidarity of LGSM and the NUM, the latter's vote was definitely cast on the pro-equal rights side of the debate.

This factor was reinforced a few weeks later at Labour Party Conference in Bournemouth. The debate on the motion organ-ised by LCLGR had deliberately been placed on the final morning, and the National Executive had asked for it to be remitted to them without vote. LCLGR members at conference not only rejected this, but also asked for a 'card vote' – that is, every part of conference would vote by handing in a card marked with the number of votes it represented. I was a delegate and part of the LCLGR team, and we made this request for a card vote because the entire week had

been spent lobbying, especially focused on delegations from affiliated trade unions, whose combined votes outweighed the rest of
conference by a large margin. The solidarity of the NUM, who
spoke in support of the motion during the short debate, was critical
in swaying undecided delegates. Sufficient union votes were cast in
its favour to ensure the motion received more than 58 per cent of
the vote share.[23] Within a few weeks, the governing bodies of the
trade union movement and of the Labour Party had adopted lesbian
and gay rights policies. Turning conference votes into action would
take much longer in the party than in the unions, but the work was
strengthened on both sides by being more joined up than previously.

These conferences are significant because of what they represented and what they meant for the future. Most union conferences
are necessary elements of a union's democracy but can sometimes,
in truth, be fairly irrelevant to the lives of their members. However,
the NUT and NALGO conferences of 1983 and the TUC and
Labour Conferences of 1985 were different. Building on the victories achieved, but now with a much broader range of allies than ever
before, lesbian and gay trade union campaigners were able to advance
from a much higher starting point. A few years previously, many had
been gathering in someone's front room wondering how to move an
organisation of tens or hundreds of thousands of members, many
of whom were entirely unconcerned (at best) about the reality of
LGBT lives and were certainly not likely to consider it a trade union
concern. Now, in the mid-1980s they were – in some cases already,
and others would follow in the near future – in a position to talk to
union leaders about next steps, to command union resources, and to
demand action. The result of the miners' strike was devastating for
whole communities and it significantly weakened the resistance of
the labour movement to Thatcher – but the solidarity the strike itself
generated through the work of a few hundred NUM, TGWU and
LGSM activists would resonate for a long time in the history of the
struggle for LGBT equality.

EXTENDING SOLIDARITY

It can sometimes be hard to visualise just how many struggles took
place during this grim decade of continuous government attacks
on people's rights. During 1983, local newspaper owner Eddie

Shah had been the first to use Thatcher's new anti-union laws; he sacked unionised printworkers from his papers and then called mass police mobilisations to break up subsequent demonstrations by the printworkers' unions. The same method was followed by Rupert Murdoch, whose corporation News International published *The Times*, *The Sunday Times*, *The Sun* and the *News of the World*. In 1986, he moved News International to new, computerised facilities in Wapping and sacked 5600 unionised workers from the old plants in Fleet Street. The unions were facing a straightforward battle for existence and voted for strike action. The subsequent struggle lasted even longer than the Miners' Strike, running from January 1986 to February 1987, and became known as the Wapping Dispute. The Electrical, Electronic, Telecommunications and Plumbing Union (the EETPU) willingly provided strikebreaking labour to take over the printworkers' jobs, and thousands of police were used to break up union demonstrations and pickets, to ensure that production continued uninterrupted. This combination of factors led to Murdoch winning against the strikers in February 1987.

The widespread solidarity with the printworkers included the work of Lesbians and Gays Support the Printworkers (LGSP), which was directly modelled on LGSM and attracted many of the same individuals. An important member was Cath Booth, who was also a print worker and member of the National Graphical Association (NGA). LGSP organised regular planning meetings at the London Lesbian and Gay Centre, turned out for every demonstration, took their banner along to picket lines and collected money at lesbian and gay venues, gathering over £2000 in support of one of the striking union branches (the Society of Graphical and Allied Trades, SOGAT). LGSP also published nine bulletins to promote forthcoming actions and to spread support, including by challenging opposition from within the LGBT community itself. The low point of this was an article in the widely-read monthly, *Gay Times,* in July 1986, which attacked printworkers, arguing that they were as responsible as the owners for anti-gay press coverage. LGSP wrote a point-by-point rebuttal to this piece, but the editor, Alex McKenna, refused to publish it.

In the print unions, attitudes were changing to LGBT rights. The GLF leafletting campaign ten years earlier had strictly limited effectiveness (as discussed in Chapter Two). This time, with practical solidarity being demonstrated on a weekly basis as workers fought for their jobs, the response to an LGBT presence was more positive. The crunch came when lesbian and gay members of the National Graphical Association (NGA) moved a motion at the union's London region 1986 annual conference; they demanded support for anti-discrimination and for establishing an advisory group. There was much positive support from members who were on strike (the conference was for representatives of all those in the region, not just those in dispute) but the union officers stated they could not support setting up a special interest advisory group. The union officers won the vote, although by a very small margin: tellers had to be used because it was so close.

At the 1986 Labour Party Conference, SOGAT had voted for the motion organised by LCLGR. The vote was won by more than the two-thirds majority – 79 per cent – which was the amount required to put the issue on the agenda for inclusion in the next election manifesto. NGA delegates reported they had also wanted to vote for the motion, although their leaders denied this.[24] In this sector, which contained very traditional craft workers, progress was therefore also being made towards equal rights for LGBT members.

UNIONS AND AIDS

One of the unions affected by the Wapping Dispute was the National Union of Journalists (NUJ), which instructed its members not to work for the Murdoch papers while the strike continued. Many of the members followed this.

Throughout the 1980s, the NUJ had an active lesbian and gay group who worked with the union – they organised a meeting jointly with the Campaign for Press and Broadcasting Freedom (CPBF), under the heading 'Gays Fight Media Bias'. The meeting took place in May 1984, and the platform included Andrew Lumsden (former editor of *Gay News*), Margaret Michie and Gill Hanscombe representing the union, and it was chaired by Ted McFadyen. By this date, a major concern for the NUJ, and for the lesbian and gay communities, was the way the AIDS epidemic was being treated in the media and by government. AIDS had reached Britain, with gay men in particular forming a disproportionate number of those who fell victim to a set of diseases that would not be properly understood, or become treatable, for some years. *The Sun*'s profoundly and distressingly homophobic 'gay plague' story (1 February 1985) was only one of many to blame the victims for their fate, in a contemporary culture that normalised such inhumane attitudes towards people enduring great suffering and grief. During this period, the government refused to put out messages about sexual acts (and certainly not gay male acts) and protection, which meant that their propaganda – distributed to every address in the country – was initially both laughably uninformative, and contributed to a sense of panic.

To their credit, most unions responded responsibly to AIDS. The NUJ was faced with the problem that as so many people got their information from the press, the homophobic approach of the gutter press was extremely dangerous. An emergency motion carried at the union's annual conference in April 1985 'expressed revulsion' at some of the media coverage and called for union members to be instructed not to use terms such as 'gay plague' and to adhere to a code of conduct.[25] Very quickly, guidelines for reporting homosexuality and AIDS were written and published at a press conference (July 1985), which was addressed by the NUJ's acting general secretary Jake Ecclestone, with Peter Tatchell, and Anna Durrell representing CHE. Separate guidelines were soon available, one on reporting homosexuality, to which appalling real examples were appended (May 1985) and the other on reporting AIDS (April 1986), with critical advice on respecting privacy. Members were urged to refer to the union equality council for further advice, and to the Terrence Higgins Trust, the community-based support and advice group through which lesbians and gay men themselves were addressing the twin issues of life-threatening disease, and social stigma.[26] Over this time, many other unions also produced their own advice for officers, representatives and members on good practice on dealing with members who became HIV positive or developed AIDS. Betty Gallagher, then the TGWU rep at a London bus garage, recalls that when a member (at Stockwell garage) died of AIDS she tried to organise a fundraiser for his family (he had been married before coming out as gay) but no one came to it. At the next meeting of the union's London Bus Conference she made a forceful speech at which she herself came out, and denounced them for their failure to support the late member, who, she said, had been a better man than any of those present. Having explained about AIDS, she then took a collection of £500 from those present. Later, a member in her own garage (Putney) contracted AIDS and the other reps and members wanted him sacked. Gallagher managed to turn the situation around by educating her members directly. These were good examples of the impact of the panic generated by the coverage of the condition, and of the ability of good trade unionists to prevent discrimination by fellow workers.[27]

The issues around AIDS inevitably had consequences for the progress of lesbian and gay rights in workplaces (even though lesbians were one of the groups least at risk), which required a number of practical responses. Some of these were hammered out at a conference organised by NALGO activist Terry Conway; AIDS as a Trade Union Issue was held in 1985, from which a pack for workplace representatives was published. GRAW came at it from another angle, producing a leaflet seeking information on 'how far Fleet Street bullshit has had an effect among workers'.[28] There were sometimes fierce debates between AIDS activists and union members about the appropriate way to proceed. Changes to negotiating policies included adding 'discrimination on grounds of HIV status' to equal opportunities policies, and, critically, the provision of proper training within the unions at branch level, where the everyday issues facing LGBT members and the concerns of heterosexual members had to be addressed.

Alongside these examples, many other unions also acted on the issue, quite independently, but always adopting the same approach. Civil service unions discussed the issues with managers, and the gay group newsletter reported a positive response; employees with a diagnosis were able to continue in work, and this was followed soon after with a circular stressing the importance of confidentiality.[29] Far from retreating from existing commitments to lesbian and gay equality in the face of hysteria and misinformation spread wide by sections of the media, unions stood up to the challenge and ensured that they were equipped to deal with their members' concerns. This included ensuring they could support members who contracted HIV (the existence of the virus as a cause of AIDS was discovered in 1983).

Workplace health and safety had always been a central trade union issue and from the very beginning of the AIDS crisis identifying the appropriate advice to give to members who might have been at risk of infection through their jobs was an early and urgent need for their protection, and that was quickly addressed. Dealing with the stigma associated with HIV was vital, and union activists responded appropriately in most cases.[30] At the TUC, which was not otherwise doing anything to take forward the 1985 Congress policy, the education department quickly set up health and safety training courses specifically on AIDS. Jon Johnson from the National Union of Civil and Public Servants (NUCPS) remembers attending a course with a very diverse mix of unions represented, at which a similar lack of awareness to that encountered by Betty Gallagher was demonstrated. His memory of this course was that two members in particular could not be distracted from talking about their fear of contracting AIDS from sharing cracked cups.[31]

OTHER SOLIDARITY AND ACTIVITY

Lesbian and gay activists' continuing campaigning inside and outside the trade union movement had won over many heterosexual allies, and during the ruthless government and employer onslaught that characterised much of this decade, this both became more widespread and deepened in individual cases. For teachers in London, when Labour leftists won control of the Inner London Education Authority, this led to a reversal of previous hostility from the authority. Alongside this, Ken Livingstone's term as leader of the Greater London Council generated massive external support for lesbian and gay community groups. The most high profile example of this was the establishment of the London Lesbian and Gay Centre in Farringdon in 1985, mentioned above, which involved making over a derelict building for community use. Tories predictably complained at the use of local taxpayers' money to fund this minority, conveniently forgetting that everyone paid taxes, including the LGBT community, often without getting anything back to address their needs. John McDonnell (now MP for Hayes and Harlington) was then deputy leader of the GLC, and he led the way in establishing the Centre.

A group funded by London local authorities for the first time in 1984, was Lesbian and Gay Employment Rights (LAGER), which was established to advise and support workers facing discrimination. The group developed out of a project run by the Central London Law Centre; Chris Beer and Jenny Poplestone produced a magazine for shop workers in London's Oxford Street. It was decided to turn this magazine and project into LAGER with a management committee and staff, funded by the Greater London Council (GLC). Shane Enright of the TGWU was the trade union representative at the Law Centre, who was then recruited to be a gay male worker representative on LAGER's staff.[32] LAGER's annual report showed how serious the problem of discrimination continued to be: in 1986/7 it dealt with 380 cases, of which sixty-six (thirty-one women, thirty-five men) involved dismissal on grounds of sexual orientation, while 212 involved harassment. Bearing in mind that these were just the cases where individuals were aware of LAGER, and felt confident enough to approach them, the true scale of discrimination must have been even larger.[33]

CONCLUSION

The battle in the unions was ongoing at the end of the 1980s, although these years had seen great steps taken. One way to judge progress during this period is to examine how union delegations (that is, of unions affiliated to the party) voted on LGBT motions at Labour Conferences. The votes in favour of LGBT rights by the print unions at the 1986 Blackpool Labour Party Conference have been noted. The other major unions backing the LCLGR motion this time were: the TGWU, NUPE, the National Union of Railwaymen (NUR), the Technical, Administrative and Supervisory Section of the Amalgamated Union of Engineering Workers (AUEW-TASS; the larger engineering section, under right-wing leadership, voted against the motion), UCATT and several smaller unions. The most significant changes to supporting lesbian and gay rights since the 1985 conference, where the first policy had been put to the vote, were the General and Municipal Workers' Union (the GMB, previously General and Municipal Boilermakers Union) and the Union of Shop, Distributive and Allied Workers (USDAW). The postal workers had yet to consolidate progress, however; the UCW had voted in favour of the motion in 1985, but now switched back to opposition, but the National Communications Union (NCU) delegation rejected an attempt by their leaders to reverse their support for equality.[34]

The foundations had however been laid. Now it was necessary to erect the structures to consolidate the gains, as new attacks rained in, with little prospect of a new and more progressive government that might legislate against discrimination.

NOTES

1. The plan to close twenty-three pits was abandoned when the NUM threatened to strike in February 1981, because there was only six weeks' supply of coal. This episode and subsequent plans to defeat the union have been discussed in many publications, including in biographies of Thatcher by John Campbell, *Margaret Thatcher Vol. 1: The Grocer's Daughter*, London: Cape, 2000 and *Margaret Thatcher Vol. 2: The Iron Lady*, London: Cape, 2003; and Charles Moore, *Margaret Thatcher: The Authorized Biography Vols 1 and 2*, London: Allen Lane, 2013 and 2015.

2. This may sound familiar to Labour supporters following Jeremy Corbyn's election as leader in 2015 and 2016.

3. See Peter Tatchell's book, *The Battle for Bermondsey*, London: Heretic Books, 1983. The bitter irony was that all three leading candidates were gay or bisexual, but the former MP, Bob Mellish (who refused to accept the local party's decision and thus split the Labour vote), and the eventual winner, Liberal Simon Hughes, were closeted at the time.

4. I am grateful to Shane Enright for providing me with a copy of the Defend Judith Williams Campaign information briefing and speakers' notes. *Nalgay News* 46: HCA/Ephemera/450 for report of the conference debate.

5. Reports in *Nalgay News* 31, (January/February 1980), 37 (January/February 1981), 44 (March/April 1982): HCA/Ephemera 450; GRAW press release: HCA/Ephemera 233; GRAW leaflets and campaign materials: HCA/Ephemera 421.

6. GRAW Committee, *Gay Rights at Work*. Written by Ted McFadyen, Richard Thorne and Nigel Young with input from Chris Beer, Paul Crane, Ian Davies, John Lindsay, John McKay, Terry Munyard, Barry Prothero, Alaric Sumner.

7. HCA/Ephemera 111 (NUPE).

8. CPSGG newsletters: HCA/Ephemera 100 and HCA/Ephemera 521.

9. GPTW newsletters nos. 3, 4, 5 and 6 (Dec. 81-Jun. 82): HCA/Ephemera/98. The newsletters were all simply stencilled and duplicated and ran to three or four pages.

10. This section has been compiled from the memories and notes of Geoff Hardy, Alan Jackson and Tim Lucas. Peter Bradley's speech was reprinted in Gay Teachers' Group, *School's Out: Lesbian and Gay Rights and Education*, published in 1983 and then again in an extended and updated version in 1987, pp.102-3 (1987 ed.). Alan Jackson's speech is

at pp.103-4. Among those not happy with these developments, apparently, were the local Jersey gay community, who were worried by all the press attention. Jersey's laws, remarkably, took a long time to catch up with the UK. Criminality for gay sex was ended in 1990 but anti-discrimination provisions were not adopted until a campaign led by local LGBT trade unionists in 2015. Civil partnership was adopted in 2012 but equal marriage will not be allowed until 2018.

11. As remembered by Jackie Lewis, interviewed August 2016, and Angela Mason, interviewed 23 January 2017.

12. Interviews with Jackie Lewis, August 2016, Terry Conway, October 2016, Chris Creegan, December 2016 and Sarah Coldrick, 31 January 2017. Carola Towle interviewed October 2016 has helped enormously in putting me in touch with activists, providing much written material and discussing more recent developments since she became national LGBT officer for UNISON.

13. When a number of motions are submitted on the same subject, they will often be merged into a single, 'composite', motion.

14. Reports in Camden NALGO, *Public Eye: Conference Special, NALGO 1984 Brighton Conference*; discussions with Jackie Lewis and Chris Creegan.

15. There is a small two-page leaflet entitled *Gay Rights at Work* published by NALGO in 1979: TUC Library HD6661, P9.49.

16. The article appeared in *The Sun* in September 1984, with the headline 'The Sun says – Top Town – Hooray for Rugby!' The article, in full, read: 'The Tory council has scrapped a guarantee that it will not discriminate against homosexuals seeking jobs. Farmer Gordon Collett declares robustly: "We're not having men turn up for work in dresses and earrings". *Dead right! The Sun* has nothing against homosexuals. What they do in private is their own affair. But they have no right to make *their* closet problems *our problems*. For years we have had to endure a campaign to cast homosexuals first as martyrs and then as heroes. Some employers have actually been bullied into giving them preference for jobs. Local authorities – notably the GLC [Greater London Council] – have rushed to hand out public money to any group on the sole qualification that it is part of a sexual minority. The homosexuals have been led to believe that they are superior, healthy and normal while the rest of the community are out of step. A society which swallows this kind of nonsense is in danger of destroying itself. Let's ALL follow Rugby in fighting back!'

17. NALGO report on the Rugby campaign, 3 September 1985 (copy provided by Chris Creegan); reports in *Lesbian and Gay Socialist*, Spring 1985. This also contains an article by Chris Smith MP reviewing the overall, substantially negative, picture but also referring to positive outcomes, chiefly of LGSM and of his coming out at Rugby.

18. This was revealed when the Cabinet papers for 1984 were released. See Nick Higham, 'Cabinet papers reveal "secret coal pits closure plan"', *BBC News*, 3 January 2014. www.bbc.co.uk/news/uk-25549596. Accessed 10 November 2017.

19. Mark Ashton, who was then general secretary of the Young Communist League, sadly died of AIDS aged twenty-seven, in February 1987.

20. Minutes of LGSM meetings 15 July, 8 August, 12 August 1984 kindly provided by Mike Jackson, who was interviewed by the author on 25 October 2016.

21. LGSM minutes 31 March 1985; interview with Mike Jackson; HCA/Ephemera/684: notes of the conference, minutes of final meeting of LGSM; letter of protest to Pride Committee.

22. TUC Congress 1985, verbatim report, pp634-36.

23. Peter Purton, *Sodom, Gomorrah and the New Jerusalem: Labour and Lesbian and Gay Rights from Edward Carpenter to Today*, London: LCLGR, 2006, pp45-49.

24. Discussion with Mike Jackson and Shane Enright, who provided copies of the LGSP bulletins 7 and 9 (December 1986 and March 1987); HCA/Ephemera/685: poster advertising LGSP meetings, bulletins 1 (March), 3 (June) and 5 (September) (all 1986).

25. I understand that one member working on the *Manchester Evening News* was disciplined by the union for using the words 'gay plague' in an article.

26. HCA/Ephemera/464: NUJ leaflets, booklets and press releases on AIDS.

27. Betty Gallagher, interviewed by the author 25 January 2017. Gallagher had moved to London in 1966, to enable her to live as an out lesbian. After a few years as a bus conductor she reached the conclusion that she could do a better job than the existing union representative, taking 80 per cent of the vote of the hundred strong workforce to become the only female workplace rep in seventy-four garages.

28. 'AIDS as a Trade Union Issue' , pack published 1986, containing eleven fact sheets on basic issues, a letter in the TGWU magazine (the *Record*, October 1985) and the survey of union activity published by *Labour Research*, February 1986; GRAW leaflet in HCA/Ephemera/421.

29. CPSAGG newsletters November-December 1985 and June-July 1986: HCA/Ephemera/521.

30. The positive responses from all major unions to the LRD survey were discussed by Terry Conway for LCLGR in *Lesbian and Gay Socialist*, Spring 1986, p8.

31. Interviewed 26 January 2017.

32. LAGER in its early days was the site of conflicts within its staff, which was not uncommon in community bodies suddenly provided with funding enabling them to have a paid workforce. It was initially divided into

a gay men's and lesbians' sections. The women staff members rejected Enright's approach that encouraging lesbian and gay trade unionists to commit their unions was key, and Shane himself was dismissed. With union support he went to an Industrial Tribunal and agreed to settle. All information gathered in an interview with Shane Enright, 1 August 2016.

33. Lesbian and Gay Employment Rights, Annual Report 1986-87 (third annual report).

34. From my report in *Lesbian and Gay Socialist*, Winter 1986/87, p7.

4

Old and new issues, continued progress and laying firm foundations

At the beginning of the 1970s, lesbians and gay men who were also trade unionists could not rely on their unions to defend them against prejudice or discrimination at work, let alone challenge the consensus among the great majority of the population, shared by their fellow workers, that homosexuality was deviant, unnatural and unacceptable. By the end of that decade, assisted and encouraged by the work of small numbers of active campaigners in organisations such as the Campaign for Homosexual Equality (CHE) or movements such as the Gay Liberation Front (GLF), a more open lesbian and gay community was visible in the UK, which had promoted virulent backlashes that also served to raise the profile of the community. Through this changing background of the 1970s, lesbian and gay trade unionists had not only come together to organise, but had in some cases already won the backing of their unions.

In Chapter Three, I described how a dominant Thatcher government had set about weakening the power of unions, and had achieved this aim. Alongside this, parts of the media chose to use support for lesbian and gay rights as a stick with which they could beat progressive Labour politicians (as in Bermondsey, or the attacks on the decision by the Greater London Council [GLC] to fund the London Lesbian and Gay Centre). This, combined with the resistance to such attacks, placed the issue of LGBT rights firmly on the agenda of the labour movement. If the traditional leadership of political parties and unions may have preferred the issue not to be treated as important at the beginning, in due course they were either won over, or replaced by new generations of leaders.

By the end of the 1980s, unions had done much to suggest that they were champions of lesbian and gay equality and that their breakthroughs were not occasional trends, but produced sustained results. This chapter traces how progress already achieved was built upon in some important unions in the late 1980s and 1990s, and notes how developments began in others. Before long, the majority of trade union members were in unions that had adopted LGBT equality policies, or set up structures to protect LGBT members. This led to the Trades Union Congress (TUC) itself beginning to take serious note and to act.

Thatcher won a third general election in 1987 but would eventually overreach herself; the attempt to replace local government rates with a poll tax produced massive popular resistance, and ultimately a challenge to her leadership by Tory 'wet' (used to refer to the more liberal 'one nation' Conservatives who opposed Thatcher in this period) Michael Heseltine. Her replacement as Prime Minister was John Major, who, to many people's surprise, led the Conservatives to their fourth consecutive election victory in 1992.

In a changed political environment in which social attitudes to homosexuality had begun to become more egalitarian, Major carried through the first positive legal change not enforced by external courts since 1967, when he legislated to reduce the gay male age of consent from twenty-one to eighteen. There were MPs in parliament who had secured a majority to vote down amendments to make the age of consent equal at sixteen – most, but not all, Labour members had voted for sixteen. This limited step was seen as scarcely worth it to campaigners, since it positively and specifically excluded equality, but the simple fact of it having happened suggested that it might be possible to win more with the right leadership. That opportunity arose with the election of a Labour government led by Tony Blair in 1997. This New Labour regime finally began full legal reform – what is less recognised is the contribution that trade unions had made before 1997, and would continue to make to ensure it happened.

SECTION 28/2A

Reactionary legislation had been enacted in 1987, when a Tory amendment to a local government bill known (ultimately) as Section 28 (in England and Wales) and Section 2a (in Scotland) outlawed the 'promotion of homosexuality' by local authorities as a 'pretended family relationship'.[1] It came as a response to the continuing development of LGBT equality policies in Labour-controlled local authority areas. Section 28/2a was successful beyond expectations; it was never once deployed, but still had a profoundly deterrent effect. Everywhere, in local authorities but even more so in schools – where it actually did not apply – it suddenly again became too dangerous to talk about policies for lesbians and gay men. Some local authorities decided (rightly) to ignore Section 28/2a, but a lot of damage was done in schools, where school leaders insisted on adhering to it, and many teachers who were not already 'out' decided to stay that way. The fight against homophobia among young people was set back for decades. Even after it was repealed, Section 28/2a left a poisonous aftermath – with continued negative consequences for generations of children and young people, especially those growing up lesbian, gay or bisexual.

The response of lesbian and gay people was also dramatic. For the only time in the history of LGBT activism in Britain, a movement took to the streets in protest. The people who were afraid to bring politics into the Pride march in 1985 saw, two years later, just how politics was an integral part of lesbian and gay lives. This late 1980s period of protests was lit up by spectacular events, such as lesbians abseiling into parliament and protesters disrupting live BBC news broadcasts. There were widely supported open letters, political rallies and three large traditional demonstrations – tens of thousands took to the streets of major cities, including many heterosexual supporters. Once the law had passed despite the protests, this movement quickly faded away, however. People went back to their clubs, and a number of community leaders formed the optimistically named Organisation for Lesbian and Gay Action (OLGA). This quickly disappeared too, however. In 1989, a number of leading out lesbian and gay figures – such as Sir Ian McKellen, Lisa Power and Michael Cashman – decided to set up Stonewall as a campaigning and lobbying group. Angela Mason was its second director (from 1992 – the first was Tim Barnett) and went on to work closely with trade unions among many other allies.

Trade unions were now part of the resistance too, and trade union banners had been highly visible on the protest marches; a cross-union campaign under the title of Trade Unionists against Section 28 (TUAS28) was launched at the initiative of Sarah Roelofs. This became the formal trade union sectional campaign of Stop the

Clause, among many that were established by activists who had been involved in bodies like GRAW. The leaders of the National Union of Mineworkers (NUM) sent a public message of support to rallies against the clause (plate 6). TUAS28 involved union activists previously involved in Lesbians and Gays Support the Miners (LGSM) and Lesbians and Gays Support the Printworkers (LGSP) and often from the left of the movement. They participated in TUAS28 as individuals, not formally as union representatives, and their time was used to organise motions about Section 28 to be submitted to union conferences, which were based on a model they had prepared. They also attempted to integrate the anti-Section 28 fight into the range of industrial conflicts then raging, and into the resistance work against another attack that was then under way on abortion rights. Some union national conferences – those at the National Association of Teachers in Further and Higher Education (NATFHE) and the National and Local Government Officers association (NALGO) occurred at the right time – carried motions demanding that Section 28 should not be complied with. But it was more difficult to put policy into practice.[2]

Union presence in the resistance to Section 28 signified another important step. Unions were looking both inwards and outwards. For lesbian and gay activists, if they were challenging prejudice and discrimination in the workplace and sometimes within their unions, the same battles were being faced outside work. These trade unionists were also part of wider communities, whether it was because of AIDS or because of the insult to LGBT identities in Section 28/2a. The continued progress within some trade unions during the later 1980s and early 1990s raised the question of internal organisation and union policy, which were increasingly connected with issues facing the wider community.

FURTHER DEVELOPMENTS IN UNION RECOGNITION

Civil service unions

Lesbian and gay civil servants' early struggles to become established had, as discussed in Chapter Two, led to the creation of a group open to all lesbian and gay members across eight civil service unions, the Civil and Public Servants Gay Group (CPSGG). The positive approach unions adopted in negotiations with civil service managers over AIDS was a good sign, but the CPSGG struggled to sustain itself and it seems that by the middle of the 1980s, it had reverted into distinct groups organising directly within each civil service union. Yvonne Washbourne, who had been a civil servant since 1974, became involved in the lesbian and gay group in the National Union of Civil and Public Servants (NUCPS) in the mid-1980s and remembers that the group published newsletters, organised seminars with the backing of the union's executive, and held successful fringe meetings at union conferences. Brian Shaw joined the Inland Revenue Staff Federation (IRSF) in 1983, where the lesbian and gay group had functioned since the late 1970s. In 1979, the union's conference had carried a lesbian and gay rights policy over the opposition of members from Northern Ireland, and the group had got going, but mainly as a social network. A conference under the name Pink Tape took place in 1989, with members from the NUCPS, the IRSF and others in attendance. The conference discussed more effective cross-union working. It had official recognition, and a joint NUCPS-IRSF leaflet was produced – this time for a more inclusive LGB audience – with supporting statements from both union executives. Both groups charged members a fee for joining. The real take off followed the merger of these two unions and the lesbian and gay groups came together, decided to adopt the name Proud, and adopted a constitution.

The Civil and Public Services Association (CPSA) remained separate until it merged with NUCPS and the IRSF in 1998, to form the Public and Commercial Services union (PCS). The Association of First Division Civil Servants (FDA) remained separate. The CPSA lesbian and gay group relaunched after the old CPSGG folded when separate groups were launched in NUCPS (formed from the Society of Civil and Public Servants, SCPS, and the Civil Service Union, CSU) and the Institution of Professionals, Managers and Specialists (IPMS). The new CPSAGG had the same secretary as previously – Don Street – until his resignation in 1989. It too had its successes within the union, winning a vote at the union conference in that year, with only a few people opposing out of a thousand. It also attracted forty people to its fringe meeting, at the same conference, where the union's deputy general secretary had spoken. The group regularly took the union banner on Pride marches during the 1980s.

However, the CPSA leadership was more right-wing than that of the other civil service unions, and the executive kept a close eye on the activities of all the equality groups. All the civil service unions had adopted equality policies by now, and the unions had engaged in constructive negotiations on anti-discrimination policies with most government departments. One of the longest-standing issues was the continuation of 'positive vetting',[3] which made homosexuality still a bar in the Foreign Office up to 1991, when the unions negotiated it away. Jon Johnson recalls attending a meeting at the headquarters of MI5 in June 1995, where Francis Kilvington, then TUC women's officer, led a vigorous attempt to convince a seminar of 'investigation officers' and security staff to get rid of positive vetting in the security services.[4]

The Transport and General Workers' Union

Britain's largest union, the Transport and General Workers' Union (TGWU), had already shown support for lesbian and gay rights by voting for the motions at the TUC and Labour Party Conferences and by producing information on AIDS, but it had no formal confer-ence policy and no structures for lesbian and gay members. Diana Holland, the officer dealing with education in Region One (that included London) in the 1980s, had already managed to get lesbian and gay issues into the regional equality course by 1984, where Barry Canfield (who later became regional secretary) led the programme. She explained this as arising from the activities and discussions of women and young members. A national mandate was lacking, however. Policy on AIDS had provided the first vehicle. A voluntary sector TGWU branch in London (branch no. 1/524) put forward a motion on AIDS and branch member Shane Enright waved a condom during the motion's debate at the union's 1987 two-yearly conference. The chair cut off Enright's microphone but the motion was carried. At the same conference, a motion submitted from my own branch of the TGWU (also in the voluntary sector, branch no 1/1007) called for a meeting to be set up for lesbian and gay members but this failed. A speaker opposed it, asking 'why should we spend union money on these people?'[5]

Shane Enright had, during the late 1980s, been working to bring together an informal network of lesbian and gay members in the region and nationally. This was a by-product of a mass recruitment campaign in the voluntary sector that saw Enright's branch expand to more than 5000 members. It was then subdivided (and there also voluntary sector branches in Glasgow, Leeds and Liverpool linked together through a national Combine Committee). This provided a crucial support network for lesbian and gay members as well. Enright himself became part of the relevant trade group committee; the union was structured regionally through branches but it also had a committee for each industrial sector, known as trade groups. These were replicated at national level, and this combination resulted in a lot – and potentially an overwhelming number – of committees for activists to take part in.

Following the setback in 1987, much more careful planning went into recovering lost ground at the subsequent TGWU conference, in 1989. Motions were submitted by several branches and a composite version of these different motions was moved by Enright during the debate on equal opportunities, which also debated motions on women's rights, black people's rights and disabilities. Conscious of the opposition encountered previously, he constructed the speech to sit within the theme the union had adopted for the event, 'stronger because we care', stating that the composite motion was about the discrimination and invisibility faced by lesbians and gay men. He emphasised his pride in his role as shop steward, former branch secretary and regional committee member – and as a gay man – and pointed out the risks associated with being honest, with no legal protection, harassment from workmates, AIDS and its impacts. He went on to assert that invisibility was the vehicle of LGBT oppression, and insisted on the importance of presenting positive images of lesbians and gay men, reminding the conference that the union (for which he thanked general secretary Ron Todd) had supported lesbian and gay rights at the TUC and Labour Party Conference, and in the fight against Section 28/2a.

The motion's seconder was Alan Scott, who spoke as a heterosexual, calling on the labour movement to oppose all discrimination and demanding that the union now take positive steps to do so. In the debate that followed, there were two speeches against the motion, one complaining about the 'misuse' of the word gay and arguing that gays were asking for privileges, the other claiming to 'have nothing against it in broad principle' but suggesting it should have been submitted to a different conference. Two more speeches were delivered in favour and then Margaret Prosser summed up (on the whole equal opportunities debate) for the national executive, recommending delegates to support this motion, pointing out how the mover (Enright) 'had touched many hearts' in demonstrating the issues lesbians and gay men faced in their everyday lives. The vote was called and the motion was carried: Britain's largest union finally had the policy to back up the actions it had already taken, but also a remit to set about more structured work.[6]

The membership of the TGWU included working people from many different trades and occupations. The initiative for winning the motion on the policy had come from white collar members, but it could only have won with the support of delegates representing blue collar workers too: and it did, easily. The debate showed how opponents now only felt able to deploy a much narrower range of responses. The argument at that particular debate, that asking for LGBT equality was equivalent to somehow seeking privileges, despite all the evidence of discrimination, rang increasingly hollow. The other opposing speaker that day felt it was necessary to state first that he had nothing against LGBT people in principle, but rather that his problem lay elsewhere. It was significant that he now felt it necessary to preface his opposition with these words.

On that occasion, the opposition's argument fell flat; the culture inside the labour movement had changed. Even though, as the supportive speakers in the debate observed, there were nudges and innuendo while Shane Enright spoke, we had arrived at the point where they no longer felt free to state their prejudices – or to vote with them. This added up to an important change for the better. If the battle to finally win everyone over to active support still had a long way to go, the first critical steps along the road had been taken. The union's leaders had publicly demonstrated their backing for equality in the union's national democratic parliament, its biennial conference, where the lay members had the final say through their votes.

Some problems did continue, however; the union only acted on the policy after another motion criticising the lack of action was carried at the next conference, in 1991. It was only then that a national working group was formed, which developed plans including one on better training provision. This was headed up by Margaret Prosser

and then national officer Bob
Eventually, in 1993, a leafle
written and circulated around

But there was still a majoı
among the hundreds of the
different industries. Diana H
for Region One, mentioned a
meetings with members and
time she did not include lesbia
was at a meeting composed e
and it was then raised by one (

LGBT in other sectors

Lesbian and gay members outside the voluntary sector had already
organised themselves into informal networks. One was London
Transport buses, where the formidable local representative Betty
Gallagher had long before made an impact in her workplace and the
union (see Chapter Three). Here, the issue of extending employees'
travel passes to same-sex partners – already available to opposite sex
partners – was being negotiated by the union and Gallagher had
demanded the union negotiate this across the whole of London
Transport as well.

In contrast, among aviation workers, also often TGWU members,
it had long been the case that being lesbian or gay was accepted, but
only if it was not public. This now changed with the appearance
of the group FlagFlyers for 'lesbians and gay men in civil air transport', which took off with regular newsletters from spring 1994, and
which produced a briefing pointing out all the areas in which British
Airways' employment policies discriminated against them. It was a
long list.[7]

It was a slow process to set up a self-organised structure in TGWU,
in which LGBT members themselves would discuss policy – despite
the fact that the union did have a long-established women's advisory
committee. Attendance at the working group was usually low, the
meetings were infrequent, and the agenda limited.[8] It was necessary to change this structure to something more democratic, and
when that happened, the TGWU would then stand alongside other
unions in genuinely representing its many lesbian and gay members

vas vitally important, but so was the great
individual workplace representatives or local
rs in representing members against discrimina-
ing equality policies with employers.

ing unions

ress was also being made in the engineering industry, although
re the lead role was taken among its technical and supervisory
staff as represented in the union AUEW-TASS (the Technical,
Administrative and Supervisory Section of the Amalgamated
Union of Engineering Workers – but a separate union from the
AUEW), under the left-wing leadership of its general secretary Ken
Gill, who was a member of the Communist Party of Great Britain
(CPGB). TASS merged with the Association of Scientific, Technical
and Managerial Staff (ASTMS), under its general secretary Clive
Jenkins, to form Manufacturing, Science, Finance (MSF) in 1988.

An interviewee for this book, Lesley Mansell's story also tells that
of lesbian and gay rights in AUEW-TASS. Having joined TASS as
a worker in a clock factory in the 1970s, and served eleven years
as a shop steward, Mansell had been encouraged by the union to
take part in the union's formal women's structures. She also went to
university, where she came out during the campaign against Section
28 (1987-88), and then took the Section 28 issue back into the union
with a great response from her branch in the East Midlands. She
had seen a contact address for lesbian and gay members but when
she attempted to contact it she received no response. She then spoke
to the national equality officer, Anne Gibson. This led to an invitation to the next national equality meeting at which she invited other
lesbian and gay members to join her to form an informal group.
This included Mansell, Martin Groombridge, Kieran Coleman and
Kate Bloor, who came together and wrote a leaflet in 1989 that was
circulated in Gibson's name. Lesbians and Gays in MSF (LAGIM)
was created in 1989, after the unions merged, with the backing of
the national MSF. It had regular meetings and ultimately morphed
into a formal committee. They focussed on both internal and
external campaigning. Externally, a LAGIM stall at London Pride
in 1990 brought in new members, while they also circulated material
through internal union mailings to all branches. Support from the

MSF leadership was strong. The MSF *Equal Opportunities Charter for the 1990s* was published by the union in 1990 and included a section on lesbian and gay issues. *Lesbians and Gays in MSF* was published in 1992. Senior officers were regularly present and showed support at group or committee meetings, and would often stay for the whole event – including AUEW-TASS general secretary Ken Gill, and his successor, Roger Lyons. National Executive member Sue Sharpe also became a member of the LAGIM committee; a cynic might have thought this was to limit the group's activities, but Sharpe demonstrated genuine support.[9]

The internal struggle for progress in MSF did inevitably encounter some resistance. Many unions organise conferences with different purposes. A separate event would take place at intervals for the purpose of deciding changes to union rules. Policy on other issues is decided at regular (usually annual) conferences. Branches of the union are invited to elect delegates and submit motions to both types of event. When a proposal for inclusion of LGBT rights issues in the union's rules was proposed in 1989 at the rules conference, a somewhat unenlightened National Executive Council (NEC) member spoke against it, saying 'we don't want perverts in the union', and the motion was not passed. But experience at policy conferences was much more positive, and the network of members was used to generate motions to go to the union conference on a regular basis, successfully.

Dave Samuel was a TASS member working for Shell Oil in Ellesmere Port where he did not come out. He described his sector of the union (the Craft Sector) as seeing itself as the elite and thus the attitude of its members with regard to LGBT people was that 'we don't have them in our sector'. But having been elected to the union's regional council (after the merger with ASTMS to form MSF) he attended a conference in London. Here, Samuel saw publicity for LAGIM and joined in 1989, although he still kept his sexuality private. He remembers the LAGIM committee holding meetings all over the country as well as at the union's training schools held in Bishop's Stortford, all paid for by the union.

Gradually, hostility died away in MSF and when Samuel came out to his work colleagues the response was 'we always suspected', but nothing hostile. Having been accepted, he then played a more substantial role in the union, speaking at events, representing them at TUC lesbian and gay conferences in the 2000s. In the early 2000s, he noted, although some people remained homophobic in private, they no longer felt able to voice their views in public. Samuel went on to chair the North West regional LGBT group for MSF, and to help staff the LAGIM helpline (originally run by Lesley Mansell – from her home, but funded by MSF before it moved to Dave Samuel's house). Through this helpline, he had to deal with calls from people not being accepted in work, people with grievances about discrimination they had faced, such as being overlooked for promotion, and other standard problems that many people were dealing with during this period. The helpline had to be formalised (there is a legal risk to the union if unqualified people offer what proves to be wrong advice) which happened in 2001 but because of this, it lost its guarantee of having another LGBT person answering a call, which might explain why it faded out of use. Samuel remembers the powerful and liberating effect of attending his first London Pride in the 1990s, an event that was 'overwhelming and fantastic', and this was something he felt was only possible as a consequence of the (recognised) LGBT structure within his union.[10]

Katie Hanson, another interviewee and member of ASTMS from 1988, followed a different path but also came to lesbian and gay rights through the women's structure within the union, where the presence of other out lesbians gave her the confidence to come out herself. She was part of ASTMS before the merger to form MSF, and discovered that there had been a gay caucus (that is, an informal network) in the union, member-led and unofficial. This may not have been the same group that interviewee Philip Inglesant attempted to work with when he joined ASTMS in 1980; he attended a meeting of three or four people in a private house, but then heard nothing more.

Inglesant later became secretary of the formal LAGIM committee when it was established, which carried out a range of functions. It ensured union presences at Pride marches (London and Manchester in the 1990s), organised motions for union conference, and developed policy positions. Weekend events were organised at the union's training school (in Bishop's Stortford) and guest speakers were invited. These were well attended.[11]

Employers continued to discriminate throughout the 1980s and early 1990s, and the response of MSF was good when this happened. The Church of England Children's Society asked one of its patrons,

Sandi Toksvig, to resign in 1994 after she came out as a lesbian. Employees of the Society were members of MSF, so LAGIM organised a picket of the organisation. The Society also decided that it would not place children for adoption with same-sex couples. When staff members came out as lesbian or gay to challenge them, the Society agreed to let adoption by same-sex couples take place, providing it was done through the local authority and not through the Society itself. This disagreement mattered a great deal, since it highlighted the old prejudice that homosexuals were a risk to children. It also prefigured the debate that would take place under a Labour government in 2003 (see Chapter Five). In both cases, the unions' response was clearly committed to the rights of lesbian and gay members and people.

LAGIM proved to be a trailblazer in another way too. At a meeting in Camden in 1990, a member came out as bisexual. This provoked a row with those who saw this as incompatible with a specifically lesbian and gay equality remit. Lesley Mansell remembers successfully arguing for inclusion of bisexual members, and that from then on there was no problem with LAGIM being LGB. Trans members were also involved and found a welcome in the group.

It would have been incompatible with the realities of the national situation for everything to have been positive. The LAGIM mailing list had a separate facility for members who did not want to risk being out about their sexualities at work. While the national leadership of MSF, and especially the equality officers and most regions of the union were supportive, not everyone was. LAGIM was therefore a hybrid structure, involving both activists who used it for campaigning alongside those people who did not wish to challenge colleagues or managers, and who chose not to come out, but who looked to LAGIM for support and information. There were still many union members who were not comfortable talking about the issues around sexuality, and were still resistant to national debates about it, along the traditional lines of 'what's it got to do with the union?' But significant progress had been achieved and as elsewhere, it went on to be sustained.[12]

Communications unions

The postal and telecoms unions the Union of Communication Workers (UCW) and the National Communications Union (NCU) merged to create the Communication Workers' Union (CWU) in 1995. When such mergers took place, they raised questions as to what should happen to pre-existing equality structures, as so many unions had developed bodies during the 1980s to meet the needs of their women, black, disabled and – increasingly, as we have seen, lesbian and gay (and occasionally also bisexual) members. Here, the NCU came in with a recognised lesbian and gay body, known as the Lesbian and Gay Advisory Committee (LGAC). This structure, rather than the Gay Post and Telecom Workers' Group that formed in 1982 (Chapter Two), took forward the banner of LGB self-organisation in this industry. With the strong backing of the NCU general secretary Tony Young, the LGAC and structures for encouraging and developing equality continued to be recognised in the new CWU.

The decision to create the LGAC in 1991 had been controversial, as is remembered by activists Mary Hanson (who had joined the NCU in 1984) and Maria Exall (joined 1988). They became chair and vice-chair of the LGAC. Setting it up in the first place resulted in resistance from certain members of the union, often depending on gender balances in different branches. Clerical branches were 80 per cent women and were usually much more supportive of the equality agenda than the engineering branches, which were 95 per cent male. Here, homophobic (and misogynist) banter was very common. At the first attempt to establish the LGAC at the NCU conference in 1990, speakers argued that the committee was not needed, and that having it would force people to come out about their sexuality in order to get elected. The national executive were also opposed to the committee and the motion failed.

The second time the LGAC was proposed, supporters had lobbied and won the backing of the union's broad left, who were firm supporters of equality, and it was carried in 1991. The new committee was elected from people nominated by their branches and was soon active. But it was evident that, with no previous work having been done to educate members on the need for lesbian and gay equal rights, it was starting from a very low level. The LGAC had to fight to get LGBT issues onto national training courses in order to begin the process of challenging ignorance.

Laurie Smith had joined the Post Office Engineering Union (POEU) in 1975,[13] as an apprentice, and became a steward in 1983.[14]

He recalled seeing a flyer for a lesbian and gay event while a delegate to the annual conference in Blackpool in 1986. His branch never discussed lesbian and gay issues (despite having Maria Exall as its chair) and he was unaware of the existence of LGAC until he came out in 1994, and then got involved with wider LGBT rights issues. On the one hand, as Smith remembers, he did not experience bad reactions to his sexuality from work colleagues, but on the other hand, there was continuing prejudice reflected in LGBT rights posters being pulled down, homophobic workplace banter and so on.

The structures for supporting LGBT members in the unions evolved, but the importance of high visibility for doing so, and for challenging prevailing homophobic cultures has been evident since they were created. There were extensive articles in the CWU magazine *Voice*,[15] and the LGAC's own journal *Outtalk*. The clerical and engineering workplaces and branches continued to have different perspectives, which were reflected in their differing levels of support for equality. The merger with the postal workers established another gap; even in the present day, the postal side is less well represented in the LGBT equality structures than the telecom side.

There is an irony in this story, in that British Telecom (BT) has long presented itself as an outstanding supporter of equality. Through the 1980s and 1990s, the NCU then the CWU successfully negotiated a range of policies such as equal pension rights and special leave for non-married partners, and lesbian and gay members benefitted from these. As an employer, BT also supported (and continues to support) staff networks including one for LGBT members. However, the LGBT network has tended to be a social gathering for managers, rather than intervening in workplace disputes; only trade unions can represent members in dealing with the employer.

Despite the sometimes challenging workplace environment, progress in LGBT representation in the post and communications unions is evidence of a number of factors that determined unions' efforts to become champions of LGBT equality. The struggles to establish groups within these unions illustrate well the obstacles arising within workforces in which ignorance and prejudices were widespread, as they were in society in general. However, the determination of individual LGBT members to fight for equal rights, combined with the support of growing numbers of heterosexual allies (and, importantly, those at the top of the union), won through against initial opposition. These members created a visible LGBT presence and structure in the unions, and in the process, they supported other LGBT members to come out, ensured the union continued to extract more equal working conditions from the employer, widened understanding and support for equality in general, and supported struggles outside the union. Not least, it helped to challenge prejudice among members.

NEXT STEPS IN OTHER PUBLIC SECTOR UNIONS

In Chapter Three, I described the historic breakthroughs represented by the lesbian and gay victories at the 1983 National Union of Teachers (NUT) and the National and Local Government Officers' Association (NALGO) conferences. These events were decisive because, unlike on previous occasions, they were followed by real action that took the issue much deeper into the respective unions and generated campaigning both inside and outside of them.

The National Union of Teachers

The 1983 NUT conference had not established new policy but this was changed with motions at the 1987 and 1988 annual conferences. The 1987 motion was submitted by the Leicestershire and City of Leicester and Hackney (London) branches. It boldly asserted in its first line that 'being lesbian, gay or bisexual is in no respect inferior to being hetrosexual [*sic*.]' (note that bisexuals had now achieved recognition in the NUT as well as in LAGIM). The motion went on to lay out areas of discrimination. It focussed strongly on the teachers' right to decide whether to be open about their sexualities. The 1988 motion thunderously denounced Section 28 and called for the union to publish guidance on how to respond to it. However, Section 28 was a serious hindrance to the part of union policy that called for the teaching of equality, and was also a challenge to LGBT members being out at work, in a way that did not apply in any other sector. It would be a recurrent theme for all teachers' unions even after the repeal of the law in 2000 in Scotland, and 2003 in England and Wales.

The NUT's first LGB conference took place in 1989 against a background of some (minority) opposition, but with the support of the union, and was then repeated annually with the title Pride in

Education. Most of the seventy or eighty regular attendees came through branch nominations, but there was a facility for people who did not wish to out themselves to attend as well. The new national NUT equality officer, Ruth Blunt, helped with the work of the task group (into which the working group had been transformed) and encouraged participation: seven of the union's eight English regions along with Wales sent representatives. Sue Sanders, who had been working in Schools Out (Chapter Three), was recruited to run workshops at the conferences and joined the task group in 1993. The task group's input helped Blunt to author the union publication *Lesbian and Gay Equality in Education – An Issue for Every Teacher* (1999), which went to every school in the UK. Blunt remembers that it was well received. Its title shows the purpose behind it, and in the context of Section 28, the need for it was pressing. During the late 1990s, Blunt recalls that members continued to report homophobic harassment in schools, problems which were dealt with by union regional officials. Their training was an important part of the task group's role and the union now organised training courses both for lay members and full time officers in which the booklet *Something to Tell You*,[16] proved a useful tool for reaching non-LGBT members to explain the realities faced by young LGBT people.

The NUT also dealt successfully with a case of discrimination on grounds of gender identity. A trans deputy headteacher in south-west England was forced to take ill-health retirement because of her gender. Ruth Blunt advised the regional officer on how to deal with the case, and how to organise the deputy head's return to work. This was successful because of a strong case made for her professional ability.[17]

The National and Local Government Officers' Association

In NALGO, progress was substantial, although Chris Eades and Jackie Lewis were unsuccessful when they stood for election to the national executive as the first out candidates in 1984/5. It took a couple of years, then the newly established national lesbian and gay conference secured national NALGO funding (the first had been paid for by branches). Early conferences, in the mid 1980s, began to address seriously the issues of diversity within the community,[18] inviting disabled lesbians and gay men onto the lesbian and gay committee from 1985 and working on the specific issues facing black lesbians and gay men from 1986. These discussions were the genesis of the future caucuses that would be built into the union's LGBT structures.

Also in 1986, there was an attempt to throw back the advances in LGBT rights with a motion at the annual NALGO conference attacking the union's lesbian and gay equality policy. Those moving the motion argued that NALGO should stop treating lesbians and gay men as 'a special category'. Peter Hunter from the North West region said he had nothing against 'these unfortunate people who through no fault of their own have been cursed by nature'. Not surprisingly, there was uproar, but those moving the motion, and opposing LGBT rights, were well organised this time, and the vote was close. However, with the backing of the national executive, the motion was defeated. This was a decisive confirmation of NALGO's commitment to lesbian and gay equality which would not be challenged again at annual conference. A motion condemning homophobic press coverage of AIDS was carried.[19]

The same successes were not found in the continuing arguments around self-organisation. Here, the main focus of attention was black members who were fighting for their right to speak for themselves in NALGO. Representatives of each of the self-organised groups – black, women, lesbian and gay and disabled members – had prepared a joint report on discrimination, explaining why self-organisation was needed, and had toured it extensively around all of the union's districts during 1985 and 1986. But the document was voted down at the national conference in 1987. An alternative version presented by the National Executive was also voted out at the 1988 conference. In the end, the Executive was given legal advice that it could support the self-organised committee structures, and proceeded to do so, including supporting the National Lesbian and Gay Committee (NLGC).

From then on, NALGO possessed both policies, and recognised and supported national equality structures. In 1993, NALGO merged with the National Union of Public Employees (NUPE) and the Confederation of Health Service Employees (COHSE) to create a new public sector union of great size, UNISON. This merger was carried out smoothly but it posed a real challenge for the now firmly established lesbian and gay structures in NALGO, which were entirely different from what existed in the other two unions. Transitional structures were put in place and seats were reserved for the other two unions on the national lesbian and gay committee.[20]

The development of UNISON's LGBT structures

The NUPE gay group, NUPEGG, never developed into the same kind of self-organised group as the NALGO gay group, NALGAY. The culture was different in the former, a manual workers' union. Ron Harley was one of twenty-six NUPE representatives at the first UNISON lesbian and gay conference in 1993. He had come out in 1986, and never met any problems with his branch colleagues (in Camden), who mainly worked for the local authority, mostly as home help for the elderly or disabled people, or doing refuse collection. When a member who was a caretaker died of AIDS, it was not a secret, and branch members collected £500 for his family. Some home helps were understandably anxious about the possible risk to them from working with people with AIDS, and one shop steward was particularly worried, until his own nephew contracted the condition and his attitude became more positive towards lesbian and gay rights. But if there was no hostility among members, nor was there any organisation. First steps towards self-organisation were taken by black members, who faced resistance from other members to their attempt to set up a structure for themselves. When it became clear that the merger between NUPE and NALGO was going to happen, officers in the London region (Phil Thompson and Alison Waylen) tried to get a lesbian and gay group together so the union would be better placed when the merger happened. After a couple of failed attempts, the group held meetings of seven or eight people every two months.

NUPE and COHSE were invited to send representatives to the last separate NALGO lesbian and gay conference, which took place in 1992 – the year before the merger. It was, as Ron Harley reported, 'an eye-opener' with the guests 'in hysterics' at the 'political correctness' of NALGO members. Marie Mulholland (the rep from Northern Ireland) refused to follow the other women when a separate women's space was announced. So at the first UNISON event, the members from NUPE were 'walking on eggshells' for fear of not speaking appropriately to those from NALGO. However, assimilation succeeded; within one year it was no longer 'them and us'. Other reps came out in the Camden NUPE branch (which merged with Camden NALGO) and Harley was elected as one of the lesbian and gay reps sent on the union delegation to Labour Party conference.[21]

Members in COHSE similarly came with no previous LGBT structure behind them, although the union had, like NUPE, adopted a positive approach to lesbian and gay issues for a long time before the merger. Just as for NUPE home helps, the arrival of AIDS and the media-induced hysteria had posed a challenge for COHSE members whose jobs involved moving patients – such as porters at St Mary's hospital in London. COHSE was one of the first to publish guidelines on responses to AIDS. Following the events at the NALGO conference in the Isle of Man in 1983, COHSE decided that it too would boycott the venue. In 1984, the union backed the campaign to defend LGBT bookshop *Gay's the Word*, and Tracy Lambert from COHSE's eastern region was a speaker at demonstrations against Section 28. The first resolution at a national conference was in the mid-1980s, and there were two motions at the 1991 conference, condemning recent changes in criminal law that impacted on gay men, and acts of discrimination, which were carried overwhelmingly.[22] The presence of many out gay men in nursing was evidently helpful in determining the positive culture within COHSE.[23]

The newly formed UNISON thus continued to promote the equality agenda both internally and outwardly during these years. One early decision in particular was of great significance: UNISON agreed to take part in the International Lesbian and Gay Association (ILGA) world conference,[24] and went on to become an active participant when its European section was set up in 1996, with Jackie Lewis acting as the UNISON representative.

WORKING ACROSS THE MOVEMENT

With lesbian and gay rights now firmly established as a workplace issue for many larger unions, and with growing recognition of the negative treatment of lesbians and gay men outside work, there was still a long way to go before every corner of the labour movement had been reached with these messages. The question arose of what might be done by this millions-strong coalition of workers.

The Labour Party

Removing the legal oppression of LGBT rights required a Labour government to introduce new laws, but despite Labour conferences voting for LGBT equality policies since 1985, Labour leaders had made repeated retreats from conference policies, requiring repeated campaigns led by the Labour Campaign for Lesbian and Gay Rights (LCLGR) to reassert them.

As a result of LCLGR's work, motions were on the Labour Party Conference agenda time and again. Firstly, there was a motion against Section 28 (1988). This was required because the initial response of Labour parliamentarians had not been to oppose Section 28, although this was quickly reversed following loud protests and Labour leader Neil Kinnock memorably described it as 'this pink triangle clause' in a message to Pride, referencing the persecution of homosexuals during the Holocaust. Secondly, there was a motion on the age of consent (1989), after deputy leader Roy Hattersley proposed dropping the Labour Party's commitment to equalising it. Thirdly, there was a motion on the recognition of lesbian and gay relationships as of equal worth with heterosexuals' relation-ships (1994). For each of these motions, the conference vote was overwhelming: in 1994, it achieved an astonishing 97 per cent of the card vote. It appeared that all the affiliated unions were now voting for lesbian and gay rights. All that was lacking was a Labour government to carry out the policies. After the 1992 election defeat, John Smith was elected to replace Kinnock as leader of the party, but Smith died suddenly in 1994. He was replaced by Tony Blair. LCLGR had already encountered Blair in his role as Shadow Home Secretary, and he had indicated, in a meeting, his support for an equal age of consent – but emphasised that did not believe same-sex relationships were equivalent to heterosexual ones.[25] Evidently the Labour Party still had some distance to go in its relationship to LGBT rights.

The Trades Union Congress

The TUC had LGBT equality policies but during the late 1980s and early 1990s, it took no action on them, until there was encourage-ment from the unions. Up to 1998, the small equalities department of the TUC did not have a dedicated staff member whose role specifically included lesbian and gay rights, so it had to be covered by other staff.

A survey was carried out by the TUC to identify progress, the results of which were published as *Unions Working for Lesbian and Gay Members* in February 1991. It listed responses from twenty-two major unions – of the larger unions, only the engineers (AUEW) and builders (Union of Construction Allied Trades and Technicians, UCATT) were missing. The survey asked about activity undertaken by unions for LGBT rights, with the most substantial activity reported by civil service unions, MSF, NALGO, and the NUT. However, many other unions had variously supported formal or informal lesbian and gay groups, issued advice on AIDS, negotiated inclusion in equal opportunities policies, and issued advice in circulars to branches. While many had responded to pressure from members, others seem to have initiated action from the top (or from equality committees). Given how recently the issue had become part of trade union agendas, the number of unions (and the number of union members who were represented by them) that were undertaking activity on behalf of lesbian and gay members themselves, or on behalf of the cause of lesbian and gay equality more broadly, was impressive. But there continued to be gaps – unions that had not yet responded to the needs of their own lesbian and gay members.[26] An updated list was published following another survey in 1996, which demonstrated that there had been further progress.

The wide variety of actions that had taken place and the rather narrow focus of most union policies, which tended to focus on each union's particular concerns, cried out for the labour movement as a whole to address its priorities and to organise collective LGBT rights campaigns. However, there was no mechanism for this to happen; this was unlike the TUC's existing women's and black workers' conferences, which could debate motions that became recommendations to the TUC. The absence of such a structure could be seen as a form of inequality in itself.

There had been intermittent efforts at cross-union organising, including the L&G workers' conferences of 1975-6 (Chapter Two), Gay Rights at Work (GRAW, now long defunct) and TUAS28 (now redundant). The next attempt to bring together trade unionists on a cross-union basis was set up by NUCPS member Jon Johnson in 1992. Calling itself the Lesbian and Gay TUC, it was a group containing the same people as had organised TUAS28, but it also attracted new activists. It focussed mainly on self-organised LGBT groups in unions rather than those unions where formal structures had already been established, such as in NALGO. This meant that most of those involved were drawn from unions like the TGWU and the NUT, which did not yet have formal structures. The group's main focus was to develop organisation and support for equality inside unions and it found very positive support from the equality officer at the TUC who was covering the remit.[27]

Indeed, responding to pressure from unions, the TUC began to move on lesbian and gay rights, beginning a programme of annual seminars. Lesbian and Gay Rights at Work was held on 25 June 1992 and chaired by Ken Gill and Anne Gibson both from the TUC's equal rights committee. The speakers were Anne Hayfield from Lesbian and Gay Employment Rights (LAGER), talking about discrimination, Paul Fairweather from NALGO, and Diana Holland from the TGWU. Other contributions were made by Jon Johnson, Lyn Stagg from IPMS, Chris Eades from NALGO (who spoke on self-organisation) and Philip Inglesant from MSF. The sixty people in attendance came from twenty-two different unions. The demand for equal representation within the TUC was raised. One of the actions arising from the seminars was the production of a TUC leaflet, a four-page publication that sold for 60p. It called on unions to negotiate inclusive equal opportunities policies, to examine collective agreements to remove discrimination, and to campaign to change laws.[28]

Work at the TUC continued. Responding to demands from the 1995 annual seminar, attended by ninety-four people (and including an address from Angela Mason of Stonewall) a major report was published in December 1995, entitled *Pensions and Prejudice: How Public Sector Pension Schemes Discriminate against Non-Married Partners*. Janice Millman in the TUC's equal rights department was responsible for it. It presented examples from the private sector wherein the problem had been overcome, and it made recommendations on simple solutions. It had involved extensive consultation with the Council of Civil Service Unions (CCSU), the Educational Institute of Scotland (EIS, the Scottish teachers' union), the Fire Brigades Union (FBU), MSF, NATFHE, the National Association of Schoolmasters and Union of Women Teachers (NASUWT), the NUT, the TGWU, UNISON and the non-affiliated Police Federation of England and Wales.[29] This report highlighted a seriously discriminatory practice affecting both same-sex and unmarried heterosexual partners – and it took a legal judgment in 2017 to resolve this (in part – see Chapter Seven). But the report also demonstrated what the TUC could achieve that individual unions could not: bringing together many affected unions to share expertise and experience, and to produce an authoritative challenge to discrimination. Campaigning included a joint TUC/Stonewall leaflet *For Richer, For Poorer*, which made the case for equality for all married and unmarried partners.

In 1996, the TUC also took the initiative to set up a telephone hotline. Working with the community newspaper *Pink Paper*, Janice Millman organised and promoted the opportunity for people to call the hotline to 'shop the bad boss' over a period of three days in August. The call log for those days shows that thirty-three calls were received, recording a range of bad workplace experiences including dismissals.[30]

Also, by the mid-1990s there was more news on the legal front. 1996 witnessed both victory and defeat. There was triumph for transgender rights when the case of P v. S and Cornwall County Council found in favour of a sacked transwoman at the European Court, in a ruling on 30 April 1996. On the other hand, a lesbian couple, Lisa Grant and Jill Percey, who were backed by Stonewall, also took their case to Europe, where they argued that they had been discriminated against by their employer South West Trains, who failed to provide partner benefits. Their case failed in February 1998 because, as the court pointed out, male partners would also face discrimination, so there was no case under sex discrimination law— and at this time there was, of course, no other law to protect them. They were invited to and took part in the TUC's 1996 lesbian and gay rights seminar/conference.

Lesbian and gay trade union activists now saw that their next step should be to persuade the TUC to give lesbian and gay struggles for rights equal status with women and black trade unionists' struggles. The TUC changed the name of its annual event from 'seminar' to 'conference' but they kept the same format: speakers and workshops. Since there were limited democratic avenues to produce structural changes, a successful motion was proposed to TUC Women's Conference by Equity, seconded by NAPO (the union for probation and family court workers), in 1996, which followed up the call from the 1996 seminar/conference for there to be a lesbian and gay conference and called for consultation on its format.[31] The TUC acted promptly but the very hurried consultation that followed only secured fourteen responses from unions, so it was necessary to extend the deadline. However, the same unions that had supported the motion for a full conference predictably continued to support the idea, while others followed the lead of the TUC itself in rejecting the motion. Frustration boiled over at the next lesbian and gay conference held at NATFHE's offices in Kings Cross in 1997. The event was chaired by Bernadette Hillon from the General Council and had just-elected out gay MP Stephen Twigg and TUC general secretary John Monks as speakers. Every workshop was a vehicle for the demand for a full lesbian and gay conference. The TUC's head of equality, Kay Carberry, deployed the arguments: that the movement was not ready for this yet; that only a minority of unions were present; that having a lesbian and gay conference would force delegates to out themselves. In fact, those represented by delegates at this conference amounted to an overwhelming majority of trade union members.

Supporters organised across the unions that backed the call for an L&G conference. Motion 93 on the agenda of the TUC Congress in 1997 called for the establishment of a full democratic lesbian and gay conference with the right to debate and vote on policy motions. It was moved by Frederick Pyne from the actors' union Equity, who reiterated the range of discrimination faced by LGBT members, and asserted their right to equality within the movement. Jackie Lewis seconded, from UNISON. She addressed the issue that some unions without lesbian and gay structures might struggle to identify delegates by urging the TUC to encourage unions to set up such networks. Sharon Allen from MSF spoke in support, illustrating it with an account of how LAGIM had achieved recognition within her union, and Nick Roe (from the small union of Halifax staff) urged how important it was to be heard by the movement.

There were also speakers against the motion: Margaret Bayley from the AUEW did not oppose fighting discrimination but asked whether setting up a resolutions-based conference was the most efficient way, while Peggy Blyth from the General and Municipal Boilermakers' Union (GMB) asked 'if it's not broken, why fix it?' and called the idea of a conference a 'straightjacket'. A powerful speech in support was then made by Tony Young, general secretary of the CWU.

The response to the debate (delivered by Donna Covey) stressed that the General Council welcomed lesbian and gay members asserting their voices but repeated the argument that not enough unions were as yet involved. Fred Pyne delivered a stirring right of reply ending with:

> Please pick up the piece of paper that was left on all your desks during lunchtime. It is called The Right To Be Heard. That is what we are asking for. Please support the most disadvantaged groups in our movement by giving them the chance to help themselves, and support Motion 93.[32]

Winning the vote on the motion had not been left to chance. It was known that the General Council (GC) had endorsed the arguments against it from TUC head of equality Kay Carberry and it was also known that many union delegations had a default position of following the lead of the GC. Supporters had been lobbying union general secretaries all week. Arthur Scargill, told that the General Council had opposed it, responded 'of course I'll support it'. Jimmy Knapp of the National Union of Railwaymen (NUR) answered in similar fashion. Well-known Equity members Tony Robinson and Susan Tully had been talking to delegates all week to good effect, but the unknown position of the largest unions left the outcome in the balance. A caucus of supporters met at breakfast on the day of the vote, 11 September 1997, and agreed to make a pitch for the TGWU, which had been backing the General Council position. UNISON's Paul Amann approached TGWU general secretary Bill Morris with a copy of the speech Morris had himself delivered at the TUC in 1987, which had moved for the creation of the black workers' conference. Morris immediately recognised the inconsistency of his union's position. When the debate was called, it was noticed that the TGWU delegation was not in the hall. With their abstention, victory was certain and the vote was not even close.[33]

READY FOR LAUNCH

In May 1997, Tony Blair became the first Labour Prime Minister in eighteen years, in a landslide election victory. The Labour Party had a host of lesbian and gay policies which had been voted through their annual conference time and again, and their spokespeople had made a number of commitments to act.

In 1997, the trade union movement had voted to establish a structure giving lesbian and gay members the same rights and the same voice as other equality groups. This meant that the time had come to bring together trade unionists to work with all those in the lesbian and gay communities who campaigned for equality, including those doing so inside the Labour Party, to finally bring an end to the legal oppression that LGBT people had suffered for far too long and to finally begin to challenge public prejudice. These were formidable challenges, requiring engagement on many fronts at the same time.

The first TUC Lesbian and Gay Conference to debate motions from unions and to elect a committee took place on 2-3 July 1998. This provided the opportunity to show LGBT trade unionists that their voices were being heard and that the TUC would act on all the many areas of discrimination that were powerfully identified on the agenda of this conference.

NOTES

1. Section 28 (2a) began as a backbench amendment to what became the Local Government Act 1988. Conservative backbenchers took the opportunity to make illegal the promotion of understanding of same-sex relations in education (hence the phrase 'pretended family relationship'). Efforts to achieve such education had been a growing trend by Labour local councils.

2. Jon Johnson, interview with the author on 26 January 2017. Johnson also provided papers about TUAS28. His history was not unusual: he had come out while a member of Militant (the far left organisation that infiltrated and took over the Labour Party youth wing in the 1970s and 1980s) and then been expelled for organising a lesbian and gay group, which was against party rules. He then become involved in the campaign against Section 28. As a member of the National Union of Civil and Public Servants (NUCPS) he took part in the union's (re)founded lesbian and gay group from 1988.

3. Positive vetting was carried out to check a job applicant's political beliefs

and to attempt to establish whether they were homosexual – if so, they could be seen as a security risk.

4. Interviews with Brian Shaw and Yvonne Washbourne, 22 December 2016 and Jon Johnson, 26 January 2017; Johnson's notes of civil service union lesbian and gay group history and of the meeting at MI5, 27 June 1995; CPSA Lesbian and Gay Rights Group newsletter, 2 June 1989: HCA/Ephemera/521.

5. This was the result of lack of coordination on my part. I had wrongly assumed that the motion would be uncontroversial, and had not even sought nomination as a delegate to be present and thus move the motion myself.

6. This narrative is derived from the interviews with Diana Holland, 26 July 2016, and Shane Enright, 1 August 2016, and my own memories of being a delegate at the 1989 conference. The union recorded its proceedings on tape, and I am deeply grateful to Shane Enright for recovering this tape and digitising it for use in this work.

7. *FlagFlyers: Brief*, November 1994. This leaflet also contained the policy motions passed at union conferences, to confirm that the LGBT workers had the union's backing.

8. I regularly attended these meetings, as it was easier to do so for a London inhabitant.

9. Lesley Mansell, interviewed 26 November 2016.

10. Dave Samuel, interviewed 30 January 2017. After a change of jobs he ended up helping to establish a LGBT committee for UNITE in Cardiff. He has now retired.

11. I attended one of these union training schools in 1994 as a speaker from the Labour Campaign for Lesbian and Gay Rights (LCLGR).

12. From interviews with Lesley Mansell, 26 November 2016; Philip Inglesant, 29 December 2016; and Katie Hanson, 11 January 2017. The 1990 Charter spelt out MSF's support for the role of LAGIM externally and internally.

13. The Post Office Engineering Union (POEU) merged with the postal and telecoms group of the CPSA in 1985 to form the National Communications Union (NCU).

14. From interviews with Laurie Smith, 23 November 2016, and Maria Exall and Mary Hanson, 13 December 2016; between them they described the processes and events covered in this paragraph. *Kiosk*, the NCU Westminster branch newsletter, July 1991, reported the decision to create LGAC to branch members, as part of a report of the union conference.

15. *Voice*, June 1995. This particular issue of the union newspaper *Voice* contains a well-written feature challenging standard myths about lesbians and gay men and explaining that the problem for the unions was not lesbian and gay people, but their prejudiced colleagues.

16. Lorraine Trenchard, Hugh Warren, *Something to Tell You: The Experiences and Needs of Young Lesbians and Gay Men in London*, London: London Gay Teenage Group, 1984.

17. Information from interviews with Sue Sanders, 8 August 2016; Tim Lucas 10 August 2016; and Ruth Blunt, interviewed 10 November 2016. Helen Hill at the NUT kindly provided copies of the 1987 and 1988 conference resolutions.

18. At the first conference in 1983, insurers for the venue refused because it would be like 'insuring a brothel' – the union's own insurers stepped in (information from interviews with Jackie Lewis 24 August 2016 and Chris Creegan, 31 October 2016). But this illustrates the difficulties faced by LGBT activists.

19. Account of conference in *Public Eye,* Camden NALGO 1986 annual conference report.

20. This account is from interviews with Jackie Lewis, 24 August 2016; Chris Creegan, 31 October 2016; and Carola Towle 16 December 2016. Further details were taken from the internal NALGO committee papers and reports kindly shown to me by them.

21. Interview with Ron Harley, 11 November 2016.

22. The COHSE conference motions focussed on another current government attack through a criminal justice bill that increased penalties for 'procurement' of homosexual sex and a new wave of police entrapments. There had been particular targeting of clubs offering S&M. A new community campaign was formed as the Lesbian and Gay Rights Coalition, launched at a conference of seventy people in Birmingham in 1992.

23. Information from Michael Walker, interviewed November 2016.

24. ILGA was set up in 1978 and continues to flourish. It is organised through continent-wide regions and holds four-yearly world conferences (see Chapter Seven).

25. LCLGR (represented by Sarah Roelofs and I) met Blair when he was shadow home secretary in 1994. He affirmed both his support for an equal age of consent but also his doubts about the broader claim that same-sex relationships were equal with heterosexual. The commitment on the age of consent was in the Labour manifesto for the 1997 election.

26. TUC, *Unions Working for Lesbian and Gay Members,* February 1991 (TUC Library).

27. Interview with Jon Johnson, as above.

28. TUC, Report of Seminar *Lesbian and Gay Rights at Work,* 25 June 1992 (TUC Library, HD 6661); TUC, *Lesbian and Gay Rights at Work,* March 1994 (TUC Library).

29. The report also reproduced motions carried at individual union conferences dating back to 1981. Issues around pensions for non-married partners had been a recurrent theme even in unions where there was no LGBT structure.

30. This call log, the promotional leaflet and correspondence is recorded in papers held at the TUC, which are awaiting archiving (2017). I am grateful to Andrea Peace at Congress House for arranging access to this material.

31. TUC, Report of TUC Women's Conference, 13-15 March 1996, composite motion 4 'Lesbian and gay seminar'. The motion was carried.

32. All from the verbatim *TUC Congress Report*, Thursday 11 September 1997, pp176-79.

33. Discussion with Paul Amann, 3 November 2016. Paul was a member of the black caucus in UNISON's lesbian and gay structure. I was part of the campaign from my desk in the equal rights department at NATFHE, and had taken an active role in the TUC conferences/seminars.

Hello!

The NALGO Gay Group is for all homosexuals, bisexuals, transvestites, transexuals, or any other sexuals who do not fit into Society's accepted standards of sexuality (It is not for child molesters or rapists etc.) and who belong to the National and Local Government Officers trade union.

Through the NALGO Gay Group we can show our colleagues that homosexuality is not something apart from heterosexuality but part of a spectrum of sexual orientation. We can show them that homosexuality means love and affection between quite ordinary people, except that the people concerned are the same sex. There are millions of 'gay' people in this country. Independent experts reckon that 1 person in 20 is mainly homosexual, although more recent figures would point to 1 in 12, and many more are bisexual.

The young homosexual at work, i.e. those under 21, must really suffer as homosexuality is only legal in England and Wales for two consenting adults over 21 and in private. This law does not cover the Armed Forces or Merchant Navy or Scotland or Northern Ireland where homosexuality is completely illegal. The criminal law does not affect female homosexuals who are just ignored although the civil law tends to be unfair to women generally and lesbians in particular.

Adults at work also may find themselves isolated and unable to meet other homosexuals

The NALGO Gay Group exists to show the Union just how many homosexuals there actually are with the Union and works to try to change attitudes within the work situation. It will support those who may be victimised in any way due to their sexual orientation and bring pressure to bear within NALGO.

1. The contents of the first trade union gay group newsletter, *Nalgay News*, No. 1, October 1974. (*Hall Carpenter Archives, with permission from UNISON*)

2. *Tower Power,* newsletter of National and Local Government Officers' Association (NALGO) Tower Hamlets branch, September 1976, announcing an official strike in support of sacked gay member, Ian Davies. (*Hall Carpenter Archives, with permission from UNISON*)

what pansies want is a lecture on self discipline...these creatures
who children should be warned against"(News of World)

- It is editorial policy never to write about GLF(Sun)or to accept any
advertisement containing the word gay(IPC)

- No letters mentioning homosexuality may be discussed on the advice page
(Sun)

- Aristocracy pervaded with,"fornication,sodomy,and drunkenness"(M.Star)

- Times and Guardian frequently print without comment items on 'chemical
castration'They don't print,without insulting comment any activity of
GLF,nor report on the work of the counter-psychiatry group.

- Lord Arron rants on at queers(E.News)

- GLF presence at the recent lock-in of councillors in Notting Hill was
either ridiculed or ignored

- Spectator publishes celebrations of Noel Cowards death

In spite of this revolting nonsense,we are glad to be gay,and nothing will
alter that.But many of our sisters and brothers are very isolated,and they
are especially harmed by the press.

     DO YOU REALLY WANT GAY PEOPLE TO BE DESCRIBED IN THESE WAYS ?
Is that how you feel about your gay colleagues,your gay daughters and sons,
your gay brothers,sisters,aunts,uncles and neighbours?

We think you could help to change the way the press insults and abuses
all gay people.
          By challenging the instruction.
          By asking why
          By complaining to union or management
          By getting something favourable published.
          By not using gay to abuse,humiliate,insult
          By getting this demonstration reported.

We're not asking you to risk your jobs.Just to think about it and do what
you can.
We try to think about your problems,especially those of your work;we'd
like you to think a bit about ours

3. Leaflet produced by a Gay Liberation Front (GLF) working group
and distributed to trade union print workers in Fleet Street, 1973.
(*Hall Carpenter Archives*)

c/o Mike Notcutt,   OR   Lilian Lishman,
  9A, Clarendon Road,   9, Edward Place,
  Holland Park,   Newcastle.
  London, W11 4AP.

  Phone 01-727-9613   Phone Newcastle 30507

INFORMATION SHEET

We have recently formed a Gay Group for members of the
National Union of Public Employees with the principle aims
of campaigning to end discrimination on the grounds of
sexual orientation in the employment field; to bring
together homosexual or bisexual men and women who are
members of N.U.P.E.; and to assist any member of N.U.P.E.
who feels that he/she is being discriminated against/
victimised by his/her employer, or for that matter by the
Union on the grounds of his/her sexual orientation.

There are over ½ million members of N.U.P.E. in Great
Britain, two-thirds of whom are women. So using the minimum
accepted ratio of one in twenty, it produces a probable
gay N.U.P.E. membership of a minimum of 25,000 men and
women in Great Britain.

Most N.U.P.E. members are of a working class background,
and as a result would find it exceptionally difficult to
'come out' to their friends and colleagues, yet alone to
their employer and/or Union. N.U.P.E. Gay Group is the
first working class Union based Gay Group to be formed.

The T.U.C. has sent to all its affiliated organisations
a model clause on equal opportunities in employment which
it hopes unions will seek to get included in all relevant
agreements with employers. In this model clause there is
a section devoted to promote equal opportunity in employment regardless of workers' sex, marital status, creed,
colour or ethnic origins. There is no mention of 'sexual
orientation' in this section of the equal opportunity clause.

We would be grateful if you could inform the members of
your organisation of the N.U.P.E. Gay Group and if any
member of N.U.P.E. is interested in joining this group,
they should contact Mike Notcutt or Lilian Lishman at the
above addresses or 'phone numbers for further information.

GAY OPPRESSION IS CLASS OPPRESSION

Dear Geoff,
Can you thank Mike for sending me the WAGS Newsletter and tell him
that the address was correct. Is there any chance of you
including some of the above info. in your next newsletter. I am sure
you must have some N.U.P.E. members amongst your suscribers. The
N.U.P.E. journal has refused to publish any info. on the Gay Group,
so we are heavily relying on help in publicity.

Much love,

Mike.

4. The National Union of Public Employees Gay Group (NUPEGG)
announced itself with this newsletter in 1975(?). (*Hall Carpenter
Archives, with permission from UNISON*)

GAY PEOPLE IN NATFHE

a statement by TFHE Gay Group

5a. The cover of the pamphlet produced by the gay group in the National Association of Teachers in Further and Higher Education (NATFHE), 1982. (*Hall Carpenter Archives, with permission from the University and College Union*)

5b. CHE/GLG letter to trade unionists, 1975/76. (*With permission from* CHE) See p.46.

CHE / GLG

TRADE UNION GAY GROUPS
CENTRAL CLEARING SCHEME

administered by:—
GAY LABOUR GROU
37 Eastbourne Avenue
London, W3 6JR.

Dear Sister/Brother,

The Trades Unions are an important and powerful part of the economic and social fabric of this country. We believe that Trades Unions have an important role to play in gaining gay rights, not only in fighting against individual cases of discrimination but in lending their weight to the campaign for full social justice, legally, socially and economically.

Many gay people are not open about their sexuality and this fact has drastically reduced the ability of gays to campaign on their own behalf. We believe that the formation of Trade Union Gay Groups — groups of Trades Unionists committed to both the T.U. movement and to gay rights, operating within the framework developed by the T.U. movement itself — can perform a valuable service in redressing the balance.

If you would like to join or support a gay group for your Union please fill in the attached registration form and return it to Gay Labour Group. There is a voluntary registration fee of 50p. (Cheques, P.Os. payable to G.L.G.) to help with the costs of running the scheme, If you cannot afford it, please register just the same.

Overleaf you will find details of how the scheme works and information about Gay Labour Group so that you will know who is running the scheme.

I hope you decide to register.

Yours fraternally,

Mike Rowland

Mike Rowland
Secretary:
Gay Labour Group

Gay Labour Group is affiliated to the Campaign for Homosexual Equality and to the National Council for Civil Liberties.

NATIONAL UNION OF MINEWORKERS

ST. JAMES' HOUSE, VICAR LANE,
SHEFFIELD, SOUTH YORKSHIRE S1 2EX

President A. SCARGILL   Secretary P. E. HEATHFIELD

Telephone: 0742 766900

Please quote our reference in reply:

Your Ref:

Our Ref: NO11/RW/JMA/88

19th April 1988

Rebecca Flemming.
Stop the Clause Campaign.
c/o ULU.
Malet Street.
LONDON.
WC1E 7HY.

Dear Rebecca Flemming.

Clause 28 – Local Government Bill

I am in receipt of your letter dated 22nd March 1988 and would like the following message of solidarity to be passed on to the Rally to be held on April 30th.

> The National Union of Mineworkers deplores the proposals contained in the Local Government Bill that are designed to outlaw the "promotion" of homosexuality by a local authority.

> This legislation represents a further attack on those freedoms which should be enjoyed within any civilised society. Under the guise of "restoring traditional values" the powers of this Bill will undoubtedly be used in order to discriminate on the basis of a person's sexual orientation and has already led to threats being made against homosexual teachers and their employment placed in jeopardy.

> The NUM calls upon all decent people to resist this further erosion of basic human rights and fears that unless we are prepared to defend such rights the words of Pastor Niermoller in Nazi Germany will be as true today as then and when indeed "they come for me" there will be "no one left to speak for me".

Please accept our best wishes for a successful rally on 30th April.

Yours fraternally.

P. E. Heathfield.
SECRETARY.

6. The letter of solidarity from the National Union of Mineworkers (NUM) to the Stop the Clause campaign against Section 28, 1988. (*Hall Carpenter Archives*)

7. Trade union banners at London Pride in recent years
Photos: Laurie Smith

GMB, ASLEF
(train drivers'
union) and
UNISON

Communication Workers Union (CWU) and UNISON.
Also visible here are Trades Union Congress (TUC) t-shirts and flags
worn or carried by many of the marchers.

8a. Trade unions at Pride London, here showing the banners of the CWU, UNISON and the Union of Shop, Distributive and Allied Workers (USDAW). (*Photo: Laurie Smith*)

8b. International solidarity: members of the Rail, Maritime and Transport (RMT) union and the Out and Proud Diamond Group (LGBT people of African origin) picket the Lithuanian embassy against a proposed anti-LGBT law in the Lithuanian parliament, 2014. The author is second from the left. (*Photo courtesy of Paul Penny*)

5

Trade union champions of equality

When the Labour government was formed after the election of 1997, lesbians, gays and bisexuals faced inequality in so many areas of the law that it would be easier to state the few where they did not. As the result of the ruling of a European court, rather than any national institution, trans people had their right to be protected by the Sex Discrimination Act asserted (see Chapter Four). Otherwise, however, they remained far from real equality. The Labour Campaign for Lesbian and Gay Rights (LCLGR), working with UNISON (the combined public services union), had published a 'charter', a *Manifesto for Lesbian and Gay Equality* in 1995. This set out a programme of demands, responding to a multitude of legal inequalities. The Labour government came into office with a large majority and a host of lesbian and gay equality policies, which had been voted through with increasingly massive support at party conferences over the past decade (see Chapter Four).

Despite this apparently strong start, however, it proved necessary to mobilise the strength of a strong pro-equality lobby to push Blair's first government into going beyond its limited manifesto commitment to equalising the age of consent. In several areas, it took further action in Europe to prompt developments. Blair called another election in 2001, and was returned with a strong majority again. For trade union priorities, this second government would prove to be more fruitful. However, even this progress involved both use (again) of European law, and a trade union legal challenge to the Labour government's laws. It was only under the third Labour government, elected in 2005, that positive legal changes were introduced without such difficult battles.

One important reason for this – and it is the same reason that allowed David Cameron to legislate same-sex marriage under a Conservative-Liberal Democrat coalition government in 2011 – was that there had been a big change in public opinion. The British Social Attitudes surveys (carried out every year since 1983) were beginning to show a change in public views of homosexuality during the late 1990s and early 2000s, and politicians would have been aware of this. In 1983, when Peter Tatchell was losing the Bermondsey by-election, 50 per cent of people who completed the survey saw homosexuality as 'always wrong' and only 17 per cent saw it as 'not wrong'. This latter group had dropped down to a mere 11 per cent at the height of the AIDS panic (as measured in 1987). By the 2000s, the figures were beginning to show significantly more favourable attitudes to homosexuality, and these developments continued; more than 60 per cent support for same-sex marriage was recorded in 2013.[1]

Why this change had happened has not been measured. People who were once hostile were not asked why they were now more accepting. It is likely that there were a range of reasons, possibly including greater visibility, which meant that more people knew someone who was LGBT so they were no longer hidden and therefore perceived as threatening. The BSA also demonstrated a generational divide with younger people being more positive, and an urban/rural split related to the greater visibility of LGBT communities in many cities (although neither of these distinctions were absolute – there continued to be lots of prejudice among young people and in the cities, and plenty of acceptance among older people and in non-urban environments).

These surveys, however, show that the support being offered by trade union activists, officers and ordinary members throughout the 1980s and 1990s (as discussed in previous chapters) was well ahead of public opinion. Lesbian, gay and bisexual workers who stood up in front of their colleagues, declared their sexuality and argued for equal rights, believed that it was an obligation to be open about one's sexuality in pursuit of progress. The alternative, which many others continued to follow, was to keep it a private matter, but to therefore be unable to publicly challenge the forces that oppressed LGBT people. This was a choice, of course, that unions quite rightly insisted members be allowed to make for themselves. They tried to ensure that workplaces were as comfortable as possible for people to make such a decision in.

There were also heterosexual supporters who stood up against prejudice, and many of them chose to put themselves in the firing line on behalf of their LGBT colleagues; this speaks volumes for their sense of fairness and social justice. For union leaders to do the same was evidence that unions were working to champion equality. In 1988, when Labour leaders had once again faltered in their support for equality in response to the Section 28 announcements, the general secretaries of two large general, manual worker, unions, Ron Todd (Transport and General Workers' Union, TGWU) and John Edmonds (General and Municipal Workers' union, GMW)[2] put out a public statement aimed at their Labour colleagues:

> You can't cut people out of fair and equal treatment simply because you think some people in the electorate are too prejudiced to support you if you take a just line.[3]

From two heterosexual trade union leaders it was a powerful signal that these fundamental principles were now entrenched in parts of the trade union movement.

Given the reluctance on the part of ministers in the first Blair government, it was fortunate that, in the late 1990s, the Trades Union Congress (TUC) was in a position to coordinate trade union action, in order to form part of the coalition of progressive forces that came together to pressurise the government. But the establishment of a TUC lesbian and gay structure (as it was at the outset) also helped the movement. Through this, the TUC could call on the experiences of a wide range of activists in their unions, merging these into a common approach and allowing them to respond to many further issues facing LGBT people. Part of that process also involved extending the remit of the lesbian and gay structure to positively embrace trans and bisexual workers (see below). At the same time, there was continued development of new self-organised structures inside unions that may have had positive policy, but that did not have a structure through which the voices of their LGBT members could be heard, and there was further consolidation of these groups in those unions where they already existed.

CHANGING THE LAW: THE AGE OF CONSENT, SECTION 28 (ROUND ONE)

The 1997 government's public commitments were to equalising the age of consent, and to repealing Section 28. Both of these pieces of legislation were highly emblematic symbols of the oppression of lesbian and gay people. Both demonstrated the profound prejudices that continued to proliferate in society. Resistance to equalising the age of consent was chiefly based on the argument that boys at sixteen could be trusted to decide to engage in heterosexual sex but not gay sex. This clearly suggested a pervasively derogatory attitude towards homosexuality, making it illegitimate in relation to heterosexuality. Both this and the Section 28 debate always turned to the same issue: the risk of young people being 'corrupted' by deciding to explore a same-sex relationship, or even being told about it.

The timidity of Blair's government on issues of sexuality was demonstrated when an amendment to the Crime and Disorder bill was proposed, which would change the age of consent to sixteen while leaving the other criminal provisions of the 1967 act intact. The weakness of the amendment was reinforced by the successful prosecution in March 1998 of the 'Bolton Seven', for breaching the 'privacy' provisions of the law. In June 1998 the Commons voted the change to the age of consent through with a large majority. But the Lords, marshalled by Baroness Janet Young, Thatcher's leader there from the early 1980s, rejected it. The government had to drop the amendment in order to save the rest of the bill. It was reintroduced in the following session and met the same fate in the Lords in the spring of 1999. This time, Blair showed his commitment by invoking the rarely-used Parliament Act (that asserts the supremacy of the elected House of Commons) to force the measure through.

Baroness Young and her allies led similar opposition to overturn the repeal of Section 28 in July 2000. In the same year, Section 28 was repealed in the Scottish parliament despite a well-funded opposition campaign, because there was no House of Lords. For England and Wales, the misguided government decision to introduce the proposal in the Lords rather than the Commons meant there was no alternative route and this would have to wait another year and for another bill.

Stonewall, under the leadership of former National and Local Government Officers' association (NALGO) activist and Gay Liberation Front (GLF) member Angela Mason, played the central part in lobbying and putting pressure on ministers during these parliamentary battles. But this time, it did so with the active engagement of trade unions organised through the new TUC structures. Trade unions were no longer simply backing someone else's campaign, they were now partners in the LGBT struggle and they did their own campaigning and lobbying on both these bills, which were central to the LGBT equality agenda.

MAKING DISCRIMINATION IN EMPLOYMENT ILLEGAL

Trade unions played a lead role in establishing protection against discrimination in employment, which was a key union policy, and this chapter will examine some of the key struggles in this period of the late 1990s and early 2000s. However, it is essential to bear in mind that for this group of workers, complete protection and total equality have still not been won.

The agenda of the first official TUC lesbian and gay conference in 1998 was dominated by motions submitted by unions on employment discrimination. Unions were only permitted to put one motion each to this conference, so their choices are a clear signal of what was most important at this time – and it continues to be a major issue now. At this conference, eight motions called for protection against employment discrimination and three additionally called for an end to discrimination in employee benefits. This especially related to pension survivor benefits for same-sex couples. Speakers at this first conference included Baroness Turner of Camden, who was trying to introduce an anti-discrimination bill in the Lords; Angela Mason; and Lisa Grant, whose fight for employee partner benefits to be extended to her partner was documented in Chapter Four, and who was therefore able to speak from her own experience about the discrimination that needed to be challenged.

However, in 1998, the government refused to consider legislation on employee benefits and workplace discrimination against LGB people, arguing (and this was to be heard repeatedly) about possible 'burdens on business'. It never satisfactorily explained what was burdensome in being told not to discriminate against your workers on grounds of their sexuality. For a long time, all the government offered was a Code of Practice, and its implementation was to be voluntary. Given the reality of the problem, this response was rightly seen as very inadequate: employers who already had good practice would not need it, and those that discriminated could continue to do so without redress.

This frustration at the limitations of the government's proposal was the view not only of the TUC but also of the alliance of organisations that gathered around the campaign to end employment discrimination. Stonewall, Liberty and the TUC worked closely together and found strong support from LCLGR, the National Union of Students (NUS) and groups like the Lesbian and Gay Christian Movement (LGCM) and Lesbian and Gay Employment Rights (LAGER). It was important that the Equal Opportunities Commission (EOC), chaired by Julie Mellor – which had been charged by the government with drawing up the Code of Practice – made a public statement expressing a similar sense of the policy's inadequacy.

With the backing of the TUC L&G committee, the TUC had organised a campaign conference to plan the next steps towards winning legal protection. The conference took place at Congress House on 21 May 1999, where more than 150 delegates heard speeches from: TUC general secretary Brendan Barber; Ann Keen, MP; two union general secretaries, Rodney Bickerstaffe of the public service union, UNISON, and Judy McKnight of the probation and family court workers' union, NAPO; Angela Mason of Stonewall; a representative of Rank Outsiders, the group campaigning to end the ban on lesbians and gay men serving in the armed forces. A third union general secretary, Ed Sweeney of the Banking, Insurance and Finance Union (BIFU), who had been the first chair of the TUC L&G Committee, chaired the whole event. The conference also gave a warm welcome to Cheryl Carolus, the South Africa High Commissioner in London, who was able to point out that a ban on discrimination on the grounds of sexuality had been incorporated into the constitution of the new post-Apartheid South Africa.[4]

This meant that although nothing had been achieved through government channels by the time of the second TUC L&G conference a few weeks later in June 1999, it was possible to respond to the large number of motions criticising the government approach that were there voted through. The TUC and its allies then went on to organise a full-scale campaign to exert pressure on government through as many channels as possible.

However, it was recognised at the TUC L&G conference that it was firstly important to assemble the evidence that discrimination really was a problem at work – and following that, to demonstrate to ministers not only that there was a genuine problem to deal with, but also that they would not alienate public opinion by doing so. The latter issue was riskier, as it was not a certainty.

This campaign to raise awareness of workplace discrimination included distribution of pre-printed postcards for people to send to their members of parliament. A large number of people who sent out the cards received replies from their MPs which were forwarded to the TUC. Many responses were supportive – from those MPs already on side with the TUC's demands – and others were verbatim copies of the standard government response, i.e. we must wait to see what happens with the (voluntary) Code of Practice.[5] No attempt was made to identify responses not forwarded to the TUC, but there were probably many, because many activists took part in this aspect of the campaign.

The TUC also organised a survey that was distributed through existing union lesbian and gay groups over the winter of 1999-2000. The resulting report – *Straight Up! Why the Law Should Protect Lesbian and Gay Workers* – was launched on 19 April 2000. It reported that 450 lesbian, gay and bisexual workers had returned the questionnaires and that no fewer than 44 per cent had suffered discrimination. It included thirteen detailed case studies, including that of Shirley Pearce, the teacher driven out of work by harassment because she was a lesbian; she took her case through an Industrial Tribunal (IT) and Employment Appeal Tribunal (EAT) only to find (like Lisa Grant and her partner) that however great the injustice, she currently had no legal protection.

The second part of the report covered the results of an opinion poll commissioned by the TUC from the British Market Research Bureau Ltd (BMRB), which interviewed 964 people aged over fifteen and asked three questions. 74 per cent of the interviewees believed it was wrong for an employer to sack someone because they were lesbian or gay, 78 per cent believed it was wrong to treat someone less favourably on these grounds, while 71 per cent (of whom a larger proportion than for the first question – 13 per cent – only 'tended to agree') believed it was wrong to deny long-term same-sex partners access to the same benefits as opposite-sex partners or spouses.[6]

The press release of *Straight Up's* launch attracted widespread media attention.[7] The headline figure of 44 per cent of LGBT people who had experienced discrimination at work appeared, in my experience, genuinely to shock many people. Rather than hostility, the response was more that people had been entirely unaware of discriminatory practices. The increased visibility of the basic unfairness of someone being sacked because of their sexuality made a significant impact.

The survey and report were my responsibility, and they were not without their problems. The survey was entirely self-selecting: and around two-fifths of the respondents were from UNISON, not surprisingly given the size of the union and its established lesbian and gay structures. It was also more likely that people who had faced a problem would respond. It could not therefore be said to have been compliant with standards for a scientific analysis. However, other surveys – one carried out by Stonewall in 1993, another by Social and Community Planning in 1995 – produced comparable findings on the level of discrimination faced by lesbian and gay workers. It was also notable that while the worst outcomes involved workers being sacked (or forced to move to another location), the vast majority of cases reported workplace harassment. Every subsequent survey (and there have been many through to the present day, carried out by universities and voluntary organisations such as Stonewall) reported the same, and after the law was changed, the overwhelming majority of complaints made to Industrial Tribunals were for harassment as well.

Despite the pressure and the evidence, and the results of the opinion poll – set up by Mike Power of the TUC campaigns and communications department – the government still refused to change its stance on the Code of Practice.

Meanwhile, in 1999, the ban on gays and lesbians serving in the military was overturned by the European Court of Human Rights, and this forced the British government to act, and the ban was lifted in the UK in January 2000. The Ministry of Defence vigorously defended the ban right up to the end. This showed that certain parts of government were not on the side of equality based on sexuality. The unions had supported the case, in which Stonewall played the lead role, although members of the armed forces were not able to join unions.

It took another European measure to finally drive the second Blair government to act on employment discrimination. The European directive, introduced to implement the 2000

Amsterdam Treaty, for the first time included sexual orientation as grounds for unfair discrimination. Therefore Britain was now obliged to transpose this obligation into UK law. How they did so was left largely to the national government's discretion, as with other member states of the European Union. Alongside sexual orientation, protection on grounds of religion or belief was also introduced. The coincidence of these two extensions happening together would also foretell many future problems for LGBT equality in British society.

THE 2003 REGULATIONS AND THE CHALLENGE TO THE EXEMPTIONS

The government was constitutionally able to implement different laws in different ways, by using secondary legislation called 'statutory instruments', which bypassed the need for parliamentary bills. This is what it did with the new laws on discrimination from Europe. The new regulations were therefore laid before parliament, agreed and brought into force on 1 December 2003. They attracted widespread attention and many organisations rushed to issue guidance to employers on what they were now required to do. The TUC produced posters and information leaflets, thousands of copies of which were distributed through unions, advising members on their new rights, which protected against discrimination on grounds of sexual orientation and religion. Many unions published their own advice in their journals or by briefings.

This should have been a cause of great rejoicing – finally, there could be legal recourse in cases similar to those affecting people like John Warburton (refused employment because of his sexuality in 1974, Chapter Two), John Saunders (sacked from his job in a children's camp in 1979, Chapter Three), Susan Shell (sacked by Barking Council when she mentioned her sexuality in 1981, Chapter Three), or the many others right up to Lisa Grant and her partner and Shirley Pearce (mentioned above and in Chapter Four). But while they were, of course, welcome, and welcomed by campaigners, the new laws were flawed. The TUC had pointed out the problems in its initial response to the government's pre-legislation consultation,[8] and other equality organisations had made similar points in their briefings and responses. James Purnell MP led a debate on these problems in the

Commons in January 2003, while Lord Lester challenged them in the Lords in June of the same year.

The regulations as legislated contained two significant exemptions. Regulation 25 allowed governments (and therefore also public bodies) to discriminate in the provision of benefits dependent on marital status. This exemption meant that public sector employers could opt to discriminate against same-sex partners in pension survivor benefits. Although many private sector pension schemes had long since abandoned this discriminatory approach, millions of workers were in public sector schemes, which meant that the partners of many thousands of lesbian and gay public sector workers would suffer pension poverty after their partners' deaths. (This also applied to unmarried heterosexuals, but as marriage was not available to same-sex couples at this time, it was a much more severe form of discrimination in their cases.) Despite the challenges in parliament, and despite vigorous campaigning and lobbying inside and outside government, this exemption remained.

Regulation 7(3) allowed organisations of a religious character exemption from the ban on discrimination on the grounds of sexual orientation. It impacted on anyone who worked for an organisation that could claim to be founded on a religious ethos. This particularly affected numerous charities, but potentially the most troubling effect would be in the growing number of faith schools. The teachers' unions protested vigorously over this exemption, with detailed evidence of the likely impact. However, this was all to no avail against the similarly vociferous lobbying of faith groups, including the largest churches, who wanted to be able to discriminate. Regulation 7(3) was added to the regulations after the close of the consultation period, without the knowledge even of the minister responsible for the legislation, and it was widely believed (including by Labour ministers) that it was introduced at the behest of the Prime Minister himself (Tony Blair) as a result of lobbying from the bishops.[9] Parliamentary procedure does not allow for amendments to draft regulations: one votes either to accept or to reject them. Supporters of equality therefore had no option but to vote them into law.

It was not usual for trade unions to challenge a Labour government over the wording of laws through the courts, and it was unheard of for them to do so on an issue of lesbian and gay rights. But that is what happened in 2004.

There was only one way to challenge the exemptions legally and that was by judicial review – in this case, that meant inviting a judge to rule that the exemptions were *ultra vires*, that is, they went further than was permitted in the original legislation (the European directive) and should be struck down. Such challenges are expensive, so this required unions to agree the approach and to share the burden of cost. Fortunately, Lucy Anderson was on the staff at the TUC equal rights department, and she had legal training and experience organising trade union legal cases. Anderson was therefore in a position to broker a cost-sharing deal with the seven unions that agreed to be part of the challenge: Amicus (the merged Amalgamated Engineering and Electrical Union, AEEU and Manufacturing, Science and Finance, MSF); the National Association of Schoolmasters and Union of Women Teachers (NASUWT); the National Association of Teachers in Further and Higher Education (NATFHE); Public and Commercial Services union (PCS); the Rail, Maritime and Transport union (RMT); and UNISON. The National Union of Teachers (NUT) lodged a claim on just one ground but the cases were all heard together. The case was known as 'the Amicus case' simply because their name came first alphabetically. A TUC press release announced the legal challenge on 16 March 2004, which was picked up by the national media and dozens of local papers and local radio.

The case was heard in the High Court of Justice Queen's Bench. It was presented by Rabinder Singh QC and Karon Monaghan, instructed by Thompsons Solicitors, who were the trade union firm of solicitors; the TUC worked with solicitor Nicola Dandridge on this. Aidan O'Neill QC and Sandya Drew represented the NUT. It was defended by equally high-ranking lawyers on the government side – Monica Carss-Frisk QC and Dinah Rose. Those groups that were opposed to equality and that supported the exemptions to the law recognised the significance of the case, so interventions were made in support of the religious exemptions by lawyers (James Dingemans QC and Paul Diamond) representing Christian Action Research Education (CARE), the Evangelical Alliance and the Christian Schools Alliance.

The three days of the hearing were dominated by legal argument but the union case was presented based on the impact on individual trade union members.[10] The Honourable Mr Justice Richards gave judgment on 26 April 2004. Superficially, the unions lost on both grounds, but the real outcome turned out to be much less clear and much more beneficial.

Mr Justice Richards' ruling on Regulation 7(3) made it explicitly clear that its terms must be interpreted very narrowly – in effect, the legal right of a religious organisation to discriminate was to be restricted and would only apply where it was 'for the purposes of an organised religion', which usually only meant ministers of religion. The ruling spelt out that people working for faith *organisations*, whether as cleaners, schoolteachers, or in some other role, were protected against discrimination under the new laws. This ruling was of great importance. In the years ahead, there would be numerous attempts by religious organisations to discriminate against lesbian or gay employees. In every case that went to tribunal, the judge's interpretation in 'Amicus' was called upon and the employee won.

On whether a government was allowed to discriminate on grounds of marital status, Regulation 25, the judge upheld the argument that this fell within the scope of the state's discretion, but he stated that this finding was 'troubling' and gave permission for the unions to appeal on that judgment.[11] Carefully examining the findings of the judgment, the group of unions decided to take the pensions issue to the Court of Appeal. However, the appeal did not reach its conclusion, because another opportunity arose to test the government's resolve on keeping the exemption in place.

This was fortuitous. Not long after the judgment, government ministers announced their intention to legislate to create civil partnerships, so that same-sex couples could formalise their relationship in a way that the government claimed would be almost indistinguishable from marriage. This was welcomed by unions and equality campaigners. The TUC also saw that it would be possible to take further the provision in the civil partnership bill that was intended to equalise pension benefits from the date at which civil partnerships became law. Pensions formed a significant part of the TUC response to the public consultation on the bill in April 2004; the argument was that these rights should be backdated in order to achieve equality, recognising that many same-sex couples had lived together in the same way as heterosexual couples for many years, but unlike them were not permitted to marry, so were excluded from the financial benefits. As the bill to create civil partnerships proceeded through parliament, the TUC helped supporters in parliament to put questions and put down amendments to secure this backdating. Anne Maguire MP and Angela Eagle MP led such attempts with powerful speeches.[12]

Progress in persuading ministers was encouraged by the imminent hearing of the unions' appeal on the ruling in the Amicus case on Regulation 25 of the employment regulations. Unions had discussions with government ministers and officials. TUC general secretary Brendan Barber wrote to Jacqui Smith MP, the minister responsible for the bill, on 4 October 2004, stating that if the government were to introduce amendments removing the discrimination in Regulation 25, the unions would withdraw the legal challenge.

The government did decide to introduce its own amendment to the bill, which backdated the provisions of the civil partnership bill to 1988, making civil partners' rights equivalent to the rights of widowers.[13] The Department of Work and Pensions (DWP) announced this in a press release on 27 October 2004 and amendments were duly made in parliament at this late stage. Surviving attempted wrecking amendments by Tory MPs and peers (for example, trying to include siblings in the rights), the bill passed into law and became an Act in November 2004.[14] The trade unions involved in the Court of Appeal action withdrew the appeal.

As is so often the case, this result was a compromise: dating access to benefits back to 1988 was not equality, but it was much better than them being cut off at 2005, and would make a meaningful difference to many people's lives. There had been substantial and continuous lobbying by a range of groups backing equality, and unions had done a great deal of work both directly and through supporters in the Commons and the Lords. But it would be difficult to deny that the unions and the appeal case had an impact here, given that the ministers' agreement to insert an amendment for backdating took place towards the end, not the beginning of the bill's several-month-long progress through parliament.

THE UNIONS AND EQUALITY LAWS UP TO 2010

Other legal battles over this period also engaged trade union action, organised through the TUC. This included (at last) the repeal of Section 28, where the TUC lobbied the substantial group of (former) trade unionists who had become peers in the House of Lords. Education unions also collated evidence of the negative impact Section 28 was having in schools. An immense coalition of organisations, including the TUC and UNISON, formed an alliance to make sure that this time the House of Lords would not wreck the repeal. The House had been reformed, with many of the hereditary peers removed, and this combination of factors meant that in 2003, Section 28 was repealed.[15]

Unions also played a significant role in debates over the measures introduced by the government to extend adoption rights to same-sex couples. The problem here was that some Catholic adoption agencies demanded to be exempt from this extension of rights, and asserted that if they did not secure the right to be able to discriminate, the organisations would shut down rather than be forced to offer children for adoption to same-sex couples. There was never any question that such couples would have to comply with all the many checks that prospective adoptive parents had to undergo; this was simply an ideological stance, not based in any way on concerns for children's wellbeing. Well aware of the risk that government ministers would make discriminatory concessions (as over the employment regulations), the TUC joined a consortium of organisations to campaign against such an outcome. Working with the Lesbian and Gay Christian Movement (LGCM), and particularly with its Catholic caucus, I assembled a powerful dossier of evidence proving that: same-sex couples were as capable of providing the same loving and quality care as heterosexual parents; that adoption by same-sex couples had no negative impacts on children; and demonstrating that the religious views of others should be irrelevant to adoption issues. This dossier was widely circulated as a briefing and sent to government ministers. In order to reinforce the message, we set up a meeting with the minister, Ruth Kelly MP. The trade union delegation was led by TUC general secretary Brendan Barber. A forthright but friendly meeting ensued. It was rare for the TUC to take such high-level action on issues not connected with the workplace, and it would once have been exceptional for them to do so around lesbian and gay rights, but this was clearly no longer the case. In the end, the legislation was achieved without any exemptions. Most Catholic adoption agencies continued to provide their services, rather than closing down.

Other legal steps were taken by the Labour government of 2001 to 2005, in which the unions and the TUC played a full part, whether in lobbying to strengthen draft laws or in mobilising supportive parliamentarians to defend the government's proposals through the legislative process.[16] It proved necessary once again to collect evidence through union equality and LGBT structures when legal protection was introduced against hate crime. The TUC had meetings with Maria Eagle, MP, to present the argument for new laws, and on this it largely succeeded – the question of hate crime laws has always had to find the appropriate definitions to distinguish what amounted to criminal behaviour.

However, the issue of religious exemptions to anti-discrimination laws persisted. It returned over the introduction of laws to protect against discrimination in the provision of goods and services, which arose through an equality bill, which had not been completed by the time parliament was dissolved for the 2005 election. The government had decided to introduce regulations to extend this to protect people from discrimination in this area on the grounds of religion or belief. Once the 2005 election was over, the bill was reintroduced. The TUC joined with Stonewall and others in campaigning for it to cover sexual orientation. LCLGR took it to debate on the floor of Labour's 2005 conference and won an overwhelming victory (again). At the start, ministers adopted the extraordinary argument that it would be too difficult to introduce such protection but that it could be done through future legislation. But this was contested – with good reason – and the government conceded. The protection was introduced into the bill, although there was further argument about providing religious exemptions. This time, supporters of equality were prepared (remembering what happened over the employment regulations in 2003) and ready to counter the lobbying from Catholic bishops, determined to secure exemptions for (Catholic) adoption agencies. Angela Eagle, MP, directly confronted the Prime Minister on this issue, pointing out that to agree to such an exemption would be comparable to the effects of Section 28. Working with the minister responsible for this, Alan Johnson, MP, and Baroness Cathy Ashton, Eagle and her allies ensured that there was a majority within the Labour team working on the legislation to reject any such exemption, and indeed this was the outcome.[17]

Legal equality continued to improve under this third consecutive Labour government, culminating in 2010 when the Equality Act was implemented, which successfully brought together the by now large accumulation of laws and regulations dealing with equality. The unions and the TUC played a constructive role, uncompromising on all areas of equality. The Act included sexual orientation and gender identity in the list of characteristics that were protected from discrimination, finally consolidating LGBT rights as being on a par with the other grounds for protection against discrimination. The Equality Act was passed with little parliamentary (or media) opposition, demonstrating rapid progress that had taken place in popular and parliamentary support for equality. The Act has survived the Conservative-Liberal coalition that took office after the 2010 election, and has so far seen no attempt to row back on its main provisions under the Conservative governments elected in 2015 and 2017.

However, the Act has also not remained unscathed. The TUC and unions had fully supported the part of the law that made it a duty for public sector organisations to positively promote equality; this approach was a result of the inquiry by Sir William Macpherson into the murder of black teenager Stephen Lawrence in 1993, which found in 1999 that the Metropolitan Police was 'institutionally racist'. This demonstrated that it was not enough to outlaw discrimination, but that progress required positive measures to root out prejudiced cultures within organisations. Having initially been focused on racism in its first incarnation in 2005, the Act had next incorporated discrimination against disabled people, and had been extended to the other areas of equality and discrimination in 2010.

However, the real potential of the extended Act has never been tested, because the coalition government of 2010-2015 refused to implement those sections of it that had not come into force before their election. It went on to reduce the list of obligations for public bodies, and, as most public bodies were subjected to repeated and severe cuts during this period, it became increasingly difficult for them to spend money on equality provision and support.

The Labour government of 2005-10, while bringing together all equality legislation, had also decided to merge the existing equality commissions: the Equal Opportunities Commission (which worked on gender), the Commission for Racial Equality, and the Disability

Rights Commission were merged into a single body called the Equality and Human Rights Commission in 2007. The TUC response to this proposal was broadly welcoming, while recognising what might be lost in such a merger. However, from the viewpoint of LGBT people it was another great step forward in being recognised as a group with an equal voice, since no previous national statutory body had existed for supporting their fight for equality. The commissioners included someone from a trade union background. Kay Carberry, then TUC assistant general secretary, was nominated successfully by the TUC in the first commission in 2007. Sarah Veale – at that time head of equality in the TUC – was appointed for the subsequent term in 2013. But for the seat representing religion and belief communities, the government appointed the chair of the Evangelical Alliance, Joel Edwards, in 2009. Since the Evangelical Alliance had consistently lobbied against LGBT equality, this decision caused great dismay, and there was uproar on the TUC committee. Another vigorous campaign was launched, including a packed fringe meeting held at the next TUC Congress in 2009. This took place in Brighton; having been actively advertised through the local LGBT community, there were probably more openly gay vicars at this event than ever seen at a trade union event. It was not possible to overturn Edwards's appointment but the potential conflicts were well highlighted and he was not appointed for a second term.

BECOMING INCLUSIVE AND GETTING HEARD

Another major step taken by the 2001 Labour government was the introduction of the first legislation on trans people's rights. What became the Gender Recognition Act of 2004 went through a long process of consultation in which ministers, civil servants and the trade unions undertook a rapid course of new learning. The law allowed people who underwent or wished to undergo gender reassignment the right to be recognised in their acquired gender. The TUC worked closely with trans organisations, the Gender Trust and Press for Change, in preparing its response to the government consultations. Alex Whinnom, then vice president of Press for Change, wrote to me in 1998, when I was the newly appointed TUC lesbian, gay and disability officer, urging the TUC to develop policy on trans rights.

In responding (as the TUC and other unions did) to government consultations in the early 2000s, unions were confronted with the fact that while many openly trans people wanted to be included under a common 'LGBT' heading, in reality they had rarely been considered by L&G groups unless they also identified as lesbian or gay. The absence of recognition of trans people also extended frequently to anyone who identified as bisexual, although unlike trans people, bisexuals were protected by the employment regulations. The processes by which both bisexual and transgender people were recognised and included in LGBT groupings, perhaps not surprisingly, tended to run congruently. The discussions around these issues were important.

Anyone who was part of the sometimes outspoken debates that raged across many lesbian and gay organisations across the 1990s and into the 2000s will recall the argument frequently presented by supporters of inclusion: perpetrators of violence (queerbashing) are unconcerned whether their victims are L, G, B or T. Other arguments that were frequently presented proposed that gender identity was unrelated to sexual orientation, or – an argument used by some radical feminists – that gender is socially constructed rather than about sexual organs. Some sought to exclude transwomen from certain women's spaces on these grounds. This was the same argument originally noted by trans activists at the time of GLF (see Chapter Two) and it continues to be voiced today.

Bisexuals faced different problems: commonly, ignorance. Some people thought that because a bisexual could be in a relationship with someone of the opposite sex they should not be part of a lesbian and gay group. Growing amounts of research from organisations of bisexual people demonstrated that many bisexual people faced as much and sometimes more prejudice even than those identifying as lesbian or gay – and that much of it was in fact from lesbians and gay men themselves, making it often very difficult to take part in union or other networks or groups.[18]

These debates around bisexual and trans identities were taking place across lesbian and gay organisations, which included lesbian and gay trade union groups. As already shown, a few unions, such as MSF and the NUT, had already resolved the debate in favour of inclusivity. The discussion ultimately reached the TUC with motions and amendments at L&G conferences.

At the very first L&G conference in 1998, a motion from the union for senior civil servants (FDA) referred to lesbians, gays *and* bisexuals, and an amendment from NAPO to exclude bisexuals from this provoked a very closely-fought debate at this conference. The amendment was defeated by just three votes, but another motion, from PCS, explicitly calling for the addition of bisexuals to the conference remit was withdrawn. At the 2000 conference, MSF and the Chartered Society of Physiotherapy (CSP) proposed amendments to add trans people to a motion from UNISON, but these were defeated.

The issue was finally resolved the year after, at the L&G conference in 2001. MSF (supported again by FDA) proposed a motion that the exclusion of trans people from the L&G conference was unacceptable, and criticised the failure explicitly to include bisexuals. A motion from the NUT was supported by Equity, and called for a forum to enable trans trade unionists to elect delegates. This time, both were carried.[19]

The L&G committee and the TUC had already anticipated this and had invited a representative from Press for Change to observe at meetings of the L&G committee. Claire McNab performed in that capacity, offering advice that was of great benefit to the committee members. By 2002, the conference was transformed into the TUC LGBT conference. In order to ensure that the voices of groups facing particular exclusion were heard, the L&G, now the LGBT committee, had secured the agreement of the TUC General Council to modify its constitution to allow the creation of additional seats reserved for black and disabled delegates elected at the conference. This provision was extended to create seats for bisexual and trans delegates and in future years went on to be further extended to ensure a voice for young LGBT delegates as well.

2001 was also a significant year in extending democracy within other TUC structures. The governing body, the General Council, was elected every year at TUC Congress according to a complex voting system that took into account the size of affiliated unions. Large unions were represented by having a number of set places; small unions had to fight it out amongst themselves in elections. The outcome was usually that the General Council was (and is) populated by union general secretaries and key figures from the executive committees of larger unions. This often led to a male-dominated council, so to improve gender balance they had agreed long before to create additional seats for women representatives. This was now extended to black, disabled and lesbian and gay (and then LGBT) representatives. So far, the person who occupies this space on the council has also been the chair of the respective TUC committee; that role has to be filled by a member of the General Council (and is elected at Congress), and the chair performs an important function in linking the committee and the ruling body (i.e. the General Council). In a body which has many and disparate concerns to address, dealing with national and international politics and workplace issues, having a direct voice for representatives of equality groups was important.

PROGRESS IN THE UNIONS

The TUC LGBT structure had an impact on the rest of the trade union movement, with mutually interacting progress. Unions were being challenged to take part in a TUC structure, so had to find ways to identify LGBT members to do so. There was no rule requiring delegates to be LGBT – who to send was each union's decision. However, conference monitoring confirmed that the great majority of delegates were either LGBT and/or were officers from a union's equality department. Year by year, more unions began to take part, and to develop their own structures when they saw the benefits other unions gained by supporting the development of their own LGBT members.

UNISON

UNISON had been debating inclusion in parallel with other unions and the TUC. The self-organised L&G structure had quickly become embedded inside the new union after the merger of various public service unions with their own structures.[20] The resources to service it were established inside NALGO's full-time staff from 1990 when Kursad Kahramanoglou was that union's lesbian and gay officer. UNISON set up a Membership Participation Unit, and Carola Towle was appointed to be UNISON's national lesbian and gay officer in June 1993. There were already self-identified bisexual and trans members within the UNISON lesbian and gay committees and conferences but they were not explicitly recognised or given a specifically distinct voice at the beginning. When the national committee decided to remedy this, there was at the outset a sense that inclusion would happen, without doing much conscious work to bring it about. This proved to be an illusion. Changing the constitution (as usual with organisations) required a two-thirds majority in favour, and the first time a UNISON lesbian and gay national delegate conference voted on extending the remit, a trans member spoke against, on the basis that she was not gay. This contributed to the defeat of the proposal, which, while it did receive a simple majority, did not reach two-thirds. The national committee and Carola Towle organised a year-long campaign to win inclusion at the next conference, encouraging branches and regions to discuss the issue and to submit rule change motions; Philippa Scrafton, a trans member, wrote a powerful account of the progress she made in her local branch.[21] At the following conference the rule change was agreed and from now on the UNISON structure was fully inclusive: not just L, G, B and T, but also inclusive in terms of gender, race, and (dis)ability; the rules dictated a fully representative structure and established specific seats for each 'constituency' to ensure this.

UNISON therefore arrived at an inclusive self-organised LGBT structure within the union. The inclusivity was and is reflected in the UNISON delegation at TUC events, including the LGBT conference.

Sometimes activists ask a very good question about such well-resourced and comprehensively inclusive self-organisation: what does such a structure do to actively challenge the discrimination and prejudice that are the reasons for establishing them in the first place? The evidence from UNISON continues to be that working for LGBT equality is well integrated into the work of the union as a whole, and there are LGBT activists involved in every part and at every level of the union. More than 200 branches had their own LGBT officers in 2016.[22] All UNISON training includes modules on equality, and well-resourced LGBT groups at regional level ensure that equality is a mainstream part of the union's concerns and activities.[23]

UNITE

Other unions also saw significant progress in their structures, policies and actions for LGBT equality. UNITE is a union on a similar scale to UNISON, formed from a succession of mergers culminating in the coming together of Amicus and the TGWU in 2007. The latter had developed a lesbian and gay committee structure in the 1990s but it had no formal status, even though it was entirely supported by the union leadership and by the lead UNITE official on equality, deputy general secretary Diana Holland. As a result, the TGWU had played a full part in TUC LGBT conferences, organised presences at Pride, and included LGBT rights in training courses. More important still, the union supported members in the workplace – not just Betty Gallagher on the London buses, but also across the whole disparate union and its hundreds of thousands of members. One of the consequences of the merger with Amicus was that a far more sophisticated and integrated structure was developed across the equality groups. This was ironic, because apart from those coming from MSF into Amicus, that union had no LGBT structures. Diana Holland has described how in advance of merger there was great concern on the TGWU side to ensure that equality was properly part of the new union. There was a working group that focused on structures, which counted 2017 general secretary Len McCluskey among its members. This established a format that gave equal status between the equality structures and the industrial sectors into which the union was organised (e.g. aviation, cars, health etc), with national and regional conferences and committees and rights for union equality representatives established in the new union's rule book. The pressure for these outcomes was driven strongly by the organised left within the union. From the official merger in 2007 to 2009, when the process was completed, Amicus and the TGWU progressed towards becoming UNITE in tandem, and both UNITE-Amicus and UNITE-TGWU delegations were registered for TUC equality conference until 2009, when it became necessary to decide who was going to represent the new merged union in a single delegation and who was going to be nominated for election to the TUC committee. The story of progress within this trade union, one of the most powerful and influential in the country, was linked with the continuous activity of the TUC on LGBT rights.[24]

Public and Commercial Services Union

In the civil service, the creation of PCS Proud accompanied the establishment of the merged civil service unions in 1998. The development of Proud, like that of UNISON's L&G (then LGBT) set-up, brought together different unions' cultures and traditions. Proud elected its own steering committee – Yvonne Washbourne was chair, Brian Shaw secretary – and organised annual seminars, attended by upwards of a hundred members. Proud also ensured training for LGBT workplace representatives through national courses with LGBT trainers. These were well subscribed. But the steering committee was conscious that (one of the potential risks of self-organisation) many LGBT members were active only in Proud structures, not in the wider union, and deliberately set about challenging this culture by successfully supporting LGBT members in developing the skills and confidence to play a part inside PCS at all levels. The union's national executive appointed two of its members to serve on the Proud steering committee, which cemented links between the self-organised group and the national union.

Of course there were problems. One was that – especially among members coming from the Civil and Public Services Association (CPSA) – Proud was seen as left wing. There were also workplaces where the culture was still homophobic. Proud therefore faced issues of politics *and* prejudice. By a patient strategy which included consciously leaving factional politics off the agenda, Proud began to overcome these challenges. The election of Mark Serwotka as general secretary in 2002 not only repositioned PCS as a more left-wing union on the national stage, but also saw greater support for equality from the top. It was he who ensured PCS took part in the Amicus case in 2003, challenging exemptions to equality law.

In the same year, Proud finally dropped the joining fee that had lasted since the early days of self-organisation in the civil service. It has a mailing list of many hundreds and maintains its own website.

Proud was able, through the PCS, to meet directly with employers in government departments to help managers implement the equality employment regulations, to negotiate agreements and to establish joint working parties in some departments. Sadly but predictably, much of this progress has been undermined by the devastating impact of relentless cuts and redundancies since 2010. The civil service has shown some worrying retreats from good practice on equality during this period (see Chapter Seven).[25]

Communication Workers' Union

The new TUC structures and greatly increased activity brought visibility and greater legitimacy to trade unionists arguing for acceptance of LGBT issues in member unions. And, in the merged structure represented by the Communication Workers' Union (CWU, see Chapter Four), the determination of its elected Lesbian and Gay Advisory Committee kept equality issues on the agenda. The CWU continued its tradition of highlighting significant issues in its communications to members. On the back of the *Straight Up!* report, for example, the union journal carried a whole page report reinforcing the message that prejudice was a trade union issue, and focussing on Duncan Strivens's account of his personal experiences of coming out after twenty years. As an officer in a branch (South East London) with 1100 members, he attended a training course where he first became aware of the existence of the Lesbian and Gay Advisory Committee, and decided to go to its next seminar, which he did without telling anyone else. His feelings reflected those of many other trade union LGBT members – 'every roundabout on the journey was an invitation to turn around and go home'. But he didn't and when he got there, having nothing but stereotypes in his mind, 'everyone seemed so normal. Suddenly, the whole world opened up'.[26] He later put himself forward for election to the committee and came out gradually – to his branch chair then his closest work associate, and found both had long suspected he was gay. Having come out and started to become a firm advocate of equality, Duncan Strivens reported none of the hostility from colleagues that he had anticipated and feared. However, the CWU also printed a story in the journal explaining why it supported the repeal of Section 28, which was then in parliament – this led to letters in subsequent months both for and against, demonstrating that prejudice continued but also that some members were ready to challenge it.[27]

The advisory committee originally fed into the CWU's national leadership through an indirect route: minutes of meetings were presented by non-voting L&G Advisory Committee (LGAC) representatives to the union's Equal Opportunities Committee (EOC, composed of members of the national executive). Now, they go direct to the National Executive Committee (NEC). Here, the continuation of prejudice at a relatively low level reflected that the battle had not yet been wholly won inside the membership. LGAC member Maria Exall remembers three occasions over fourteen years (up to 2016) when hostility to proposed LGBT actions was voiced on the NEC. However, backing from union general secretaries (particularly Tony Young (1995-97), Billy Hayes (2001-15), and Dave Ward (2015-date) has helped the cause of equality. Branch activist and TUC LGBT committee member Laurie Smith reported that at the 2016 CWU national conference earlier items on the agenda overran, and the whole section on equal opportunities was dropped. He lodged a complaint and received a personal telephone call from the general secretary in response.[28]

In the CWU, therefore, a combination of self-organised activism among LGBT members and political support from the leadership had helped establish LGBT equality on a strong basis within the union, and had given sufficient support to enable many members to find the confidence to come out, and to establish themselves within the union's structures as workplace and as equality activists.

GMB

There are – evidently and not surprisingly – similarities in the stories of how LGBT rights issues came to be taken up inside unions, and how unions were won over to recognising that the argument for equality was necessarily a core part of a union's purpose. This process is most powerfully illustrated in the unfinished story of how the GMB, the country's third largest union after UNISON and UNITE, now known by this acronym, came to participate in the movement.

There is no hiding from the fact that, for many years, this major union had not pulled its weight on LGBT equality. With an excellent record of support for women members, the GMB made an unusual decision in 2002 to recognise sex workers as workers; this established a still unresolved difference with many other unions, in which certain feminist arguments about women's oppression lead to a denial that those engaged in this occupation should be seen as workers as opposed to the recognition of paid labour in any role. Despite this, and despite sometimes supporting motions on lesbian and gay rights at TUC or Labour conferences, no group of LGBT members was recognised within the GMB structures. Instead, there were often conflicts between local GMB and NALGO (then UNISON) branches operating in the same workplaces (such as in local authorities), in which the GMB representatives during the 1980s sometimes made arguments against LGBT equality.

This was not to say that GMB LGBT members necessarily lacked support locally; the first elected chair of the TUC Lesbian and Gay Committee in 1999 was David Lascelles,[29] who was an openly gay GMB member working in a steel works in Lincolnshire. His account confirms the positive support that the union provided to lesbian and gay members from the 1980s onwards. Lascelles had served in the Royal Air Force as a telegraphist since 1968 but remained in the closet, homosexuality still being illegal in the armed forces – he remembers escorting a gay colleague to be court-martialled for that 'offence'.[30] He left the armed forces to find a life where he could be more open and ended up on contracts at British Steel in Scunthorpe. His branch secretary publicly revealed his sexuality so that he would help to make connections between the GMB and the local LGBT community, where Lascelles was already active. This encouraged members who were facing discrimination to take their issues to the union, which organised 'open evenings' across the region from Hull to Peterborough. From this start, Lascelles joined first the regional, and then the national Equal Rights Committees. The national committee was chaired by executive member Donna Covey who got him to attend the first TUC Lesbian and Gay Conference. But there was no internal structure for LGBT members of the GMB.[31]

An LGBT group was established in 2004, however, and came to be called GMB Shout! It was set up following a fortuitous meeting between Brian Shaw, John Keates (both of whom worked for PCS) and Sandie Maile (who worked for Prospect); they were all GMB members who met through PCS Proud and were encouraged by a lesbian GMB officer, Kelly Rogers, to set up a network. The national context encouraged this, with a Labour government, employment protection, and civil partnerships. None of them knew whether the GMB was involved in these important developments and none of them knew David Lascelles, because there was no channel of communication for GMB LGBT members.

The result was the creation of Shout! in the London Region in 2004. Carl Banks joined up; he had previously been a member of PCS Proud and had been encouraged by PCS activist Zita Holbourne to join the equality forum in his workplace (the Department for Trade and Industry, DTI). Through attending the LGBT network then being developed in the TUC's southern and eastern region, Banks, Shaw and Maile met GMB members from the union's southern region. Between them, and with the support of GMB officer Kelly Rogers and her manager, Rihanna Azam (now a GMB national secretary), the Shout! network was established during 2005, helping to find people to attend as GMB delegates to the TUC LGBT conference. They advertised through the regions and established a database of interested members.

Shout!'s first AGM was held in March 2006 and a constitution drafted. Sandie Maile was elected chair and Carl Banks served as secretary. While the union leadership was suspicious of potential factions developing, they decided to let it be, and the new officers met with the London regional secretary of the GMB, Ed Blisset, to ask for money to enable Shout! to take part in the London Pride march. He was happy to agree.

Sandie Maile also delivered a presentation at the GMB's regional council. The union had previously established women's and race advisory committees but nothing for LGBT. With the development of Shout!, however, this began to change. A new GMB national equalities officer (Kamaljeet Jandu, formerly of the TUC) oversaw the creation of a national equalities forum, on which three of the twelve members were LGBT (Brian Shaw, Tony Hughes and Nick Day). The forum first met in 2007. The same year, Sue Hackett became GMB regional equality officer in London and actively promoted self-organised equality groups on the model of Shout! with the full backing of the regional secretary.

Shout! looked inwards and outwards at the same time, quickly generating a large membership through social media (there were 400 members by 2011). It carried out an exhausting range of activities: training for branches; producing training packs on specific issues; publishing newsletters and placing articles in the union journal; organising union presences at Pride events across the two regions in which it was active (London and southern); organising motions to take to national conferences; holding fringe meetings at the TUC LGBT conference; hosting social events for members; and all the while, it was also raising money to pay for these activities. The achievements of this small group of activists included running a campaign called Putting the T in LGBT which included producing an educational pack addressing trans issues in trade union language, and making a short film (GMB activist Sarah Hurley led this project) that was shown at the GMB national conference and helped Shout! London and the region win a President's Award (one of the prizes awarded at national conference to recognise outstanding achievements – in this case for work on equality).

The wider impact of this initiative has been to encourage greater recognition and inclusion of equality in general, and LGBT equality in particular, across the GMB nationally. Most GMB regions now have equality forums, there are Shout! groups functioning in five regions and following a debate at GMB national congress in 2016, the Central Executive Council has agreed to set up an equality task force to take forward its proposals, including for reserved seats for equality groups who are not currently specifically represented on the executive.

The impact of Shout! London on the rest of the union in the wider region has been substantial; it made people aware that it was essential to reach out. The profile of all the self-organised groups (e.g. for women, black people and disabled people as well as those who are LGBT) has been raised by continuous communication through all channels with other branches, including through the recently established annual regional equality conferences. These are run by the regional equality forum, on which Shout! is well represented, and well supported by GMB regional equality officer Sue Hackett. 800 members responded to the survey done for the Putting the T in LGBT project.

Inevitably, in a largely manual workers' union, with little tradition of self-organised equality groups, some members continue to experience discomfort with talking about LGBT issues. However, there is also growing engagement, discussion and exchange, and little negativity. Despite the major challenges to trade unions in the present, such as cuts and austerity measures, the GMB now represents impressive progress on the equality agenda, although it has not yet reached its final form. GMB Shout! has demonstrated, as we have seen before, how success can be achieved by playing to the strengths of the trade union movement. In establishing the group, GMB activists understood the importance of self-organisation and activity, but also how vital it was to win active backing from the union's leadership – former general secretary Paul Kenny played a highly visible supportive part and general secretary since 2016, Tim Roache, has done the same. GMB Shout! worked hard to show the relevance of LGBT rights to the rest of the equality agenda and to trade union workplace issues in general.[32]

Rail, Maritime and Transport Union

Another blue-collar union with a left-wing leadership but no tradition of LGBT organisation was the National Union of Railwaymen (NUR) which after merging with the National Union of Seamen (NUS) became the Rail, Maritime and Transport union (RMT) in 1990. There had been previous history of union support for lesbian and gay members in the NUR. Activist Mark Beresford recalls how it won partner travel rights from British Rail in the 1980s (as it was called at the time – after privatisation the successor companies agreed to maintain the policy) when NUR member Mark Robinson's same-sex partner secured them on the buses in Newcastle. British Rail accepted the argument that partner rights should also apply to same-sex partners of people working on the railways.

An internal LGB support structure was initiated by Janine Booth in November 1997; she was a member of the RMT's Holborn branch, who got a motion carried in that branch calling for the establishment of a lesbian, gay and bisexual advisory committee alongside the existing women's and black members' committees. As this was a constitutional issue, it had to be debated at the union's annual general meeting. However, union leaders agreed first to explore the views of members; general secretary Jimmy Knapp issued a circular to all branches, but only four actually responded. This was a sign that the existing culture of the union did not encourage members to be open about their sexuality or discuss related issues in a union setting. Assistant general secretary of RMT at the time, Vernon Hince, had been delegated responsibility for progressing the issue. He organised and attended a special conference in November 1999, which was widely advertised among members, to discuss what role the proposed lesbian, gay and bisexual advisory committee might play. The discussion was positive and led the union's leadership to organise a further meeting which took place on 2 March 2000. These events provided an opportunity for LGB participants to discuss the problems they faced at work, the attitudes of other members, and the bigger picture of changes going on around them. Following a third meeting in April 2000, the RMT agreed to take part in the TUC presence at that year's London Pride and again considered how to reach LGB members. The proposal to create the LGB committee was carried at the AGM and the first meeting took place in May 2001, with fourteen people in attendance including the union's national president, with (now) acting general secretary Vernon Hince, three other members of the executive, and the equality officer, Pat Wilkinson. Pete Heyes was elected chair of the new committee at the second meeting, and an annual LGB conference was established.[33]

Mark Beresford (who is now chair of the RMT LGBT committee) and RMT activist Paul Penny reported that the culture in the RMT has improved remarkably since the committee was established in 2001. In these early days, it was a matter of acute embarrassment to discuss the topic of sexuality at all, and allegations of special treatment were commonplace. There are still sometimes problems, but the leadership of the union, who had initially been reluctant, had embraced the cause and actively supported LGB members. Former general secretary, the late Bob Crow, frequently attended the LGBT conference and was taken to gay clubs afterwards. He personally intervened to deal with cases of harassment of LGBT members, and marched with RMT members at London Pride (although Beresford recalled that he politely declined the offer of a pink RMT cap). The current general secretary, Mick Cash, has also shown his support by marching on Pride. The LGBT advisory committee is well attended (nominations to it are made from branches) and the annual conference attracts forty delegates, with a steady flow of new delegates each year. Taking part gives members the confidence to become involved in their branches and outside too.

The RMT recognises a role for workplace equality representatives (even though they do not have statutory rights) and LGBT rights (the T was added at the LGB conference in 2007, the change endorsed at the union's AGM that year) are regularly part of the union's national and regional training programmes. The current equality officer, Jessica Webb, is a strong advocate, and the union (Mick Cash is often to be seen wearing the badge produced by the committee) takes an active role in TUC LGBT structures both nationally and regionally.[34]

Fire Brigades' Union

An unofficial network of (mainly gay male) members of the Fire Brigades' Union (the FBU) came into being as a result of workmates meeting each other in LGBT places outside work, mainly in London. This happened at about the same time that the Stephen Lawrence inquiry (leading to the Macpherson report in February 1999) was creating awareness of institutional prejudice in the police, but also raising concerns in other public bodies such as the fire service. The latter set about investigating racism, sexism and homophobia in the organisation. FBU general secretary, Ken Cameron, learnt of the informal equality networks in his union, and invited representatives of these groups to a meeting where he expressed support for formalising the groups. It was agreed at the FBU conference in 1998 to create new sections (alongside the existing industrial sections) for women, black, and lesbian and gay members. Women and black members also received elected seats on regional and national executive committees but, because they could not publish membership lists of lesbian and gay groups without betraying confidentiality, the L&G section did not have this presence. This problem was overcome by 2002, and the fact that the position was always unopposed removed the need for election anyway. Stewart Brown was the first to hold the L&G position on the national executive. Meanwhile, the union was participating in the new TUC structures, and Pat Carberry was the first FBU nominee to sit on the TUC lesbian and gay committee.

Carberry describes the continuing problem of the sometimes exclusionary macho culture in the FBU, which is 96 per cent male. Despite equality training provided by the fire brigades which has challenged the problems of sexism and racism, homophobic 'banter' remains a significant issue and is a serious impediment to encouraging LGBT members to come out at work. The LGBT committee continues to battle with such problems and strives for high visibility. It regularly submits its full entitlement of three motions to the union's annual conference, always well supported by members, and it organises an annual training school. The FBU has regularly brought motions on international issues to the TUC LGBT conference because of its belief that equality cannot be won in any country on its own. It has also overcome initial reluctance by fire brigades to ensure a presence of uniformed officers complete with firefighting appliances at many Prides, always making a dramatic impact on the public and other LGBT marchers, as well as setting an example to other uniformed services, and challenging stereotypes. With significant cuts to the fire brigades since 2010, meaning a freeze on new recruitment for five years, and repeated industrial conflict with the fire brigades (especially over pensions) there have been setbacks for equality too. The current general secretary of the FBU, Matt Wrack, has carried through changes that have removed all the equality reserved seats from the executive. In 2017, a joint union/employer review of equality strategy has shown that some people among management are still uncomfortable with even talking about LGBT people's genders and sexualities.[35]

CONCLUSION

The FBU is a good example of how the trade union movement had championed LGBT equality over the decade, and more, after the election of a Labour government in 1997 made legislative progress possible. The TUC itself was now firmly established as a coordinator and initiator of activity to promote the equality agenda as a whole. The distinction had disappeared between 'bread and butter' work-place issues that had been the traditional raison d'être for unions and the practice of supporting equality both at work and outside the workplace for any section of society. That trade unions also had a duty of solidarity with workers across the world had long been an accepted principle. The FBU example confirmed that this solidarity now included LGBT people in other countries. That is the subject of the next chapter.

NOTES

1. The surveys, produced NatCen, can be read on line at http://natcen.ac.uk/our-research/research/british-social-attitudes.
2. Today, this is the GMB, no longer an acronym but a title deriving from one of its earlier name, the General, Municipal and Boilermakers' union.
3. The statement was reported in some of the LGBT community press and is cited here from Purton, *Sodom, Gomorrah and the New Jerusalem: Labour and Lesbian and Gay Rights from Edward Carpenter to Today*, London: LCLGR, 2006, p.51.
4. TUC General Council Report, 1999.
5. Documents and letters in the TUC records.
6. Equal Rights Department, TUC, *Straight Up!*, April 2000. The details

of the campaign had been organised through a working group of committee members – Lesley Mansell, Brian Shaw, Maria Exall, David Lascelles, and me as the officer, who had drafted the plan of campaign in December 1999.

7. I had back-to-back interviews with local radio stations all day on the launch.

8. TUC Response to Government Consultation on Draft Regulations, January 2003.

9. I am grateful to Angela Eagle, MP, who discussed the way this happened with me (26 October 2017) and explained the role of the Prime Minister's office in bypassing the normal government channels.

10. I sat in the court throughout the proceedings so much of the forthcoming narrative comes from my own experience.

11. The judgment is 2004 EWHC 860(Admin), 26 April 2004. The press cuttings and many letters, briefings, and consultation responses are in store at the TUC where I was able to read them prior to them being archived.

12. *Hansard*, House of Commons, 12 October 2004 cols 249-50 and 26 October 2004 cols 181-2.

13. The cut-off date for backdating survivor pensions for widowers was 1988. There was no such limit for widows. This remains unchanged in 2017 (see Chapter Seven).

14. I reported this to the TUC LGBT Committee on 10 October 2004, and the TUC Executive Committee on 16 March 2005.

15. The tragedy was that the prejudicial attitude encouraged by Section 28 had long since worked its way into the education system, where the law itself never actually applied. LGBT staff and students continue to suffer from this to the present day.

16. Many unions retain links with Labour MPs, originally through a process whereby the MP was 'sponsored', a connection now reduced in weight to 'supported'. This does not force the member to follow the union's advice, but it does provide a regular channel of communication. There are many peers in the House of Lords who were once union leaders themselves, and the TUC retains regular contact with them.

17. Discussion with Angela Eagle, 26 October 2017. Angela Eagle and Alan Johnson received Stonewall's equality award that year in recognition of their work.

18. Debates on inclusion in unions were reported in bisexual community media, for example (from 1995) www.bicommunitynews.co.uk/5353/bisexuals-in-unions. K. Roen, *Bisexuality Report for ILGA-Europe*, ILGA, 2002. Exclusion and discrimination faced by bisexuals from all sides continues and is reported and challenged by organisations such as BiUK. For a powerful study from 2012, see M. Barker, C. Richards, R. Jones, H. Bowes-Catton and T. Plowman, *The Bisexuality Report*,

at https://bisexualresearch.wordpress.com/reports-guidance/reports/thebisexualityreport/. Accessed 6 November 2017.

19. Reports of the TUC Lesbian and Gay Conferences 1998, 2000 and 2001.
20. The development of the self-organised structure was explored in depth and through interviews with a number of lesbian and gay members in Fiona Colgan, 'Recognising the lesbian and gay constituency in UK trade unions: moving forward in UNISON?', *Industrial Relations Journal*, 1999, 444-63.
21. *Out in Unison,* issue 55 (Spring 2015), p.5.
22. This is out of a total of 900, but represents a higher proportion of the membership because it covers the larger branches, some of the others being small (information from Carola Towle).
23. Information from Carola Towle, interviewed 31 October 2016, and in subsequent email communications. When I was working in the equality department at NATFHE (1994-98) and as TUC LGBT Officer from 1998 to 2016, I was routinely in communication with Towle and with UNISON activists nationally and regionally and I take the view that these UNISON structures were powerfully effective in working for LGBT equality.
24. I am very grateful to Diana Holland, UNITE assistant general secretary in 2017, for these insights. Holland was interviewed 26 July 2016. The LGBT in UNITE work is now part of Siobhan Endean's role as national officer for equalities with whom I worked closely for many years.
25. Brian Shaw and Yvonne Washbourne, interviewed 22 December 2016.
26. Duncan Strivens, interviewed in CWU's magazine, *Voice,* June 2000, p.5
27. CWU, *Voice,* March, April, May and June 2000 and *Outtalk,* June 2000 (kindly supplied by Laurie Smith).
28. Interviews with Maria Exall, Mary Hanson and Laurie Smith, November-December 2016.
29. When the conference and committee were first created there was no opportunity for an election (see next note) so the TUC General Council appointed Ed Sweeney, General Secretary of BIFU, to be the chair in the interim.
30. As discussed above, the chairs of equality committees were those elected as representatives of the equality groups on the TUC General Council. When the TUC L&G Committee was set up, there existed an agreement among the biggest unions to share these seats. As UNITE(-TGWU) and UNISON had the women's and black members' seats, GMB had the newly created L&G seat. The system broke down when Lascelles had to stand down through illness in 2003, and Maria Exall of the CWU won the election at Congress to take the LGBT seat. She has held it since then.

31. Communication with David Lascelles, March 2017.
32. Interview with Carl Banks, 15 December 2016. I also served on the London Shout! committee for many years until retirement and can testify to the contribution and hard work of not just the chair, vice chair and secretary (Sandie Maile, Brian Shaw, and Carl Banks – some roles changed in 2017) but also of the other committee members who took on many other tasks. Regional officer Sue Hackett has always provided tireless advice and practical backing to Shout! for agreed projects.
33. I was invited to speak at this meeting about the TUC's *Straight Up!* campaign and to give information about the experiences of other unions in establishing such structures.
34. Paul Penny and Mark Beresford interviewed 6 February 2017. Jessica Webb kindly facilitated the meeting and supplied copies of the papers relating to the Holborn motion and minutes of the special conferences and early meetings of the advisory committee.
35. Pat Carberry, interviewed 30 January 2017. There has always been a FBU nominee serving on the TUC LGBT committee.

6

Global outreach

Trade unions have long demonstrated awareness of the importance of international workers' solidarity. The Trades Union Congress (TUC) is part of an international global federation of free trade unions (now known as the International Trade Union Confederation – ITUC) and has an active international department, which has worked for LGBT equality and has made possible many of the initiatives described in this chapter. The TUC also plays an active part alongside European unions in the European Trade Union Confederation (ETUC), based in Brussels. In addition, since it was created in 1919, a TUC employee has been involved in the Workers' Group of the tripartite (i.e. employer, government and worker) International Labour Organisation (ILO), which is (now) part of the United Nations and based in Geneva. Through this structure, and assisted by a member of the TUC LGBT committee at the time (Stewart Brown of the Fire Brigades Union, FBU), the ILO formulated, debated and agreed to a progressive convention on HIV/AIDS. Alongside this work by the TUC, the central body of British unions, many UK trade unions play a role in their respective global trade union federations. Finally, since the 1990s, there have been LGBT organisations that work internationally, in which some UK trade unions have also played their part.

The need for solidarity with LGBT communities globally has always been evident but has never been more urgent than it is in the second decade of the twenty-first century. The progress towards legal equality linked to the growing acceptance of LGBT people in society, culminating in the recognition of same-sex marriage in many countries in western and northern Europe, and north and south America, has been in stark contrast to the legal persecution and social stigmatisation of homosexuality in much of Asia and Africa, and in the Caribbean. The 'world map' published by the

International Lesbian, Gay, Bisexual, Trans and Intersex Association (ILGA) on its website,[1] has shown an increasingly polarised world in terms of LGBT people's rights (and even right to live). The contrast has increased rather than decreased over the first years of the twenty-first century. Regional conflicts, the rise of jihadist groups like ISIS, and reactionary appeals to 'national traditions' as in Putin's Russia have all served to render being LGBT in a growing number of countries profoundly dangerous. Nor is the risk of the imposition of newly regressive legislation limited to states outside Europe: the election of right-wing governments in many countries in the European Union has seen anti-LGBT sentiment strengthening. In some countries the threats of discriminatory laws (even though they are incompatible with EU directives and therefore ought to be incapable of enactment) has confirmed the fragility of LGBT rights in countries where a pre-existing hostile culture and slow social progress have not yet matched laws imposed from outside, such as in some of the Baltic states or Poland.[2]

There have therefore arisen far more calls for solidarity than it is possible for any single organisation (even one as large as the TUC) to be able to respond to effectively. The scope for action that might make a difference is seen to be smaller than might appear, and indeed some actions, however well-intended, can be actively counterproductive.

In this chapter I will summarise some of the initiatives taken by the UK trade union movement and their impact; this shows that there is substantial scope for solidarity action – providing it is the right sort of solidarity. British trade unions need to recognise the responsibility of living in a country where legal protection for LGBT rights is (probably) secure, and to use this privilege to do what they can for the cause of global LGBT rights. Equality and freedom will not be secure until it is achieved everywhere.

UNION RESPONSES TO INTERNATIONAL PROBLEMS

Unions have long used the opportunity of submitting motions to the TUC LGBT conference to raise issues of oppression in many countries, and sometimes, in reality, there has been very little practical that could be done to put them into practice. Calls for solidarity with LGBT people in countries so ravaged by war as Afghanistan, for example, leave one struggling to identify any practical way of offering support – especially as one consequence of decades of foreign interference and reactionary insurrection has been that there is no trade union movement in the country, which would be the natural first place for the TUC to start such work. Important work can be done to support people fleeing the country, and raising awareness of the international issues around LGBT rights and giving a platform to representatives from LGBT communities facing oppression is part of the TUC's agenda. A major conference was organised at Congress House entitled Stamping Out Homophobia All Over the World on 6 February 2006, with speakers representing the British government (Ian Pearson, MP), Amnesty International (Nora Cranston), the international trade union movement – Fred van Leeuwen (Education International, EI), Rebecca Sevilla (Public Services International, PSI), Carol Beaumont (New Zealand Trade Union Congress) – and more. Most importantly, however, there were speakers representing LGBT people in Bosnia, Dubai and Uganda, although they were no longer resident in their countries of origin. This was one of a number of events designed to highlight and give a voice to global persecution and trade union solidarity.

Two years later, on 29 January 2008, a different type of trade union event took place at the headquarters of the ETUC in Brussels. Called *Extending Equality,* its purpose was to share the good practice of European trade union confederations and seek to deepen this across the continent. The ETUC commissioned a report under the same title that summarised the state of play across European unions. It highlighted very different stages of development in different countries, and showed that the strongest examples were based in the west and north of the continent (Spain, Portugal, Italy, France, Belgium, the Netherlands, Scandinavia and Britain). The influence of western trade union support for LGBT rights on developments elsewhere was also evident; the Polish confederation OPZZ (which would subsequently host another European LGBT trade union conference in Warsaw) had appointed the first LGBT officer in any eastern European union. Adam Rogalewski was a Polish gay man who had been working for UNISON in London. The representative of the Turkish LGBT organisation KAOS GL, Kursad Kahramanoglou, had previously been UNISON's first national lesbian and gay officer. He was also responsible for organising a well-attended joint

union/LGBT community conference in Ankara in 2015, supported
financially by Dutch union federation FNV.

The 2008 *Extending Equality* conference led to the organising of a training week for representatives from unions in eastern
European countries. This was hosted in Paris by the French General
Confederation of Labour (CGT), in February 2011, and training
was delivered by a group of LGBT officers and tutors from Britain
and France.[3] This also offered an important networking opportunity, providing contacts and ongoing support for people in less
developed unions pressing for more attention to be paid to LGBT
rights. During 2015, the French CGT with financial support from
the European Commission organised a major campaign, *Contre la
Homophobie*; this included four large regional conferences, at which
representatives of the TUC (myself, and Jan Baxter from PCS Proud
– the LGBT group of the Public and Commercial Services Union)
were invited to talk about the UK experience. A delegation from
the CGT came to London and met a range of British LGBT trade
unionists.

It is very hard to measure what impact these international
campaigns actually have, other than to consider the changes and
work that was sustained or inspired by them subsequently.

This has certainly been reflected beyond Europe in the continuing work of two international trade union federations already
mentioned, Education International (EI) and Public Services
International (PSI).[4] Their involvement began following the international lesbian and gay conference attached to the World Gay Games
in Amsterdam in 1998.[5] The EI and the PSI set up a working group
in 1998, and have since been involved in promoting equality among
the 50 million workers (in 950 unions) around the world that belong
to the federations. UNISON provided the resources to publish the
working group's first booklet, *Working for Lesbian and Gay Members*,
in 1999 and also helped produce a more substantial document, *Trade
Unionists Together for LGBT Rights!*, in 2007. The latter presented a
succinct account of the issues for LGBT communities and the role
that unions can play, setting out examples of where unions have
supported communities under attack as well as defending their own
LGBT members facing victimisation. One striking example given
was the action by thousands of members of a Polish teachers' union
who demonstrated in defence of a gay member sacked by the govern-

ment in 2006. EI and PSI have been instrumental in ensuring there is a trade union component at each international LGBT event since 1998. Large numbers of LGBT trade unionists from every continent are taking part in the human rights conferences attached to the games, although they are inevitably dominated by Europe and North and South America. Again, important connections have been made, and information exchanged, and best practice shared.

Trans people, whose rights, or lack thereof, have rapidly climbed the agenda in recent years (see Chapter Seven) also now have international structures in place: there now exists a European Transgender Council (TGEU) at which UNISON is represented.[6]

ILGA has developed into an authoritative international voice for LGBT people, with member organisations in 110 countries. Once again, UNISON has played the leading role among British unions in developing a relationship with ILGA through continual engagement with ILGA-Europe (the body operates at both a world and a regional level). But it is a fact that few other British unions have yet affiliated to this important organisation or committed resources to supporting it; they have not taken part in its conferences or backed its campaigns.

The still narrow international base for LGBT rights – when so many countries still have homophobic legislation and cultures – is a big obstacle to progress. Alongside its work in the ETUC, the TUC has also worked to promote a clear policy in the global trade union movement. In 2016, at the four-yearly world congress of the ITUC, the TUC collaborated with other supportive federations to present an amendment to the draft conference platform explicitly supporting LGBT equality. It also organised a fringe event with an international platform of senior trade unionist speakers to discuss the amendment with delegates. The proposal was carried without any dissent.

However, many trade unions around the world still do not support LGBT rights. There are many countries where it could have a substantial impact, if the trade union movement stood up for the rights of the LGBT community or campaigned for legalisation. When at the TUC, I tried to make contact with union federations in Russia, but obtained no responses. In making contact with Uganda, where the old Commonwealth connection established strong and friendly relations with Ugandan unions, union leaders could not be persuaded to stand up to the increasingly virulent attacks on the

LGBT community carried out under the government of president Museveni. The attempt to legislate the infamous 'Kill the Gays' bill aroused wide global condemnation from world leaders and in the end it was vetoed,[7] but the bill was essentially incidental to the persistent suffering of LGBT people in the country.

What kind of solidarity can be effective in these desperate circumstances? For a long time, the TUC supported and helped run a programme around AIDS in Africa. TUC staff sought to raise gay and bisexual rights with partner unions in Nigeria through this route, but with limited success.

J-FLAG

There is also the route of fundraising. For several years, the TUC tried to develop practical support for the NGO Jamaican Forum for Lesbians, All-Sexuals and Gays (J-FLAG). In Jamaica, a violently homophobic media is linked to relentless preaching against LGBT people by US evangelicals, and combined with a widespread macho gang culture and a number of popular reggae performers whose lyrics explicitly called for gay people to be murdered. This led to precisely this outcome, with many deaths of LGBT people in the country in the past decade, leaving other LGBT people in genuine fear for their lives. A campaign organised by Peter Tatchell (*Stop Murder Music*) in Britain did lead to some of the singers with violent lyrics having invitations to perform abroad being cancelled, and some to sign up to a statement renouncing homophobia.[8] Meanwhile, the TUC raised several thousand pounds in donations from trade union branches but this actually made little impact: the then leaders of J-FLAG have now mainly obtained asylum in countries like Canada. The organisation still functions and there have been occasional promises of reform by ministers in Jamaica, which continues to apply Britain's repealed anti-gay laws from the nineteenth century, but it is not yet clear whether the reforms will happen.

Rulers of countries with homophobic and exclusionary policies and cultures, such as Zimbabwe's president since 1987, Robert Mugabe, denounce efforts by British governments to protest about many things, including LGBT rights, as the attempts of an imperial power to influence the decisions of a former colony which is now an independent country.[9] Ultimately the only solution is to change the culture from inside the country, as LGBT movements have had to do in western countries.

THE LGBT STAKEHOLDER FORUM

A number of Commonwealth countries impose legal penalties (usually inherited from the British) on LGBT people. Under the British Labour governments elected since 1997, some progress was made when two government departments, the Government Equalities Office (GEO) and the Foreign and Commonwealth Office (FCO), set up a LGBT stakeholder forum (2007) which met occasionally to discuss how best to deal with this issue. These were productive discussions, sharing much information and suggesting the approaches that would work best, with positive responses. The TUC and UNISON were regular participants in these forums.

One focus of the discussions at the forum was the two-yearly Commonwealth Heads of Government Meeting. At the meeting in 2015 in Malta, a coalition of LGBT organisations, including the recently established LGBT lobby group Kaleidoscope, the intergovernmental Commonwealth Foundation and the TUC, planned a programme of activities, seeking to raise the profile of LGBT rights. However, until there is a change of approach within many of the Commonwealth member countries, there is no chance of the issue being raised at the formal meeting sessions without risking negative responses from many African heads of government. Therefore, for the time being, progress is limited to discussions on the fringe, such as at the large 'peoples' assembly' that gathers outside the main forums.

The UK coalition government elected in 2010 suspended invitations to trade unions to take part in the LGBT stakeholder forum, and since 2015 the forums appear to have been suspended altogether.

SANCTIONS AND ASYLUM

Another problem is the kneejerk reaction when the latest news story breaks about another homophobic murder, such as sixteen-year-old Dwayne Jones in Jamaica in 2013, or another 'kill the gays' parliamentary bill, such as in Uganda from 2009, or the legislation in the Russian parliament banning promotion of homosexuality to young people in 2013. People often argue in response to such events that the UK should impose sanctions, or (in the case of African countries) withdraw aid. There are two real dangers to this approach, however. The first is that sanctions risk harming those who benefit most from any overseas aid, the poorest. The second is that those in power can very easily turn the blame for any negative impact against the LGBT community and hold them out as being responsible. It would be preferable to maintain support for local communities while targeting governments, but this is difficult to achieve. When asked by the TUC, Russian LGBT groups said they did not want western countries to impose sanctions.

There are three practical areas where trade unionists and others can support international LGBT rights directly: by promoting understanding in the trade union movement within specific countries (making reference to the pro-LGBT policy adopted by the ITUC in 2016); by supporting activists in these countries with money raised by trade unions; and by supporting those fleeing persecution and seeking asylum in western countries.

The issue of LGBT asylum seekers has of course become entangled with current xenophobic and racist responses in the UK to human catastrophes across the world, but even before the civil war in Syria and before the impact of ISIS, the simple task of offering refuge to those fleeing persecution – as Britain and other states are obliged to do by international law, and by solidarity – has proven to be just as much of a challenge for Labour governments as any other. Because of its history of empire and international exploitation, Britain has become an obvious potential place of refuge for LGBT people facing persecution in former colonies. But those applications for asylum on the grounds of persecution for sexuality which have been refused have often made the headlines,[10] and were frequently raised in motions to the TUC LGBT conference. I frequently drafted letters for the general secretary of the TUC to send to the current home secretary, raising both individual cases and the general issues. It became clear that immigration officers were either challenging applicants' stories of persecution, or proposing that they could remain safe in their own country if they just kept their sexual orientation hidden, or – and this was the most alarming response – they were demanding that applicants prove they were LGBT.

As these actions by immigration officers took place, government ministers were simultaneously responding to public concern about the plight of LGBT asylum seekers, by stating that it was government policy to welcome those fleeing persecution on the grounds of sexuality. In 2010, the new Prime Minister, David Cameron, announced that the practice of demanding that applicants for asylum prove their sexuality would cease. He thus claimed credit for abandoning these prejudicial practices, which had been carried out under Labour ministers, but the truth was a little more complicated. Immigration officers were under instructions to keep numbers of accepted asylum seekers as low as possible. They therefore needed to find reasons for refusing applications. Offers to ensure that immigration officers were adequately trained to deal with LGBT applicants were made by suitably qualified trainers in the LGBT community, but these were refused (training is expensive and staff time limited).

Meanwhile, any progress under Tory rule has been minimal and stories still emerge showing the continuation of the same practices. It is thanks to the actions of specialist immigration lawyers, often acting pro bono, public campaigning generating media coverage and pressure on politicians, that some applications for asylum on these grounds have been successful.

RAINBOW INTERNATIONAL FUND

Some trade unionists have taken more direct action to provide international LGBT solidarity. Paul Penny, a member of the Rail, Maritime and Transport union (RMT), was frustrated by the slow progress of action on international LGBT issues through traditional trade union channels – this required submitting motions to one's branch then onwards through various higher levels up to annual conferences, all of which had to take place before union leaders might be asked to even write a letter. Penny decided to set about organising direct support in 2013. The situation in Russia was rapidly deteriorating; several cities and regions, including St Petersburg, banned 'public displays' of homosexuality in 2011, which rapidly led to the measure becoming national law. This, in addition to the first outing of the 'kill the gays' bill in Uganda in 2009 led Penny to make contact with activists in Uganda and to set up the Rainbow International LGBT Activists Solidarity Fund, which was launched at a well-supported event in December 2013.[11]

Direct union contact generated some of the actions that were mobilised by the Rainbow International Fund. RMT activist Janine Booth had been in Lithuania in 2013 when an anti-LGBT bill had been proposed in the Lithuanian parliament, and she made contact with the local LGBT organisation there, LGL. Back in London, Paul organised an urgent Rainbow International campaign to respond to these events and staged a picket of the Lithuanian embassy on 27 November 2013, which was supported by trade unionists and campaigners from London-based Out and Proud Diamond Group (LGBT people from African countries) (plate 8b). Such solidarity works both ways; initially, the Vilnius LGBT group had not seen any purpose in establishing a trade union link, but they now saw the potential impact of doing so. By 2017, the proposed law had not so far been taken forward.

The Rainbow International Fund raises money to provide direct support for LGBT activists working in a number of countries – it works with people in Uganda, Cameroon and Nigeria. Following the 2016 election in Uganda that returned president Yoweri Museveni to power, numbers of LGBT Ugandans sought refuge in neighbouring Kenya and were placed in a refugee camp near Nairobi by the United Nations High Commission for Refugees (UNHCR). But the UN had not anticipated what happened next: having been placed in a separate section, the LGBT people were subjected to homophobic attacks by other refugees, and Rainbow International had to work with the UN officials to find a satisfactory solution.

Penny spoke of his experiences of trying to work with the FCO, suggesting that he found an absence of urgency in responding to these challenges. This echoes the experience the TUC has had in trying to re-establish the working relationship between the TUC and the FCO that prevailed before 2010.

As a result of RMT support for Rainbow International, the union's new general secretary, Mick Cash, raised the question of LGBT rights at the International Transport Workers' Federation (ITF, the equivalent of PSI and EI in the transport sector) and urged them also to set up an international transport LGBT trade union committee. So far, this proposal has met with resistance.

Rainbow International takes the approach of working directly with LGBT activists and groups on the ground and trying to sustain them financially. Working with them on this is a positive way in which

British trade unions could demonstrate practical solidarity – and at the same time show that unions are allies of those struggling for equality.[12]

LOOKING FORWARD

Despite the awful international situation prevailing in the twenty-first century, the basis exists for British trade unionists to build on good foundations to support LGBT people across the world. The current Conservative government is not hostile to arguing for equality abroad, and this provides openings for further work.

The international trade union movement has an explicit policy that all unions could use to raise LGBT equality issues to a significant level of support and action in many more international trade union federations than the two that already have such a focus. Many unions have developed direct links with unions abroad and could promote the agenda for equality through such connections.

There also remain the opportunities to show support closer to home, by taking part in occasional pickets and protests at embassies or consulates, by making financial contributions to campaigns like Rainbow International, and by inviting speakers to union meetings and conferences from the many campaigns based in Britain that represent LGBT people from countries in which persecution continues. It is vital that we help to make it possible for those who wish to return home to do so, and recognise that the breakthrough towards greater equality can only ultimately be brought about from within each country itself.

NOTES

1. The map is at http://ilga.org/what-we-do/lesbian-gay-rights-maps/. ILGA has existed since 1978, and employs a small staff based in Geneva thanks to funding from several governments and income from many affiliates. The map is updated yearly along with reports on the current legal status of LGBT+ people in each country. In 2016, homosexuality was illegal in seventy-eight countries with the death penalty in thirteen. Almost exactly the same number of countries had laws protecting against discrimination although there is a wide variety of different levels both of legal rights, and also differences in social acceptance of LGBT communities in each country.
2. While (in line with European Union law) discrimination against LGB

people is illegal in employment in Poland, attempts to introduce civil partnerships were rejected in parliament in 2014 and again in 2015. In September 2015, Amnesty International reported that in Poland there is 'widespread and ingrained discrimination' against LGBT people. Politicians from the ruling Law and Justice Party have made frequent reported statements critical of LGBT people. Pride marches have taken place each year in Warsaw but were banned by the city government in 2004 and 2005. The Eurobarometer (an annual survey of public attitudes on a wide range of issues) has identified that more than half the population surveyed is hostile to equal rights for LGBT people and particularly strongly opposed to equal marriage, in part because of strident opposition from the Catholic church in a country where that institution is exceptionally powerful. For attempts to outlaw LGBT rights in Lithuania, see p156.

3. I was involved in these events, which provided a great opportunity to share experience with trade unionists from other European states.

4. National unions in particular sectors (e.g. transport, education) can participate in global federations that address issues facing unions in that sector at an international level. EI and PSI have long included a focus on equal rights for LGBT people, as described in this chapter.

5. These international gatherings have been held since 1982 in host cities around the world, organised by the Federation of Gay Games. A split took place in 2006 because of irreconcilable differences over the budget, leading to the creation of the separate International Gay and Lesbian Sports Association which organised the Outgames in Montreal 2006, Copenhagen 2009, Antwerp 2013 and Miami 2017. International human rights conferences have been attached to these games, organised by groups from the host country, including trade unions.

6. UNISON National LGBT Committee, *Annual Report*, 2016, pp14-17. The report from EI/PSI's first international LGBT forum held in Brazil in 2004 was presented to the British TUC LGBT Committee in October of that year and was used to encourage discussion on how to develop unions' international solidarity work.

7. The bill, which originally contained the death penalty for 'repeated offences', was introduced by David Bahati MP in October 2009. Prior to this, US evangelicals had held workshops and encouraged an attack on homosexuality which culminated in the publication of the names of many gay Ugandans in the press (April 2009). Intense international pressure delayed consideration of the bill which was eventually carried (modified to replace the death penalty with life imprisonment) in December 2013, signed into law by the president in January 2014. However, there had not been a quorum present for the vote so the Constitutional Court struck it down (August 2014) and in 2017 it had still not been reintroduced.

8. The campaign, which worked in Canada and the UK where it was run by Peter Tatchell's organisation OutRage and the Black Gay Men's Advisory Group (BGMAG), gained the support of the Green Party, and J-FLAG. Gareth Thomas MP (then development minister) spoke in support (reported 22 November 2004). In 2007, a number of stars signed a statement renouncing homophobia, although one of the signatories subsequently denied doing so.

9. The response to US President Obama's attempt to link financial aid from the US to Zimbabwe with civil rights met with similar contempt in 2013. In that year, Mugabe repeated many times at his election rallies the assertion that lesbians and gays were no better than pigs or dogs (first made in 1987) and that homosexuality was alien to African values, norms and traditions. He used the same words in his address at the UN General Assembly on 28 September 2015.

10. For example, see Saeed Kamali Dehghan, 'UK may deport man facing persecution in Morocco for being gay', *The Guardian*, 26 October 2017. www.theguardian.com/world/2017/oct/26/man-may-be-deported-from-uk-despite-facing-persecution-in-morocco. Accessed 10 November 2017.

11. I delivered a supportive speech from the TUC at this event.

12. Paul Penny, interviewed 6 February 2017. The Rainbow International website is at www.rainbow-international-fund.org. Donations of all sizes are always welcome.

7

LGBT+, trade unions and new challenges

The recession that followed the banking crisis of 2008 has had profound, negative effects on equality. The long duration of the recession, and the way governments and economies responded to it, were different from previous cases. When some economic recovery happened, it was at the expense of working people, millions of whom are now struggling in precarious employment. The gap between the wealthy and the rest of the population did not shrink, but reached levels not seen in a century. Real wages in Britain fell 10 per cent between 2007 and 2015, and persistently failed to keep pace with inflation.[1] The economic crisis has helped fuel a rise in right-wing political forces that has significant implications for many people, not least for LGBT communities.

During this period in Britain, trade unions have been challenged at every level. Repeated government cuts to public spending have devastated the services that are relied on by growing numbers of people. This has also reduced trade union membership which was disproportionately concentrated in the public sector as a result of earlier devastation to the former manufacturing industry union heartlands. I will argue that the cuts have also had disproportionately negative effects on LGBT communities.

In many ways, the LGBT equality agenda remains incomplete, in terms of both social attitudes and legal rights. The trade union movement has continued to support these ongoing struggles, including since the recession and the general elections of 2010, 2015 and 2017. It has worked to challenge the political consensus that working people and the poor should carry the cost of neoliberal capitalist crisis, which has been decorated with the lie that 'we're all in it together'. In the 2015 general election, the Labour Party was unable to convince voters that it possessed either a real political alternative to the Conservatives, or an adequate record of economic competence. David Cameron thus ushered in a new Conservative majority government, taking over from the 2010-2015 coalition government.

The change in leadership of the Labour Party after the 2015 general election led to a new political agenda, but it has been significantly challenged by the disjuncture between the leader, backed by most party members, and the majority of Members of Parliament. After 2015, Jeremy Corbyn's leadership at first appeared to face a mountainous task to convince voters of the party's agenda and electability, in the face of persistent criticism from the press. The rise in Labour support and Theresa May's loss of a Tory parliamentary majority at the snap election in June 2017, which appeared to be called in order to exploit Labour's perceived weakness, and to strengthen the Conservative majority for the Brexit negotiations, has created continuing political instability and uncertainty. It remains to be seen how this will turn out, but one consequence for LGB people was immediately apparent: as soon as May concluded a deal with the Democratic Unionist Party of Northern Ireland to prop up her weakened government, the prospect of extending equal marriage to Northern Ireland disappeared off the agenda.

Many disabled people took to the streets in protest to voice their anger at a range of devastating cuts to their essential services; actions organised by Disabled People against Cuts (DPAC) included blocking London streets, invading Conservative Party events, and holding a picnic on minister Iain Duncan Smith's lawn. Impoverished black young people led riots on inner city estates, and, supported by the Trades Union Congress (TUC), women organised campaigns through workplaces and parliament for equal pay and on issues such as domestic violence. However, during this period the voices of the LGBT community have been rare in the resistance to government policies. One reason for this was Cameron's remarkable decision (announced to an astonished Conservative Party conference in 2011) to legislate for same-sex marriage. Carried into law despite the disagreement of many Tory backbenchers and of grassroots Tory supporters, this legal step ensured the government appeared socially liberal, while, at the same time, they cut support services, which were relied on by many in the LGBT community.

Equal marriage legislation was welcomed by many LGBT rights

supporters, including the TUC,[2] which intervened in an effort to ensure continued access to civil partnerships for those preferring that option, and to minimise the impact of exemptions granted to churches and of continued inequality in survivor pensions. The Labour Party had long been seen as the only party of government that would bring about equality for LGBT people, and this was evidently no longer the case. Ten years earlier – when David Cameron, like most Conservative MPs was voting against most of the Labour governments' equality laws – such legislation being led by the Conservatives would have been inconceivable.[3]

THE TUC

Progress inside the unions working for LGBT rights has continued. In 2002, the TUC incorporated into its rules that all TUC affiliates must have an explicit commitment to equality. Since then, it has commissioned from the Labour Research Department a two-yearly Equality Audit, which is published for public access and is reported to TUC Congress. The audit checks on progress but also serves to highlight examples of good practice, to encourage others to follow. Frequent union mergers have continued, which complicates interpretation of the simple percentages that are presented in the audits. However, it remains particularly significant that half of all unions have routinely published up-to-date guidance on LGBT issues to their officers and representatives. In recent years, more and more have also published separate materials on trans issues. The percentage of unions organising seminars or conferences for LGBT members grew from 22 per cent in 2007 to 42 per cent in 2014. The number with a national LGBT committee roughly remained steady at around half of all unions between 2003 and 2016. However, these statistics are somewhat misleading and partly conceal real progress: they include all unions, from the very small to the large, merged unions (thus where two merged unions each recognised a LGBT structure, they now only count as one). This means that the actual percentage of union members who benefit from these provisions has actually grown.

The TUC encouraged unions with detailed advice on the law, workplaces issues and issues like monitoring with its *Negotiator's Guide: LGBT Equality in the Workplace* (of which I was the author), first published in 2006, with updated new editions published both in hard copy and available to download from the TUC website in subsequent years. Many thousands of these booklets have been taken up by trade union members over the years.[4]

One of the more complex questions on which TUC policy evolved was whether, and how best to monitor for sexuality, i.e. to ask members or employees for information on their sexual orientation. Detailed discussion with UNISON's Carola Towle in 2006, who had already taken part in a thorough exploration of the issues and pitfalls in that union, produced very cautious policy, which laid down a set of conditions that union negotiators needed to work through before proposing that an organisation undertake a monitoring exercise. The reasons for caution on this question (in contrast to better established systems of monitoring for gender and ethnicity designed to identify possible discrimination) were that asking anyone to identify their sexuality on an employer's form raised many issues that would not generally apply to gender or race, for example, with invisibility and thus the right to confidentiality being a key difference. With progress in terms of legal protection and better understanding among employers, unions and members, the TUC advice is now to monitor sexuality, subject to certain conditions being met.[5] As of 2014, 31 per cent of unions monitored their membership to establish members' LGB status, in contrast to just 6 per cent in 2011. Monitoring of trans status raised different questions, including the elementary point that someone changing their gender will generally thereafter want simply to be recognised in their acquired gender. (Non-binary and genderqueer rights will be discussed below.) These questions were also addressed in the TUC advice following consultation with trans organisations, but the wording of appropriate questions for monitoring is an ongoing debate.[6]

ONGOING SELF-ORGANISATION

Self-organisation continued among unions. This was often the result of members observing the benefits obtained in other unions and raising the call for development of similar structures within their own unions. One such example was the education union the Association of Teachers and Lecturers (ATL),[7] which began to develop self-organisation in 2008, led by Julia Neal, a prominent activist in the union.

At the time that the TUC was helping to organise the European TUC (ETUC) LGBT conference (see Chapter Six), Neal was a member of the union executive, and served a term as union president, but had not publically come out. She decided it was time to get involved and persuaded the ATL to take part. She convinced them to allow her to travel to Brussels as part of the TUC delegation. Neal encouraged the union to take big steps forward in organising for equality, appointing its first national equality official. Wanda Wyporska, who had previously worked at the TUC, secured the post and was able to draw on advice from her former colleagues to set up dynamic equality structures in ATL for each of the equality strands, including LGBT. ATL has therefore provided equality organising for its LGBT members, and plays a full part in the TUC's equality structures.

In a very different sector, the large shop workers' union, the Union of Shop, Distributive and Allied Workers (USDAW), has a small team of equality officers. They discussed with the TUC how best to reach their own LGBT members and organised a network for them. As a result of this, the union has successfully regularly nominated a candidate for election to the TUC's LGBT committee.

The National Union of Teachers (NUT) appointed an officer charged with organising its LGBT members. David Braniff-Herbert, who was then also a member of the TUC LGBT Committee, has successfully brought hundreds of the NUT's LGBT members into activity since 2015.

CHANGING CIRCUMSTANCES: TRANS RIGHTS

Unions have also continued to respond quickly to changes within the communities. Among the many developments of recent years, transgender people and issues around trans rights have secured high and not always welcome visibility. The change since the days of the Gender Recognition Act in 2004 has been remarkable. Back then, civil servants working on the bill estimated – with very little to go on – that a very small number (at most, they thought, a few thousand) of people would be affected by the Act. The public emergence of a flourishing trans community across Britain since 2004 has confirmed that this was wrong.

Within a few years of this Act, trans people won a particular battle for equal inclusion, along with LGB people, as a 'protected characteristic' in the Equality Act of 2010. In 2015, an alliance of trans groups, organised within the LGBT Consortium, put together a manifesto of key demands.[8] Central to this was an emphasis on the need to revise existing legislation and address transphobia. Currently, for example, an existing spouse has the right to veto a trans person's right to obtain a gender recognition certificate (which enables that person to change their name, records etc). The TUC was among several organisations that rapidly added its name to back the manifesto. It made a detailed submission to the formal inquiry that was then carried out by the parliamentary Women and Equalities Committee. It is a remarkable signal of the progress made on LGB and T issues that the committee, under a Conservative chair, took on the manifesto. Even more astonishing was the committee's report, which recognised the validity of most of the manifesto in strongly positive terms.[9]

Another element of this change in attitudes towards trans rights is the growing challenge to gender norms in a broader sense, which is now taking place. It has now become a subject of legitimate public debate, discussing whether to offer alternatives to the gender binary on monitoring forms – or to abandon it altogether – and to ask before assuming what pronoun someone prefers. At the TUC LGBT conference in 2016, a panel discussion took place with young trade unionists, who raised such changes in self-definition, and the simple shorthand formula 'LGBT' at the TUC has now been rendered more inclusive to a wider range of non-binary, genderqueer and other queer identities by adding a '+': LGBT+.

In the public domain, the response to the developments in rights for trans people has not always been positive. The language used by a number of newspaper columnists against trans people has been dangerously violent – and indeed the number of transphobic hate crimes has soared (see below).[10] Alongside the relentless targeting of this group across the world, these events have mobilised many unions to recognise the international trans day of remembrance each 20 November. Unions organise activities to highlight this persecution, which is no less virulent than that faced by many LGB people, but which even continues to occur in countries where legal equality has been gained, such as in Britain, the USA and countries in Latin America. The horrible attacks launched against trans rights in the British press reflect the language used by a particular current in radical feminism, which was exclusionary to trans people even as the liberation movement first emerged (see p28).

REPRESENTATION FOR ALL

Phyll Opoku-Gyimah is the founder of UK Black Pride (UKBP), and is currently an official working for the Public and Commercial Services union (PCS), having earlier been the black representative in PCS Proud. Opoku-Gyimah explicitly recognised, along with many other LGBT people of colour, that the British LGBT movement (insofar as there is one) was dominated by white voices and that there was rampant racism in the community: 'we don't want white people stealing our voice'. Her response was not just to criticise, but to challenge this problem, arguing that this had to be the work of black members of LBGT communities because 'you can't empower people who've lost hope'. Working with Black Lesbians UK (BLUK), Opoku-Gyimah organised an outing to Southend in 2005 for black lesbians, and invited some gay men. The event was a success and led to the creation of UK Black Pride, which in eleven years has gone from strength to strength, organising annual events (open to everyone) usually around the time of London Pride, but free of commercial sponsorship and with the enthusiastic and generous support of the TUC and trade unions. As Opoku-Gyimah put it: 'trade unions are the bedrock'.[11]

UKBP is not about separation. On the contrary, it is a vehicle that enables black LGBT+ people to work collectively to promote inclusion in the white-dominated LGBT+ community, and to challenge homophobia in black communities. UKBP has had excellent coverage in the black community paper *The Voice*, and works with groups like Operation Black Vote and the Runnymede Trust. It now works with London Pride, where the board that runs it began almost totally white but which has understood the importance of becoming more representative. UKBP reflects precisely the same principle that lesbians and gay men in the 1970s recognised: to achieve anything, we need to work together and to insist on having our own voices heard.

IMPACTS OF CUTS ON LGBT+ COMMUNITIES

There has been a significant problem, as suggested above, with the absence of protest from LGBT+ community leaders to recent austerity cuts. The economic crisis has been particularly felt by young LGBT+ people in the areas of mental health and homelessness – which are sometimes connected problems. The course followed by so many generations of young people of leaving home—sometimes as a result of parental homophobia—for the big city has collided with a housing crisis. When this is combined with rapidly increasing poverty and homophobia, the recession has had a disproportionate impact on young LGBTs. The TUC published briefing materials on the statistics, which show the estimates for homelessness and the figures for mental health problems. In its most extreme form, the latter leads to twice as many young LGBT+ people attempting suicide as their heterosexual peers.

At the TUC in February 2016, equality officers, with the support of all four equality committees, organised a conference on the equality aspects of the mental health crisis. At the confer- ence, there were first-hand accounts of the traumatic experiences of young lesbian and trans people.[12] For the speakers, becoming active members of trade unions had helped provide support and, literally, a lifeline.

The trade union movement has attempted to mobilise support for an alternative to austerity and did much work to research impacts and mobilise resistance, including several immense national marches.[13] The TUC LGBT committee played its part as well, giving support to the creation of a campaign group similar to Disabled People against Cuts. However, despite efforts to reach out to communities, Queers against Cuts (QAC) never involved more than a small number of committed members.

The TUC commissioned research into the impact of cuts in the LGBT voluntary sector, and Fiona Colgan of London Metropolitan University carried this out. The TUC published the report as *Staying Alive* in 2014, which showed how cuts to a sector, which already only represented 0.4 per cent of voluntary sector spending, had closed down many LGBT community groups, or forced them to replace paid staff with volunteers, and reduce the scope of their already limited operations. These same organisations had provided vital support precisely to those homeless young LGBT+ people, or those with mental health problems, or supported people with usually hidden problems such as same-sex domestic abuse, and who found statutory services less able to deal with their specific issues.[14] At the same time, UNISON published its own survey of these impacts, seen from the perspective of its members dealing with the issues. The message was the same. An already significantly under-resourced sector was suffering disproportionately.

The purpose of publishing these findings was both to alert people to what has happening, but also to encourage more activity against the cuts. It did not. Protests did take place, however, when rocketing house prices in London led to landlords shutting down well-known gay pubs in order to redevelop the space, and local LGBT+ community voices were raised in protest against this. Such venues have always been important as safe spaces as well as recreation and places to meet others. Their loss is another blow for the community. However, the absence of joined-up resistance has reduced the prospect of any one service or venue being saved.

PRIDE IN THE TWENTY-FIRST CENTURY

It is a sign both of growing confidence and increasing support from outside the community that many towns and cities now regularly host Pride every summer. There are not many routes for unions to reach the LGBT+ community, and Pride celebrations are often the only opportunity. For many years, individual unions had taken their banners and set up stalls at LGBT+ community Pride events. However, once the TUC had established a national structure in 1998, it became easier to focus some of this engagement on the biggest events and particularly on the parade and festival in London, which continues to strive to make sure it is the biggest Pride in the country (plates 7 and 8a).

Unions supported Pride for a number of reasons. For a group whose default position is safety in invisibility, taking part in Pride was a direct challenge to the ongoing homophobia in society saying clearly 'we are here and we are not going away'. Also, Pride has been banned in increasingly reactionary Russia under Putin. Even in countries in the European Union that are bound by their treaty obligations to respect LGBT equality, this has still been attempted, such as in Riga and Warsaw (see Chapter Six). This makes participation in Pride, even in the UK, an important sign of resistance to marginalisation. Further, by taking part, unions are able to deliver messages to other participants, to explain what unions do, to recruit members and to meet members who may have been unaware of their union's commitment to LGBT+ rights.

Prides have often had problems with their inclusiveness (or often lack of inclusiveness) towards everyone in their communities, but they remain an important celebration of LGBT+ lives. However, Pride has also historically been a campaign and a protest, and this must continue. The first Pride marches organised by the Gay Liberation Front (GLF) were about challenging exclusion, oppression and invisibility. But as early as the middle of the 1980s, as we saw with the experience of Lesbians and Gays Support the Miners (LGSM, Chapter Three), later generations of London Pride organisers disagreed with the suggestion that Pride should in any way be 'political'. By the 2000s, when the TUC began collecting financial contributions from unions to enable it to sponsor London Pride (and in due course UK Black Pride) and thus win a voice in the preparations, the equality agenda had not been achieved. Delighted to receive the money and willing to reward unions by giving them desirable positions in the parades and opportunities to have speakers at rallies, Pride boards continued to emphasise that Pride should be a 'party', rather than being ('small p') political – that is, to campaign for all the rights still missing, at home and abroad. Representing the TUC in these debates, I never proposed Pride should not be a celebration, but failed in pressing for a stronger profile for campaigning.

An opportunity to convey the international solidarity agenda did come, however, when London won the right to host World Pride in 2012. The TUC worked closely with the first (and so far, the only) black chair of the Pride board, Patrick Williams, who was also a trade unionist who had served on the TUC LGBT committee. Great plans were made (including for an international conference on the eve of the Pride parade) but financial mismanagement by those responsible combined with an inflexible attitude by some suppliers led to a crisis in the last week. The whole World Pride event was nearly called off, and a simple march had to be substituted for the usual carnival-like parade.

Many in the LGBT+ community were up in arms about this last minute change to plans. The TUC took the initiative to address issues raised by the problems of Pride 2012 by organising a series of public meetings, attended by London LGBT people concerned for the future of Pride, at Congress House over the following months.

The meetings adopted a platform of principles including: account-ability of the organisers of Pride to the community (for the first time); inclusion for all; and delivering a campaigning message. One of the new consortia of people wishing to take control of Pride London from 2013 agreed to them all and this helped them secure the funding on offer from the Mayor of London.

Over the next four years Pride became bigger, more colourful and more diverse; it made serious attempts to enable disabled people to participate and to strive for diversity among speakers and performers, and it allowed TUC speakers on the platform at the Trafalgar Square event that has been the culmination of the parade.

In 2015, it was suggested by various people in the wake of the success of the film *Pride* (2014) around which LGSM had reformed, that it would be good if LGSM led the parade, in recognition of the thirtieth anniversary of the Miners' Strike. The Pride board first agreed, but retracted this when it learned that LGSM expected to march with the trade unions. I was told by organisers that this would have meant too many people in the lead group. LGSM confirmed their solidarity with the wider labour movement by giving up the front and joining the TUC in the middle. The trade union section of the march, complete with NUM banners, marching bands, dozens of union banners, hundreds of marchers and three union floats, was spectacular. However, the following year the unions were placed right at the back.

The first Pride march had carried banners demanding an end to oppression and demanding liberation. These messages continued to be conveyed by trade unions, and some other marchers, in the 2000s, and were of course still relevant. What was different was that large corporations, which have historical records of exclusionary policies on gay rights, had, by the 2000s, realised not just that many of their most valued employees were LGBT+, but also that Pride offered the chance to buy (for a modest price) the longest mobile advertising hoarding (and plenty of social media spots) ever seen in Britain. Many have therefore jumped at the chance.[15] With the acceptance of this sponsorship, Pride's message has become inextri-cably tied in with corporate advertising. Pride London has a good statement of its own principles (as agreed back in 2012/13) which is highlighted on its website but the reality is that being committed to diversity and campaigning is put at risk by its reliance on corporate money: analysis of participation in the 2016 parade showed that half of the contingents were from commercial organisations, rather than LGBT+ community groups.[16] The Community Advisory Board (CAB) was set up after 2013 to offer independent advice to the Pride board on fulfilling its commitment to accountability. I advised the CAB that it should adopt a set of ethical principles for sponsors, but this was not accepted. In 2017, the CAB report on that year's Pride was critical of the lack of diversity across the event. The board's response disagreed. But the issue is not going away.[17]

Big events like London (or Manchester, or Brighton) Prides require massive financial backing. That is not the issue. However, corporate messages run the risk of diluting or obscuring the ongoing need for resistance and protest against exclusionary and marginalising politics – particularly given the otherwise glaring lack of work being done by these corporations for LGBT+ rights. Sadly, however, the corporate takeover of Pride is not limited to London and is continuing apace. The banners expressing the views of LGBT+ community organisa- tions (which include LGBT+ trade unionists) are less visible amidst the advertising for organisations that were not previously part of the struggle for equality. Their support is welcome, but Pride must be both for, and of the diverse LGBT+ communities.

ATTITUDES IN SCHOOLS AND COLLEGES

Aside from (but sometimes connected to) the cuts issues, unions have been continuing to challenge on a whole range of issues affecting LGBT people, which have not been narrowly confined within workplaces. If promoting such issues was unproblematic when the political environment was friendly and the economy prosperous, to do so when neither of these conditions applied has been much harder.

An ongoing issue ever since the first battles of the Campaign for Homosexual Equality (CHE) and GLF has been how children are educated about sexuality and gender. It is a real test of the progress that has been achieved for equality, and attitudes to teachers being LGBT+ is often indicative of ongoing homophobia and transphobia.

Even when it has been national policy to teach that LGBT+ iden- tities are equal and valid, the message has not been received. The regular *School Report* produced by Stonewall since 2007 has quantified the level of homophobic intolerance continuing in classrooms and playgrounds. The 2017 *School Report* showed an improvement since 2012 – now the figure for LGB pupils facing harassment is down from 55 to 45 per cent – for trans pupils it is 65 per cent.[18] These figures are shocking. Voluntary groups like Schools Out have spent years campaigning for decent policy and on the way have produced education materials, provided training, and given wide-ranging support to achieving an inclusive curriculum. However, Schools Out co-chair Sue Sanders believes that even now there continues to be a fear among school leaders of parental responses to teaching LGBT+ equality, which prevents the schools from taking action.[19] For a long time, governmental responses, under different parties, was to pretend the issue did not exist.

In 2006, the TUC called together a coalition of education campaigns, including Schools Out, other voluntary groups, such as anti-bullying campaigns, and academics to press the Labour government to take appropriate action. It took years to get an education minister to listen, and when there was finally a response in 2009 (minister Kevin Brennan MP attended a meeting at the TUC) the general election meant that this campaigning had to start again with a new government who were, once again, disinclined to address the roots of the issue, and little progress has been made since then.

Where governments have taken notice, they have restricted themselves to the too narrow focus of trying to prevent bullying. However, important though this is, it fails to address the basic question of why homophobic bullying happens in the first place, and does not promote understanding of difference and diversity, and alternatives to traditional gender roles. Ofsted added bullying to its inspection regime from 2012, which has been a mixed blessing. Sometimes, the more ham-fisted interventions simply stir up hostile newspaper headlines,[20] and this alarms headteachers and inhibits future progress.

This is an all-school issue, not just in the classroom, so includes non-teaching staff, and education unions have struggled to turn policy into action. Many teachers still have fears about being out at work, and many heterosexual colleagues do not feel supported, or trained, to adequately challenge prejudice.[21]

At a time when national education policy has for many years encouraged schools run by faith groups to flourish, the additional question of cultural and religious attitudes has often been proposed as a reason for not working on LGBT+ equality in schools – or has been cited as grounds for allowing these schools to opt out of teaching LGBT+ equality. Proposals to make inclusive sex and relationships education compulsory across all schools have been made several times – with another one forthcoming. However, any law that permits an opt-out from teaching inclusion and equality will be dangerous. This would allow ministers to claim that they have resolved the problem of LGBT+ education, but those already predisposed to opt out will continue to do so. This continues the terrible harm being done both to pupils who grow up to be LGB or T, and to those who do not but instead grow up unaware and prejudiced.

OTHER ONGOING INEQUALITIES – AND FIGHTS AGAINST THEM

This is not to suggest that one can simply equate faith with prejudice. British Social Attitudes surveys regularly confirm that there is little difference in the attitude of people of faith (any faith) and those of no faith towards LGBT equality. The problem lies with those leaders of faith groups who assert that their beliefs exclude the possibility that LGBT people can be equals in their faith community. Since 2007, the TUC has supported a campaign, which was set up initially by the Lesbian and Gay Christian Movement (LGCM), to bring together people of faith (and no faith) to challenge these exclusionary claims, and to support those campaigning for acceptance in all religions. Such campaigning groups do exist in all faiths, and many of them are part of the Cutting Edge Consortium, of which TUC LGBT Committee chair Maria Exall is the chair (as of 2017). This consortium has organised large, successful conferences, events in Parliament and has gathered political allies to strengthen the argument and to demonstrate that faith leaders with reactionary views do not speak for all the members of that religion.

Another area of continued inequality is in pensions. Despite the (relative) success of the TUC campaign in 2004-5 (Chapter Five), which introduced the backdating of survivor pension benefits to 1988, this was still not equality. The issue appeared time and again on LGBT conference agendas. The TUC organised another big campaign on the issue in 2015, gathering together committee members, policy officers and union pension officers to produce a detailed dossier that was presented to the government before the 2015 election. With the dossier rightly refusing to separate out the two groups of people affected – same-sex partners and unmarried heterosexual partners – the government was persuaded through this pressure mobilised by the unions to re-visit the question. A report was produced that shows that it would be feasible to remove the inequality with the upfront cost remaining manageable. The argument was bolstered by the fact that a majority of private sector schemes had already equalised their provision, and the largest inequalities remained in most – though not all – public sector schemes. At the time the report was produced, Theresa May was Home Secretary. No action was taken. Now Theresa May is Prime Minister, and still no action was taken. In 2015, the Labour leadership, while understanding the argument, refused to make any commitment when presented with the case by a TUC delegation, for fear of being seen to make spending commitments when the party still backed austerity. It was therefore left to a determined individual, John Walker, who won a Supreme Court ruling in 2017, which stated that the exemptions in the Equality Act justifying same-sex pension discrimination were incompatible with European law.[22]

HOW SECURE ARE LGBT+ RIGHTS?

One of the many significant findings of the Equality Audits was that a number of unions have regularly reported successes in bargaining LGBT policies with employers. But one of the impacts of recession and austerity has predictably been confirmed by the most recent audits. In 2016, it reported that while five unions found that they continued to make progress with employers on the workplace equality agenda, eighteen had found the opposite, and a third of unions reported that employers were watering down the equality policies that they already had. This confirmed the widespread anticipation that when times got tough, it was equality work that would be sacrificed.

Although it has been illegal since 2003, workplace discrimination on the basis of sexuality has not gone away. In 2014, the TUC was part of the advisory group chaired by Baroness Rita Donaghy for an academic survey carried out by Manchester Business School

(MBS). This involved the largest-ever study of the experience of harassment and bullying of workers across different sectors of the economy. Thousands of people, LGB (it sadly did not cover the experience of people identifying as trans) and heterosexual were questioned. The outcome, published in 2014 as the *Ups and Downs of LGB Workplace Experience*,[23] was a real shock to any complacency that the law had ended the problem. Both overall and equally in every type of employment, lesbian, gay and bisexual people were *two and a half times more likely* than heterosexuals to experience harassment and bullying. This survey was also done before the government created additional hurdles to accessing justice, with the imposition of fees in 2013 (ruled unlawful by the Supreme Court in 2017 in a case taken by UNISON), which had to be paid before one could even lodge a case with an employment tribunal. LGB people have always been reluctant to take their cases to tribunal, even though the success record and often high awards were telling evidence that the law could work. The scale of the problem revealed by the MBS survey shows that problems of prejudice all around us have not gone away.

The British Social Attitudes (BSA) surveys show massive swings in popular opinion from hostility to acceptance across two decades. But there remain two worrying aspects to the surveys, one in the statistics themselves, and one in their interpretation. The percentages themselves confirm that at least one-fifth of the population continues to hold prejudiced views, such as in the survey in 2013. Twelve million is a lot of people. It is my belief that homophobia has become publicly unacceptable, but remains privately rife. Therefore the BSA statistics are misleading; people may deny their homophobia on the form, but privately retain exclusionary views. This is reinforced by a poll carried out by YouGov in July 2017 which found that 42 per cent of respondents believed same-sex relations were 'unnatural'.[24] The MBS study suggests this too, as does the continuing problem in education. There are also plenty of other indicators. Very prominent is the fact that in men's football (the situation is thankfully much better in women's football with a number of 'out' players), not one of thousands of professional players or officials has been willing to come out as gay or bisexual while still playing professionally, despite the good equality work and training provided by their union, the Professional Footballers' Association (PFA). Progress is being made but far too slowly and the reality of continued homophobic chanting by some fans shows that players' fears are genuine.[25]

HATE CRIMES

The figures reported by the police for hate crime consistently show that crime committed on the basis of sexuality is second highest in this list. In 2015-16, of the 60,000 or so reported offences, the large majority (78 per cent) were motivated by race hate. LGB hate crimes totalled 7194, or 12 per cent, while there were 858 against trans people. The latter figure may be only 1.4 per cent of the total, but it is a substantial proportion of the openly trans people living in Britain. These totals had risen by 19 per cent from the year before, with a particular spike after the EU referendum.[26] It is no longer plausible that, as the police have been known to caution, increased numbers may just be the result of more people reporting these attacks. On at least 8000 occasions, LGBT+ people in England and Wales were attacked. If there is any significant under-reporting, the picture is even bleaker: and the most recent Stonewall survey, based on responses from more than 5000 people, confirms that the trend is continuing to get worse rather than better.[27]

The reality is that while LGBT+ people may live freely and safely now in many places in Britain, there are also many places where they cannot. If one believes the findings of the General Household Survey (GHS) that is used to count LGB (again, not trans) people in lieu of there being a question in the census (something else the TUC campaigned for, unsuccessfully), then the total number is only around 1 per cent of the population. However, these findings seem somewhat unreliable, given that they show, for example, that there are almost no LGB people in Northern Ireland. It seems likely that there are many parts of the country where LGB people still do not feel secure enough to declare their sexuality, even to an anonymous household survey.

It is evidently not realistic to believe that all the gains made over the last two decades are secure. The horrendous increase in race hate and islamophobia that has marred vast parts of the world in the last few years is a source of great anxiety, as is the election of Donald Trump, who has joined the growing list of world leaders who appeal to 'traditional values' as opposed to 'liberal political correctness' to consolidate their electoral popularity. Trump has an echo in Britain (and Europe) with the rise of parties like UKIP. All of this poses a severe threat to even already-established LGBT+ rights, just as it does to women's rights, disabled people's rights, immigrant rights and many more.

One way to alert people in LGBT+ communities to the danger is to recover the history of these communities and their struggles. In 2006, the TUC hosted the launch event for LGBT History Month, which was created by Schools Out! TUC general secretary Brendan Barber delivered the welcome. LGBT History Month now takes place each February with growing reach across the land.

The trade unions helped to bring about many of the improvements achieved for LGBT+ people's rights in Britain. The battle for equal rights is not won, and the prospect of completing this agenda is threatened by the new world political climate post-2008. There are severe risks of a right-wing backlash of terrifying proportions driving back these historical gains – as we have already seen beginning to happen in the United States.

Whether these threats can be successfully resisted depends ultimately on the coming together of those who have an interest in social and economic justice. This requires a response at many levels, critically, the political, but also challenging bigotry everywhere. The unions can offer a wealth of experience, knowledge, and skills to support these ongoing battles, and the scale of the challenge makes them necessary participants in the struggle. In the often quoted words first used by Edmund Burke, those who do not understand their history are doomed to repeat it.

NOTES

1. 'The latest official forecasts suggest that the average worker will still earn less in 2021 than they did in 2008', *Financial Times*, 19 June 2017. Statistics on the economy are published monthly by the Office of National Statistics (ONS).

2. A number of activists saw marriage as a betrayal of LGBT liberation, which represented co-option into an oppressive institution. The TUC LGBT committee understood this but saw the step towards equality as more significant.

3. Cameron opposed the repeal of Section 28 in 2000 and 2003 (though soon after changed his mind), voted for civil partnerships but against

same-sex adoption (2002) and against in vitro fertilisation for lesbians in 2008. Stonewall's survey of voting records gave him 36 per cent in 2010. (Information compiled by Stonewall from *Hansard* and press interviews.)

4. The third edition was published in 2013 and is available from www.tuc.org.uk.

5. TUC advice is that monitoring needs to be accompanied with guarantees of confidentiality and a clear plan as to what the employer will do with any data collected, all of which needs to have been explained clearly to workers beforehand.

6. TUC, Equality Audits, 2003, 2005, 2007, 2009, 2011, 2012, 2014, 2016. The format was changed in 2011, and since then, alternate audits have examined workplace bargaining, which explains why the two year cycle changed in 2011-12. Published copies of the audits can be ordered from TUC Publications.

7. During 2017, members of both the Association of Teachers and Lecturers (ATL) and the National Union of Teachers (NUT) voted for a merger, creating the National Education Union (NEU), which has nearly half a million members.

8. At www.lgbtconsortium.org.uk/transmanifesto. Accessed 27 October 2017.

9. However, by 2017, action to follow the recommendations of this report has still not taken place.

10. In Britain, columnists like Richard Littlejohn in the *Daily Mail* routinely use intemperate language. Some long-standing feminists such as Germaine Greer and Julie Bindel (in *The Guardian*) have also argued for the exclusion of trans women from women's spaces, questioning their right to identify as 'women' (see, for example Julie Bindel, 'Gender benders, beware', *The Guardian*, 31 January 2004. www.theguardian.com/world/2004/jan/31/gender.weekend. Accessed 9 November 2017. And Matthew Weaver, 'Women-only Cambridge college to allow students who "identify as female"', *The Guardian*, 4 October 2017. www.theguardian.com/education/2017/oct/04/women-only-cambridge-college-to-allow-students-who-identify-as-female-murray-edwards Accessed 9 November 2017.) The issue continues to generate much heat but little light – there was even a brawl between trans activists and radical feminists in London's Hyde Park (19 September 2017 – reported in many newspapers).

11. Phyll Opoku-Gyimah, interviewed 10 February 2017.

12. The report was published on 9 March 2016 and can be read at www.tuc.org.uk/equality-issues/disability-issues/equality-and-mental-health-age-austerity-report.

13. There were large-scale marches and protests held in London and in several major cities simultaneously in March 2011, December 2012, and June, August and October 2015.

14. The report can be found at www.tuc.org.uk/sites/default/files/ StayingAlive.pdf. The National LGBT (Voluntary Sector) Consortium collaborated fully in the project.

15. In 2017, for example, the largest sponsors apart from the Mayor of London were Barclays Bank, Tesco, Starbucks, CMS and Price Waterhouse Cooper.

16. See the report at 'Pride in London is called to account by the Community Advisory Board', *Planet Nation*, 16 August 2017. www.planet-nation. com/lifestyle/big-bang-opinions/pride-london-called-account-commu- nity-advisory-board. Accessed 30 October 2017.

17. Edward Lord, 'Pride in London – Advisory Board report ques- tions organisers approach on diversity', 26 August 2017. https:// edwardlord.org/2017/08/16/pride-in-london-advisory-board-report- questions-organisers-approach-on-diversity; the response was on the front page of the Pride website, https://prideinlondon.org. Both accessed 29 October 2017.

18. Stonewall, *School Report*, 2017. www.stonewall.org.uk/school- report-2017. Accessed 9 November 2017.

19. Sue Sanders, interviewed 8 August 2016.

20. An example from 2017 was a Jewish junior school, failed by Ofsted for not teaching respect for LGBT people, which attracted critical reports in the *Independent, Daily Express* and *Daily Telegraph* (June).

21. Ros McNeil (NUT), interviewed 2 September 2016. Details in this section were also taken from the interview with Sue Sanders.

22. Walker v. Innospec Ltd, Supreme Court, 2017, UKSC47. Judgment handed down on 12 July 2017. The claim had been rejected at two pre- vious hearings but the decision of the Supreme Court was unanimous. John Walker's case had been supported from the beginning by the human rights organisation Liberty.

23. Available at www.mbs.ac.uk/hubs/pdf/The-ups-and-downs-of-LGBs- workplace-experiences.pdf.

24. This survey, carried out for the *Pink Paper*, was small (1000 people), and additionally showed a correlation with age (young people much more tolerant, over 65s much less so). See Chris Baynes, 'Homosexuality decriminalisation at 50: Four in 10 British people believe gay sex is "unnatural"' *Independent*, 27 July 2017. www.independent.co.uk/ news/uk/home-news/homosexuality-decriminalisation-50-gay-sex- unnatural-rights-british-people-believe-same-sex-a7862191.html. Accessed 10 November 2017.

25. This issue is yet another taken up by the TUC. A campaign was launched following a well-attended fringe meeting held at TUC Congress in Liverpool in 2009, which attracted the participation of many grass- roots campaigns. TUC affiliate the Professional Footballers Association (PFA) has done great work through its equality head, Simone Pound,

and Stonewall has been running its 'pink laces' campaign to good effect. The key body, the Football Association (FA), has been slow to respond to these campaigns and has rejected advice and offers to help from the TUC's alliance. The latter has been promoting grassroots engagement through Lindsay England's 'Just a ball game?' and the work of local branches of the Communications Workers' Union (CWU) and Unite.

26. Home Office, *Hate Crime, England and Wales 2015/16*. Most recent figures available at www.gov.uk/government/statistics/hate-crime-england-and-wales-2016-to-2017.

27. Stonewall, *LGBT in Britain: Hate crime and discrimination*, 2017, available from the Stonewall website www.stonewall.org.uk. The survey covered a twelve-month period (2016-17) and found that one in five people overall had faced hate or discrimination, but four in five had not reported it. Within the total, two in five trans people, one in three black, Asian or minority ethnic and more than a quarter of disabled LGBT people had suffered discrimination or abuse.

Index

Abse, Leo, MP (politician), 20
ACTT (film technicians' union), 73
Afghanistan, 151
AIDS (Acquired Immune Deficiency
  Syndrome)
  Appearance and popular reaction, 77-
  9, 116
  ILO Convention, 150
  Trade union responses, 76-8, 79, 87,
  90, 103-4, 155
Allen, Sharon (trade union activist), 109
Amann, Paul (trade union activist), 110
AMICUS (trade union), 125-6, 135-6
Amnesty International, 151, 161n2
Anderson, Lucy (trade union official),
  125
Anti-Nazi League (ANL), 50
Arran, Lord (politician), 30
Ashton, Cathy, Baroness (politician),
  129
Ashton, Mark (activist), 70, 83n19
Association of Scientific, Technical and
  Managerial Staff (ASTMS) (trade
  union), 95-7
Association of Teachers and Lecturers
  (ATL) (trade union), 166
Asylum seekers (LGBT), 157-8
Amalgamated Union of Engineering
  Workers-Technical Administrative
  and Supervisory Section (AUEW-
  TASS) (trade union), 80, 94-7
Azam, Rihanna (trade union official),
  141

Bahati, David, MP (Ugandan
  politician), 161n7
Banking Insurance and Finance Union
  (BIFU) (trade union), 120
Banks, Carl (trade union activist), 140-1
Barber, Brendan (trade union official,

TUC general secretary), 120, 127,
  128, 180
Barnett, Tim (director of Stonewall), 87
Baxter, Jan (trade union activist), 153
Bayley, Margaret (trade unionist), 109
Beaumont, Carol (New Zealand trade
  unionist), 151
Beaumont Society (trans organisation),
  20
Bebel, August (German social
  democrat), 14
Beer, Chris (activist), 79
Benkert, Dr (writer on sexuality), 13
Benn, Tony, MP (politician), 54, 57
Benson, Ben (trade union activist), 66
Benton, Sarah (*Spare Rib* reporter), 48
Beresford, Mark (trade union activist),
  143-4
Bermondsey by-election (1983), 55, 116
Bickerstaffe, Rodney (trade union
  official), 120
Bisexuals (inclusion of), 97, 100, 132-3,
  147n18
Black Gay Men's Advisory Group
  (LGBT organisation), 162n8
Black Lesbians UK (BLUK) (LBT
  organisation), 169
Blair, Tony, MP (politician, prime
  minister), 7, 105, 111, 115
Blick, Mike (trade union activist), 34,
  68
Blisset, Ed (trade union official), 141
Bloor, Kate (trade union activist), 94
Blunt, Ruth (trade union official), 101
Blyth, Peggy (trade unionist), 110
'Bolton Seven' (court case 1998), 118
Bonham, Steve (activist), 64
Booth, Cath (trade union activist), 75
Booth, Janine (trade union activist),
  143, 159

184

Boychuk, Louise (sacked by employer), 57
Bradley, Peter (trade union activist), 41-3, 62-4
Bramall, Sir Ashley (head of ILEA), 41-2
Braniff-Herbert, David (trade union official), 167
Brennan, Kevin, MP (politician), 175
British Rail (equality policies), 143
British Social Attitudes (BSA) surveys, 116, 176, 178
British Telecom (BT) (equality policies), 99
Broadbent, L (trade unionist), 73
Brown, Stewart (trade union activist), 145, 150
Burgess, Guy (spy), 20

Cabaret (play and film), 17
Callaghan, James, MP (politician, prime minister), 50n2
Cameron, David, MP (politician, prime minister), 115, 158, 164, 180n3
Cameron, Ken (trade union official), 145
Cameroon (position of LGBT people in), 159
Campaign (previously Committee) for Homosexual Equality (CHE)
Foundation and early work, 5, 19, 26-8
Work with trade unionists, 40, 46
Draft Bill, 21
Relations with GLF, 28
Campaign for Press and Broadcasting Freedom (CPBF), 76
Canada (LGBT rights in), 155
Canfield, Barry (trade union official), 90
Cant, Bob (trade unionist, activist), 31
Carberry, Kay (trade union official), 109-110, 131
Carberry, Pat (trade union activist), 145
Care Concern, sacks Judith Williams, 56
Carolus, Cheryl (South African diplomat), 120
Carpenter, Edward (writer, socialist, campaigner), 14-15
Carss-Frisk, Monica, QC (lawyer), 125

Cash, Mick (trade union official), 144, 159
Cashman, Michael, MEP (politician, actor), 87
Chartered Society of Physiotherapy (CSP) (trade union/professional association), 133
Chartists, the, 12
Christian Action Research Education (CARE), 125
Christian Schools Alliance, 125
Church of England Children's Society (sacks Sandi Toksvig as trustee), 97
Civil and Public Servants Association (CPSA), 59, 89, 137
Civil Service Gay Group (later CPSGG) Founded 1977, 46
Activities of, 59-60, 88
Coldrick, Sarah (trade union activist), 65-6
Coleman, Kieran (trade union activist), 94
Colgan, Fiona (academic), 170
Commission for Racial Equality (CRE), 130
Commonwealth Foundation, 156
Communication Workers' Union (CWU) (trade union), 98, 137-9
Communist Party of Great Britain (CPGB), 31, 48
Confédération Générale du Travail (CGT) (French trade union), 153
Confederation of Health Service Employees (COHSE) (trade union), 102-4
Contre la Homophobie (campaign, France), 153
Conway, Terry (activist), 78
Corbett, Martin (activist), 28
Corbyn, Jeremy, MP (politician), 81n2, 164
Corvello, Raymond (activist), 35
Coupe, Jeffrey, councillor (politician), 68
Cove, J. (trade unionist), 73
Covey, Donna (trade union official), 110, 140
Crabtree, J. (trade unionist), 73
Cranston, Nora (campaigner), 151
Creegan, Chris, *see* Eades, Chris

Crow, Bob (trade union official), 144

Cutting Edge Consortium (campaign), 176

Daily Express (newspaper)
Attack on *Well of Loneliness*, 1928, 16
Attack on NUT, 63

Daily Herald (newspaper)
Defence of *Well of Loneliness*, 1928, 16

Daily Telegraph (newspaper), 38

Dancer, David (CHE and Gay Labour Group), 46

Dandridge, Nicola (lawyer), 125

Davies, Ian (trade unionist) (dispute 1976), 36-40

Day, Nick (trade union activist), 141

Deacon, Bob (trade union activist), 56

Dee, Sally (trade unionist), 36

Deighton, Alan (activist), 35

Democratic Unionist Party (DUP), 164

Diamond, Paul (lawyer), 125

Dingemans, James, QC (lawyer), 125

Disabled People against Cuts (DPAC), 164

Disability Rights Commission (DRC), 130

Dix, Bernard (trade union official), 44

Donaghy, Rita, baroness (trade unionist, politician), 66, 177

Donovan, Dai (trade unionist), 70

Drain, Geoffrey (trade union official), 34

Douglas (Isle of Man) (NALGO conference 1983), 64-5

Drew, Sandya (lawyer), 125

Dulais (South Wales), colliery (miners' strike 1984-5), 70-1

Durrell, Anne (activist), 77

Eades, Chris [Creegan], (trade union activist), 65-6, 101, 107

Eagle, Angela, MP (politician), 127, 129, 147n9 and n17

Eagle, Maria, MP (politician), 129

Ecclestone, Jake (trade union official), 77

Edmonds, John (trade union official), 117

Education
Discrimination and prejudice in, 41-2, 101, 174-6

Education Institute of Scotland (EIS) (trade union), 107

Education International (EI) (trade union federation), 153

Edwards, Gerry (trade unionist), 36

Edwards, Joel (Evangelical Alliance), 131

EETPU (electricians' union), 75

Ellis, Havelock (writer, campaigner), 14

Endean, Siobhan (trade union official), 148n24

Engels, Friedrich (philosopher, campaigner), 16

England, Lindsay (activist), 183n25

Enright, Shane (trade union activist), 80, 83n32, 90

Equality and Human Rights Commission (EHRC), 130-1

Equal Opportunities Commission (EOC), 120, 130

Equity (trade union), 109, 133

European Court of Human Rights, 122

European Trade Union Confederation (ETUC), 150, 152

European Transgender Council (TGEU), 154

European Union (EU), 122, 153

Evangelical Alliance, 125, 131

Evening Standard (newspaper), 30

Exall, Maria (trade union activist), 98, 137, 148n30, 176

Extending Equality (report and conference, 2008), 152

Fairweather, Paul (trade union activist), 107

Falklands war (1982), 55

Feather, Vic (TUC general secretary), 30

Festival of Light (as anti-gay organisation), 29

Fire Brigades Union (FBU) (trade union), 107, 144-6

First Division Association (FDA) (trade union), 59, 89, 133

Flag flyers (L&G trade union group), 93

FNV (Dutch trade union), 152

Foot, Michael, MP (politician), 54

Football, homophobia in, 178

Foreign and Commonwealth Office (FCO) (government department), 156, 159

For Richer, for Poorer (TUC/Stonewall publication), 108

Franklin, Rosemary (trade union activist), 61

Friend (support group), 28

Gallacher, Betty (trade union activist), 77-8, 83n27, 93, 136

Gandhi, Mahatma (Indian leader), 15

Gay Games, World, 153-4, 161n5

Gays against the Nazis (part of ANL), 50

'Gays at Work' (GRAW pamphlet), 57

Gay Labour Group (GLG) (predecessor of LCLGR), 34, 46-7

Gay Legal Advice (GLAD), 52n23

Gay Liberation Front (GLF)
  Foundation and programme, 22, 28
  Functioning and campaigns, 28
  Trans people and women in, 28-29
  Work with trade unionists, 30-1, 47-8

Gay Librarians Group, 28

Gay News (newspaper), 33, 39
  Founding 1972, 28
  Trial 1977, 30

Gay Post and Telecoms Workers Group (GPTW), 60-1

Gay Pride, *see* Pride

Gay Rights at Work (GRAW),
  Founding, 49, 50
  Conference 1982, 56
  Publishes 'Gays at Work', 57
  On AIDS, 78

Gay Switchboard (London), 28, 68

Gay Teachers Group (GTG), 33, 41-3, 62-4

Gay Times (journal), 75

Gay's the Word (bookshop), 60, 104

Gay Workers' conferences (1975, 1976), 47-9

Gay Youth Movement, 68

Geldart, Jean (trade union activist), 51n23

Gender Trust (trans rights organisation), 131

General Household Survey, 179

Gibson, Anne (trade union official), 94, 107

Gill, Ken (trade union official), 94, 107

Gladstone, William, MP (politician, prime minister), 12

GMB (trade union), 12, 80, 139-40

GMB Shout! (trade union LGBT+ group), 140-1

Goodbye to Berlin (book by Isherwood), 17

Government Equalities Office (GEO) (government department), 156

Graham, K. (trade union official), 45

Grant, Lisa and Percey, Jill (discrimination against), 108, 119, 123

Grayson, Larry (performer), 42

Greater London Council (GLC), 43, 55, 79

Groombridge, Martin (trade union activist), 94

Guardian, The (newspaper), 30

Hackett, Sue (trade union official), 141-2, 149n32

Hackney Gazette (newspaper), 39

Hall, Radclyffe (writer)
  Publishes *Well of Loneliness*, 16

Hanscombe, Gill (trade union activist), 76

Hanson, Katie (trade union activist), 96-7

Hanson, Mary (trade union activist), 98

Hardy, Geoff (trade union activist), 42, 62-4

Harley, Ron (trade union activist), 103-4

Hate crime (against LGBT+ people), 129, 179

Hattersley, Roy, MP (politician), 105

Hayes, Billy (trade union official), 139

Hayfield, Anne (activist), 107

Hayward, Ron (Labour Party official), 58

Heath, Ted, MP (politician, prime minister), 26, 50n2

Heathfield, Peter (trade union official), 69

Heseltine, Michael, MP (politician), 86

Heyes, Pete (trade union activist), 144

Hillman, Barry (trade unionist), 36

Hillon, Bernadette (trade union official), 109

Hince, Vernon (trade union official), 143

Hinton, Eric (activist), 59

Hirschfeld, Magnus (German campaigner and writer), 14-18

Holbourne, Zita (trade union activist), 140

Holland, Diana (trade union official), 90-3, 107, 136

Homogenic Love (book by Edward Carpenter), 15

Homosexual Law Reform Society (HLRS), 19

Horsfall, Allan (campaigner), 19, 36

Howe, Barry (trade unionist), 37

Hughes, Simon, MP (politician), 81n

Hughes, Tony (trade union activist), 141

Humm, Richard (trade union activist), 51n23

Hunter, Peter (trade union activist), 102

Hurley, Sarah (trade union activist), 141

Hyman, Howard (trade union activist), 33-6

Inglesant, Philip (trade union activist), 96, 107

Ink News (newsletter), 29

Inland Revenue Staffs Federation (IRSF) (trade union), 89

Inner London Education Authority (ILEA), 41-2, 79

Institute of Professional Civil Servants (IPCS) (trade union), 59

Institution of Professionals Managers and Specialists (IPMS) (trade union), 89

Institute of Sexual Science (Berlin), 18

Intermediate Sex, The (book by Edward Carpenter), 15

International Labour Organisation (ILO), 150

International Lesbian, Gay, Bisexual, Trans and Intersex Association (ILGA), 104, 151, 154, 160n1

International Marxist Group, 31, 48

International Socialists, *see* Socialist Workers' Party

International Trade Union Confederation (ITUC), 150, 154

International Transport Federation (trade union confederation), 159

Isherwood, Christopher (writer), 17

Jackson, Alan (trade union activist), 42, 62-4

Jackson, Mike (LGSM activist), 70-1

Jamaica, homophobia in, 155

Jamaican Forum for Lesbians, All-Sexuals and Gays (J-Flag), 155, 162n8

James, Sian, MP (politician), 71

Jandu, Kamaljeet (trade union official), 141

Jarrett, Mike (CHE), 50

Jenkins, Clive (trade union official), 94

Jenkinson, John (trade union activist), 61

Jersey, Channel Islands
  NUT conference 1983, 62-3
  Equality laws, 82n10

Johnson, Alan, MP (politician), 129

Johnson, John (trade union activist), 79, 90, 106, 107

Jones, Dan (trade union activist), 51n23

Jones, Dwayne (murder of), 156

Kahramanoglou, Kursad (activist, trade union official), 134, 152

Kaleidoscope (LGBT rights organisation), 156

KAOS GL (Turkish LGBT rights organisation), 152

Keates, John (trade union activist), 140

Keen, Ann, MP (politician), 120

Kelly, Ruth, MP (politician), 128

Kenny, Paul (trade union official), 142

Kenya (LGBT rights in), 159

'Kill the Gays' Bill (Uganda), 155, 158

Kilvington, Francis (trade union official), 90

Kinnock, Neil, MP (politician), 105

Knapp, Jimmy (trade union official), 110, 143

Labouchère amendment *see* Laws

Labour Campaign for Gay Rights, later Labour Campaign for Lesbian and Gay Rights (LCLGR) (and *see* Gay Labour Group), 58, 68, 70, 73, 115, 120, 129

Labour Representation Committee, 13
Labour Research Department, 165
LAGER (Lesbian and Gay Employment Rights), 79, 83-4n32, 120
LAGIM (Lesbians and Gays in MSF, trade union LGBT group), 94-8
LGBT Equality in the Workplace (TUC publication), 165
Lambert, Tracey (trade union official), 104
Labour Party
  Foundation (1906), 13
  Conference 1985, 6, 73
  Conference 1986, 80
  Conference 1988, 105
  Conference 1989, 105
  Conference 1994, 105
  Conference 2005, 129
Lascelles, David (trade union activist), 140
Lawrence, Stephen (murdered 1993), 130
Laws
  Adoption and Children Act 2005, 128
  Amsterdam Treaty (EU) 2000, 123
  Civil Partnership Act 2005, 126
  Code Napoleon (France), 17
  Crime and Disorder Act 1997, 118
  Criminal Justice and Immigration Act 2007, 129
  Criminal Justice and Public Order Act 1994, 86
  Criminal Law Amendment act 1885 (Labouchère amendment), 16
  Employment Equality (Sexual Orientation) regulations 2003, 123-6
  Equality Act 2010, 130, 168
  Gender Recognition Act 2004, 131, 167
  Industrial Relations Act 1971, 30
  Local Government Act 1988 (Section 28/2a), 7, 86-8, 118
  Marriage Equality (Same-Sex Couples) Act 2013/14 (England & Wales/Scotland), 164
  Obscene Publications Act 1857, 16
  Paragraph 175 (Germany 1871), 14, 16, 18
  Public Sector Equality Duty (Equality Act 2010), 130
  Race Relations Act 1976, 25

Sex Discrimination Act 1975, 25, 115
Sexual Offences Act 1967, 7, 21, 55
Sexual Orientation regulations 2007, 129
Leaves of Grass (poetry collection by Walt Whitman), 14
Leeuwen, Fred van (trade union official), 151
Lemon, Denis (editor, *Gay News*), 28, 30
Lesbians against Pit Closures (LAPC), 7, 70
Lesbian and Gay Equality in Education (pamphlet), 101
Lesbian and Gay Christian Movement (LGCM), 120, 128, 176
Lesbians and Gays in MSF (pamphlet), 95
Lesbians and Gays Support the Miners (LGSM), 7, 60, 70-2, 172-3
Lesbians and Gays Support the Printworkers (LGSP), 75-6
Lesbian and Gay TUC (campaign group), 107
Lester, Lord (politician), 124
Lewis, Jackie (trade union activist), 65, 101, 104, 109
LGBT History Month, 180
LGBT Stakeholder Forum (government body), 156
LGL (Lithuanian LGBT organisation), 159
Liberal (later Liberal Democrat) Party, 12, 54
Liberty (formerly National Council for Civil Liberties), 37, 51n11, 56, 120
Lindsay, John (activist), 28, 32
Lishman, Lilian (activist), 44
Livingstone, Ken (politician), 55, 79
Lithuania (homophobia in), 159
London Lesbian and Gay Centre, 79
Lucas, Tim (trade union activist), 42, 62-4
Lumsden, Andrew (activist), 28, 76
Lyons, Roger (trade union official), 95

MacGregor, Sir Ian (chair National Coal Board), 69
Mackney, Paul (trade union official), 57
Maclean, Donald (spy), 20

Macpherson, Sir William (report 1999), 130, 145

Maguire, Anne, MP (politician), 127

Maile, Sandie (trade union activist), 140-1

Major, John, MP (politician, prime minister), 7, 54, 86

Manifesto for Lesbian and Gay Equality (publication 1995), 115

Mansell, Lesley (trade union activist), 94-6

Marx, Karl (philosopher, economist, activist), 16

Mason, Angela (trade union activist, director of Stonewall), 30-1, 66, 87, 107, 118, 119, 120

May, Theresa, MP (politician, prime minister), 164, 177

McAvoy, Doug (trade union official), 42

McCluskey, Len (trade union official), 136

McDonnell, John, MP (politician), 79

McFadyen, Ted (activist), 76

McGahey, Mick (trade union official), 69

McKay, John (activist), 34, 35, 65

McKellen, Sir Ian (actor, campaigner), 87

McKenna, Alex (editor, *Gay Times*), 75

Mckinley, Ann (trade unionist), 60

McNab, Claire (Press for Change), 133

McNeil, Ros (trade union official), 182n21

McNight, Judy (trade union official), 120

Mellish, Bob, MP (politician), 81n3

Mellor, Julie (EOC), 120

Mental health, 170

Merrill, George (partner of Edward Carpenter), 15

Michie, Margaret (trade unionist), 76

Militant Tendency (political organisation), 31, 111n2

Millman, Janice (trade union official), 107

Monaghan, Karen (lawyer), 125

Monitoring of sexual orientation, gender identity, 166

Monks, John (TUC general secretary), 109

Morning Star (newspaper), 31

Morris, Bill (trade union official), 110

MSF (Manufacturing Science Finance) (trade union), 107, 132-3

Mugabe, Robert (president of Zimbabwe), 155, 162n9

Museveni, Yoweri (president of Uganda), 155, 159

Mulholland, Marie (trade union activist), 103

Munyard, Terry (activist), 51n23

Murdoch, Rupert (media owner), 75

Nalgay (trade union LGBT group), 32-6

Nalgo Action group (trade union political group), 34-6, 40

NALGO Lesbian & Gay Conference, 65-6, 101-2

National Association of Local Government Officers (NALGO) (trade union), 72-3, 87,
  Conference 1976, 35
  Conference 1983, 64-5
  Conference 1984, 66-7
  Conference 1986, 102

National Association of Probation officers (NAPO) (trade union), 72, 109, 133

National Association of Schoolmasters Union of Women Teachers (NASUWT) (trade union), 108, 125

National Association of Teachers in Further and Higher Education (NATFHE) *see* University and Colleges Union (UCU)

National Communications Union (NCU) (trade union), 80, 97

National Council for Civil Liberties (NCCL) *see* Liberty

National Education Union (NEU) (trade union), 181n7

National Front (neo-fascist party), 25

National Graphical Association (NGA) (trade union), 75-6

National LGBT Consortium (of voluntary sector organisations), 168

National Union of Commercial and Public Servants (NUCPS) (trade union), 89

National Union of Journalists (NUJ) (trade union), 76-7

National Union of Mineworkers
(NUM) (trade union), 54, 88
Strike 1972, 26, 29
Strike 1984-5, 70-2, 74
National Union of Public Employees
(NUPE) (trade union), 34, 44-5, 57,
80, 102-4
National Union of Railwaymen (NUR)
(trade union), 16, 80, 143
National Union of Seamen (NUS)
(trade union), 143
National Union of Students (NUS),
51n11
National Union of Teachers (NUT)
(trade union), 41-3, 62-4, 87, 100-1,
125, 132-3, 167
Nazi Party, 17, 18
Neal, Julia (trade union activist), 166
News of the World (newspaper), 30
Nigeria (homophobia in), 155, 159
Notcutt, Mike (activist), 34, 44
NUPEGG (trade union LGBT group),
34, 44-5, 57
Nurick, Richard (activist), 59

Obama, Barack (US president), 162n9
Ofsted (government agency), 175
O'Neill, Andrew, QC (lawyer), 125
Operation Black Vote (community
campaign), 169
Opoku-Gyimah, Phyllis (trade union
official, activist), 169
OPZZ (Polish trade union), 152
Organisation for Lesbian and Gay
Action (LGBT campaign), 87
Open and Positive (GTG publication),
52n27
Out and Proud Diamond Group, 159
OutRage (LGBT organisation), 162n8
Outtalk (LGBT CWU publication),
99

Patrick, Paul (activist), 41, 64
PCS Proud (trade union LGBT group),
46, 136-7, 153
Pearce, Shirley (victim of
discrimination), 121, 123
Pearson, Ian, MP (politician), 151
Penny, Paul (trade union activist), 144,
158-9

Pensions discrimination, 107-8, 124-6,
146, 176-7
Pensions and Prejudice (TUC pamphlet),
107
Percey, Julie, 108
Pink Paper (newspaper), 108, 182n24
Pink Tape (trade union conference
1989), 89
Poland
Homophobia in, 151, 153, 161n2
Trade union organisation, 152
Poplestone, Jenny (activist), 79
Positive vetting (government policy),
46, 90
Post Office Engineering Union (POEU)
(trade union), 98
Pound, Simone (trade union official),
182n25
Power, Lisa (activist), 87
Power, Mike (trade union official), 122
Press for Change (Trans organisation),
131-2
Pride (film, 2014), 7, 70, 173
Pride, gay, lesbian/gay, LGBT (London
event)
First Pride march 1972, 22
Pride London 1985, 71, 172
World Pride 2012, 172
Pride London 2015, 173
Pride London 2016 and 2017, 174
Community Advisory Board (Pride
London), 174
Pride over Prejudice (trade union
publication), 92
Professional Footballers' Association
(PFA) (trade union), 178
Prosser, Margaret (trade union official),
92
Public and Commercial Services Union
(PCS) (trade union), 89, 125, 136-7
Public Employee (trade union
newspaper), 44-5
Public Service (trade union newspaper),
33-4
Public Services International (PSI)
(trade union confederation), 153
Purkiss, Bob (trade union official), 93
Purnell, James MP (politician), 123
Putin, Vladimir (president of Russia),
151, 171

Putting the T in LGBT (trade union campaign), 141

Pyne, Fred (trade union activist), 109-110

Queers against the Cuts (QUAC) (LGBT campaign), 170

Rail, Maritime and Transport Union (RMT) (trade union), 125, 143-4, 158

Rainbow International LGBT Activists' Solidarity Fund, 158-9

Rank Outsiders (LGBT organisation), 120

Reagan, Ronald (US president), 54

Regan, Bernard (trade union activist), 63

Reid, Sue (journalist), 63

Relph, Derek (trade union activist), 51n23

Richards, Lord Justice (High Court judge), 125-6

Riga (LGBT Pride in), 171

Rights of Gay Men and Women, The (Labour Party document 1981), 57

Riley, John, councillor (politician), 38

Roache, Tim (trade union official), 142

Robinson, Mark (trade union activist), 143

Robinson, Tony (actor, trade unionist), 110

Roe, Nick (trade union activist), 109

Roelofs, Sarah (trade union activist), 87, 113n25

Rogalewski (trade union official), 151

Rogers, Kelly (trade union official), 140

Röhm, Ernst (leader of Nazi Brownshirts), 18

Roscoe, Peter (trade union activist), 34, 36

Rose, Dinah (lawyer), 125

Rowland, Mike (activist), 34

Rugby, Warwickshire (campaign 1984), 67-9

Runnymede Trust, 169

Russia
  Abolition of oppressive laws 1917, 18
  Re-imposition of laws 1927, 18
  Under president Putin, 151, 154, 156-7, 171

Samuel, Dave (trade union activist), 95-6

Sanders, Sue (activist), 52n29, 64, 101, 175

Saunders, John (sacked by employer), 56, 123

Sawyer, Tom (trade union official), 58

Scarborough (NATFHE conference at), 43

Scargill, Arthur (trade union official), 69, 110

School Report (by Stonewall), 174

Schools Out! (LGBT publication and campaign organisation), 63-4, 101

Scientific Humanitarian Committee (early homosexual rights campaign), 14-17

Scott, Alan (trade union activist), 91

Scottish Minorities Group (L&G group), 33, 56

Scrafton, Philippa (trade union activist), 135

Section 28/2a *see* Laws

Serwotka, Mark (trade union official), 137

Sevilla, Roberta (trade union official), 151

Sex Inversion (by Ellis), 14

Sexual Offences Act 1967 *see* Laws

Sex workers (trade union policy on), 139

Shah, Eddie (newspaper owner), 74-5

Sharpe, Sue (trade union official), 95

Shaw, Brian (trade union activist), 89, 137, 140

Shell, Susan (victim of discrimination), 45, 56, 123

Shiers, John (activist), 43

Singh, Rabinder, QC (lawyer), 125

Smith, Chris (MP, now lord Smith of Finsbury) (politician), 82n17

Smith, Jacqui, MP (politician), 127

Smith, John MP (politician), 105

Smith, Laurie (trade union activist), 98-9, 139

Social and Community Planning (survey 1995), 122

Socialist Workers' Party, 31-2, 48

Society for the Study of Sex Psychology (founded by Hirschfeld), 15

Society of Civil and Public Servants (SCPS) (trade union), 89
Society of Graphical and Allied Trade Unions (SOGAT) (trade union), 75-6
South Wales Miners' Federation (supports Radclyffe Hall), 16
Spare Rib (journal), 48
Spectator (journal), 30
Spraggs, Gill (trade union activist), 63
Stagg, Lyn (trade union activist), 107
Stalin, Joseph (Soviet leader), 18
Stamping Out Homophobia (Conference 2006), 151
Starling, Lionel (activist), 34
Staying Alive (TUC report 2014), 170
Stonewall bar (New York), 22
Stonewall Lobby Group (LGBT organisation), 3, 7, 87, 118, 122, 174, 179
Stop Murder Music (campaign), 155
Straight Up! (TUC report), 121-2, 137
Street, Don (trade union activist), 59, 89
Strivens, Duncan (trade union activist), 137
Suffragettes (campaign for votes for women), 13, 17
Sun, The (newspaper), 16, 30, 68, 77
    On Rugby, 82n16
Sunday Express (newspaper), 16
Sweeney, Ed (trade union official), 120
Sweeney, F. (trade unionist), 73

Tatchell, Peter (activist), 51n11, 55, 77, 81n3, 155
Terrence Higgins Trust (HIV/AIDS organisation), 77
Thatcher, Margaret MP (politician, prime minister), 50n2, 54, 86
Thomas, Gareth MP (politician), 162n8
Thompson, Phil (trade union official), 103
Thompsons Solicitors (trade union solicitors), 125
Time Out (journal), 38
Times, The (newspaper), 31
Todd, Ron (trade union official), 91, 117
Toksvig, Sandi (performer, activist), 97

Tolpuddle Martyrs (early trade unionists), 12
Tower Hamlets, London borough of (dispute, 1976), 36-40
Towle, Carola (trade union official), 80n12, 135
Tracey, Herbert (TUC librarian), 15
Trades Union Congress (TUC)
    Congress 1868, 12
    Congress 1899, 13
    Congress 1985, 6, 73
    Congress 1997, 109-110
    Congress 2001, 133
    Congress 2009, 131
    Equality Audits, 165
    Lesbian and Gay Rights at Work 1992 (publication), 107
    Lesbian and Gay Conference 1998, 111, 119, 133
    Lesbian and Gay Conference 2000, 133
    Lesbian and Gay Conference 2001, 133
    LGBT Conference 2016, 168
    and LGBT Pride, 171-4
    Women's Conference
        1985, 72
        1996, 108-9
Trade Unions (creation of), 12-13
Trade Unions against Section 28 (TUAS28) (campaign), 87-8
Trade Unionists Together for Lesbian and Gay Rights (pamphlet 2007), 153
Transgender
    Case for NUT, 101
    Create Beaumont Society, 20
    In GLF, 28-29
    P v S and Cornwall County Council (legal case), 108
    Position in society, 11, 20, 167-8, 181n10
    and trade unions, 97, 101, 131-3, 135, 144, 165, 168
Trans day of remembrance, 168
Transport and General Workers' union (TGWU) (trade union), 12, 73, 90-3, 108, 135
    Conferences 1987 and 1989, 90-2
Trump, Donald (US president), 179
Tully, Susan (actor, trade unionist), 110

Turner, Baroness, of Camden (politician), 119
Twigg, Stephen, MP (politician), 109

Uganda (homophobia in), 154, 158
UK Black Pride, 169
Ulrichs, Karl (writer, campaigner), 13, 16
United Kingdom Independence Party (UKIP), 180
Union of Communication Workers (UCW) (trade union), 60, 80, 97
Union of Construction and Allied Trades (UCATT) (trade union), 73, 80
Union of Shop Distributive and Allied Workers (USDAW) (trade union), 80, 166
Unions Working for Lesbian and Gay Members (TUC publication), 106
UNISON (trade union), 108, 115, 125, 152, 171
  Merger of NALGO, COHSE and NUPE, 102
  LGBT structures in, 103-4
  Trans inclusion in, 134-5
UNITE (trade union), 135-6
United Nations (UN), 150, 159
University and Colleges Union (UCU) (trade union), 31, 43, 57, 107
Ups and Downs of LGB Workplace Experience (report 2014), 178

Veale, Sarah (trade union official), 131
Vietnam war, 22, 25
Voice (CWU journal), 99
Voice, The (newspaper), 169
Voluntary sector (LGBT) (and austerity), 169-71

Walker, Michael (trade union activist), 113n23
Walker v. Innospec ltd (pensions case), 177, 182n22
Wapping dispute (1986), 75-6
Warburton, John (victimised 1974), 41-3

Ward, Dave (trade union official), 139
Warsaw pride (attempts to ban), 171
Washbourne, Yvonne (trade union activist), 89, 136
Waylen, Alison (trade union official), 103
Webb, Jessica (trade union official), 144
Webster, Richard (trade unionist), 35
Weimar republic (Germany), 17
Well of Loneliness (by Radclyffe Hall), 16
What about the Gay Workers? (CHE report 1981), 49-50
Whinnom, Alex (Press for Change), 131
Whitehouse, Mary (and Festival of Light), 29, 30
Whitman, Walt (poet), 14
Wilde, Oscar (writer) (trials of), 7
Wilkinson, Pat (trade union official), 144
Wilkinson, Paul (trade union activist), 61
Williams, Judith (sacked by employer), 56
Williams, Patrick (trade union activist), 172
Wilson, Harold MP (politician, prime minister), 20, 27, 50n2
Wolfenden, Lord (report 1957), 19-20
Women and Equalities Committee (parliamentary body), 168
Woodcraft, Tess (trade union official), 66
Workers' Revolutionary Party, 32
Working for Lesbian and Gay Members (pamphlet 1999), 153
Wrack, Matt (trade union official), 146
Wyporska, Wanda (trade union official), 166

Young, Baroness Janet (politician), 118
Young Socialists (Labour Party youth organisation), 31
Young, Tony (trade union official), 98, 110, 139

Zimbabwe, 155